S0-BYV-856

THE SONGS OF ASCENTS
(PSALMS 120–134)

SOCIETY
OF BIBLICAL
LITERATURE

DISSERTATION SERIES

Michael V. Fox, Old Testament Editor
Pheme Perkins, New Testament Editor

Number 148

THE SONGS OF ASCENTS
(PSALMS 120–134)
Their Place in Israelite History and Religion

by
Loren D. Crow

Loren D. Crow

THE SONGS OF ASCENTS (PSALMS 120–134)
Their Place in Israelite History and Religion

Scholars Press
Atlanta, Georgia

BS
1445
,S6
C76
1996

THE SONGS OF ASCENTS
(PSALMS 120–134)
Their Place in Israelite History and Religion

Loren D. Crow

© 1996
The Society of Biblical Literature

Library of Congress Cataloging in Publication Data
Crow, Loren.
    Songs of ascents / Loren D. Crow.
       p.   cm. — (Dissertation series / Society of Biblical
Literature ; no. 148)
    Originally published as author's thesis (doctoral)—Vanderbilt
University, 1994.
    Includes bibliographical references and indexes.
    ISBN 0-7885-0218-2 (alk. paper). — ISBN 0-7885-0219-0
pbk. : alk. paper)
    1. Bible. O.T. Psalms CXX–CXXXIV—Criticism, interpretation,
etc. I. Bible. O. T. Psalms CXX–CXXXIV. English. 1996.
II. Title. III. Series: Dissertation series (Society of Biblical Literature) ;
no. 148.
BS1445.S6C76 1996
233'.206—dc20   95-52852
                                   CIP

Printed in the United States of America
on acid-free paper

To Cheryl

CONTENTS

ACKNOWLEDGMENTS

The present work is a minor revision of my 1994 dissertation presented to the faculty of the Graduate Department of Religion at Vanderbilt University. I wish to express my sincere thanks to the many people without whose support this project might have remained uncompleted. I am particularly grateful to the members of my dissertation committee—Douglas Knight, James Barr, Peter Haas, Robert Drews, and William Race, and especially its chairman, Walter Harrelson—who encouraged me in the work and provided incisive critiques of it. I am also grateful to a number of other mentors, colleagues and friends. Eugene TeSelle, Professor of Church History and Theology at Vanderbilt Divinity School, patiently assisted with my forays into Patristic exegesis. Shemaryahu Talmon, who was a visiting faculty member at Vanderbilt University in 1989, spent several hours of his valuable time discussing my ideas with me and prevented my chasing of several wild geese. Jon Berquist, who at that time was at Phillips Graduate Seminary, provided a before-press draft of his most recent book (*Judaism in Persia's Shadow: A Social and Historical Approach*, now available from Fortress Press), read a draft of Chapter 4 and corrected a number of mistakes, and throughout the project supplied needed moral support. The errors of omission and commission that remain are of course no one's responsibility but my own.

Thanks are also due to two agencies that provided financial support for my research and writing. The United Negro College Fund provided needed assistance during the summer of 1991, in the form of the Charles A. Dana faculty fellowship. The Board of Higher Education and Ministry of The United Methodist Church awarded me a Sam Taylor Fellowship for the summer of 1992. These fellowships enabled me to cope with the difficulty of conducting research while located at a considerable remove from academic resources.

I also wish to thank the faculty and students of Wiley College, whose patience and encouragement have been a great aid. Nkanga Bokembya, my colleague in the Religion program at Wiley College, more than once substituted in my classes when the project took me away, critiqued several drafts of papers related to this study, and reassured me that the dissertation could be completed. I wish to thank my parents, Roy and Carolyn, for their support of my efforts in myriad ways. I also wish to thank my son Nathan, who came into my life while I was in the midst of the project, for putting up with my absence and my churlishness when present, and more importantly, for being the source of such indescribable joy. Finally, the depth of my gratitude to my wife Cheryl is beyond words. No acknowledgment can describe the thousands of ways in which she has contributed to this work; every expression of thanks sounds trite when compared to the debt that I owe her. The dedication of this book to her is the best that I can do.

LIST OF TABLES

LIST OF ABBREVIATIONS

Abbreviations for biblical, deuterocanonical, pseudepigraphal, and rabbinic works, as well as for standard journals in the field, follow the standards set by the Society of Biblical Literature (Society of Biblical Literature, "Members' Handbook," in *AAR/SBL 1993 Membership Directory and Handbook* [Atlanta, GA: Scholars Press, 1993] 386-400). The following abbreviations also appear.

ET   English translation

RF(s)   repeated formula(e). Refers to the six formulae identidied in Table 1 (p. 131)

CHAPTER I

HISTORY OF INTERPRETATION OF THE
SONGS OF ASCENTS

INTRODUCTION: THE TRANSLATION OF
THE SUPERSCRIPT

From very early times the translation of the superscript שִׁיר הַמַּעֲלוֹת,
literally "The Song of the Ascents," which is attached to each of Psalms
120-134,[1] has been an occasion for speculation.[2] In fact, with few
exceptions, the meaning of the superscript has dominated the discussion
of these psalms.[3] It is axiomatic that psalm superscripts are difficult to
interpret. In the case of the superscript שִׁיר הַמַּעֲלוֹת the suggestions
for interpretation have been quite diverse.

Syntactically, שִׁיר הַמַּעֲלוֹת is problematic. The first word stands
in a construct relationship to the second, which is definite, rendering the

---

[1]Psalm 121, the superscript of which reads שִׁיר לַמַּעֲלוֹת, is the only exception.
The LXX has Ὠιδὴ τῶν ἀναβαθμῶν in all cases, including Ps 120 (MT 121).
Other elements in the superscripts, such as the ascriptions, need not figure into the
discussion here.

[2]Gerald H. Wilson has noted that the Songs of Ascents are the only one of the
explicitly named psalm-types that were collected entirely together in the Psalter. He
(in my view rightly) takes this to mean that the collection probably existed before the
Psalter was edited into its present shape (*The Editing of the Hebrew Psalter* [SBLDS
76; Chico, CA: Scholars Press, 1985] 143).

[3]A few of the individual psalms, e.g., Psalms 122, 130, and 132, have either
spawned or been part of continuing discussions in their own right. But there are few
treatments of the collection as a whole that do not give primacy to the meaning of the
superscript as a guide for the meaning of the whole.

entire phrase definite.[4] This structure is precisely analogous to that found in the superscript of Psalm 30, which reads שִׁיר־חֲנֻכַּת הַבַּיִת "song of the dedication of the house [temple?]." Unfortunately, there, as in the Songs of Ascents, the meaning of the genitive is completely uncertain. Does "song of the dedication of the temple" mean that it was sung at the temple's dedication, or that the song served a dedicatory purpose, or that it is a reflection on that dedication? And all this says nothing about the difficulties involved in the translation of the *nomen rectum* הַבַּיִת (which could as easily mean either house or temple). A very similar situation obtains with the translation of שִׁיר הַמַּעֲלוֹת, in which the meanings neither of the genitive relationship nor of the *nomen rectum* are certain. It is precisely this problem that has given rise to the striking diversity of opinion about the meaning of the superscript.

Not surprisingly, such attempts at interpreting the superscript have taken precedence over the interpretation of the collection of songs in its own right. As Moses Buttenweiser has quipped, the interpretation of the Songs of Ascents (specifically here Psalm 120) as pilgrim psalms "has no basis in fact, but…is due primarily to the bias with which the psalm has been approached because of its label…."[5] I shall argue in Chap. 3 that there are unifying factors in addition to the superscript. It is not only possible but necessary to suspend judgment about the meaning of the superscript until one has fully treated the collection as a whole without recourse to it. Historically scholarship has been, with a few exceptions, unduly influenced by the interpretation of the superscript, many proposals having been made for its meaning that either totally disregard

---

[4]The *nomen regens* שִׁיר is definite because of the definiteness of the *nomen regens*, but since it is applied to each of the fifteen songs (except Psalm 121, for which the genitive relationship is accomplished with the *lamed*), it must be translated as indefinite. GKC §127e discusses instances in which this phenomenon occurs, though the superscript "Songs of Ascent" is explained as having originally been applied to the collection as a whole, and only later to the individual songs.

[5]Moses Buttenweiser, *The Psalms, Chronologically Treated, with a New Translation* (Library of Biblical Studies; New York: KTAV, 1969) 375. He adds (375-376) that "it is a grave mistake to be guided, in interpreting either this psalm [Psalm 122] or any of the fourteen others so designated, in terms of their label, considering that nothing whatever is known about its significance…."

the songs themselves or bend the evidence to fit one's own solution.[6] This history of interpretation is the subject of the next section.

THE INTERPRETATION OF THE
SUPERSCRIPT

For the most part, as I have indicated, interpreters have subscribed to the view that to explain the superscript of the Songs of Ascents is to explain the *Sitz im Leben* of the collection (and therefore of each individual song). Ancient and modern authors may be divided into several camps vis-à-vis the meaning of the songs. Taking their cue from Philo of Alexandria, the majority of early Christian writers interpreted the superscript allegorically, relating to the individual's ascent to God. This view has been largely abandoned in the modern period, with the exception of a few devotional books.[7] Another ancient position, which has been somewhat more influential in the modern period, is the opinion that the superscript refers to the returning of the Babylonian exiles to Jerusalem, thus having a one-time historical referent.[8] In comparatively recent times several prominent scholars have proposed that the superscript has to do with a particular metrical or poetic structure. The school with the most modern adherents, however, posits that the superscript refers to a recurrent cultic reality, whether in connection with pilgrimage to the temple from outlying areas and foreign lands or in connection with the Levitical songs sung on the "steps" in the Temple. All of these readings of the superscript, to varying degrees, have ignored

---

[6]Artur Weiser appears to go in the opposite direction (*The Psalms*, trans. Herbert Hartwell [OTL; Philadelphia: Westminster, 1962] 21-23). In his discussion of the superscripts he does not even mention the Songs of Ascents. In fact, he says the word שִׁיר is used fourteen times in the Psalter headings (p. 22), apparently ignoring Psalms 120-134 altogether. He does mention the songs later on (p. 100), affirming that the collection "contains only one genuine pilgrim song," namely Psalm 122.

[7]E.g., Erik Routley, *Ascent to the Cross* (New York: Abingdon, 1962). John Bunyan's *Pilgrim's Progress* and Dante's *Divine Comedy* are certainly based on similar ideas, although I found no evidence to link either of them specifically to the Songs of Ascents.

[8]Other attempts at a one-time historical referent are discussed below (pp. 9-14).

the content of the songs in favor of the supposed meaning of the superscript.

Mystical Interpretation

In many ways biblical interpretation during the first centuries of Christianity is based on the method and orientation of Philo of Alexandria, the Jewish interpreter of the early Common Era. Philo's method is essentially to interpret biblical texts *via* a Platonic philosophic framework. The end of this exegesis was probably to make Platonic philosophy palatable to Jews in the Hellenistic world (and perhaps to give the Bible appeal among educated unbelievers). It was obvious to Jews and Christians that there was much merit in the thought of the Greek philosophers, but this was difficult to reconcile with the notion of divine revelation to Israel. The dilemma was mediated in Philo's writing. His program of allegorization allowed him to find Platonic philosophy in even the most unlikely biblical texts.[9] Later writers even argued, some quite vehemently, that the Greeks had plagiarized their wisdom from the Divine Wisdom given to Israel.[10] By the end of the first century CE Judaism (and so also Christianity) was textually grounded to a large degree. The allegorical method provided a useful tool, since believers had to square their belief with the sacred texts. Allegory allowed people to affirm the place of the scriptures as divinely inspired with a message for the contemporary world, while also providing a method whereby believers could move in a Hellenistic intellectual framework. The Songs of Ascents did not escape this method of interpretation. For many early Christian interpreters, "ascent"

---

[9]In fact, it was precisely the most difficult biblical texts that most effectively served such purposes, their very problematic nature seeming to demand allegorical interpretation. For this insight (as for many of my ideas concerning early Christian interpretation) I am indebted to Prof. Eugene TeSelle.

[10]For a discussion of this accusation and retorts to it, as well as other attempts to reconcile the difficulty, see Henry Chadwick, *Early Christian Thought and the Classical Tradition: Studies in Justin, Clement, and Origen* (New York: Oxford University Press, 1966).

became the mystical ascent of the human soul to God, with all that this implies in a Platonic framework.[11]

Origen (ca. 185-253 CE)

For Clement of Alexandria the fallen soul was placed into the world (and hence into the human body) in order to redeem it. God was eternally trying to save those rebellious souls from their own error by creating more and more new bodies in which to place them, until such time as they began their ascent back to God. When the soul was reunited with its creator this process ended; it was saved.[12]

Clement's most celebrated pupil, Origen, indeed one of the greatest scholars of the early church, developed this idea, and found it in a variety of texts. He interprets the Songs of Ascents in connection with the forty-two "stages" of the march up from Egypt (Numbers 33). These latter he interprets allegorically as the spiritual ascent of the soul from "earth" to "heaven." While the soul is in bondage here on earth (which he ties to Psalm 120) it groans under the burden.[13] In his commentary on the Song of Songs he discusses what other biblical "songs" should be understood as the group from which Song of Songs was taken. On the list he includes the Songs of Ascents:

---

[11]It may be instructive to note that very little actual biblical content is needed for such an allegorical interpretation. According to Johannes Quasten, Gregory of Nyssa (*In psalmorum inscriptiones*) argues that the five books of the Psalter "form as many steps on the ladder to perfection" (*Patrology*, vol. 3, *The Golden Age of Greek Patristic Literature from the Council of Nicea to the Council of Chalcedon* [Westminster, MD: Newman, 1960] 265). For him the LXX titles are only present to lead one to goodness. Gregory of Nyssa also speaks of the mystic ascent of the soul to God, which allows one to enter heaven immediately upon death (295-296), but he apparently does not connect this with the Songs of Ascents.

[12]See Werner Eisenhut, "Clemens," in *Der Kleine Pauly: Lexikon der Antike* (Stuttgart: Alfred Druckenmüller, 1964) 1222.

[13]Origen, "Homily XXVII on Numbers" in Rowan A. Greer, *Origen* (New York: Paulist, 1979) 250-251.

> [The interpreter] will join to the others the fifteen songs of ascents...and by examining the excellences of each of the songs he will acquire from them steps for the soul in its progress, and by a spiritual understanding will bring together the order and coherence of these matters. Then he will be able to make clear with what noble steps the bride walks through all these and arrives at the wedding chamber of the bridegroom.[14]

For Origen the fallen soul is on pilgrimage back to God. In many ways this process is more automatic than one might expect, somewhat like "moving from grade to grade in school."[15] The soul is incarnated into a human body as a result of the fall, and its lot is to find its way back to God.

Augustine of Hippo (354-430)

By far the most influential ancient mystical[16] interpretation of the Songs of Ascents was that exhibited in the work of Saint Augustine of Hippo. He interpreted the collection as songs to be sung by the Christian during one's life-journey while becoming more fully Christian, that is, more fully in communion with God.

In his Psalms commentary Augustine

> sees these "songs of steps" as encouraging the newly baptized Christian, the New Man, to yearn with his whole mind and heart for the heavenly Fatherland, to become part of the People of God ascending toward Jerusalem while singing together the Songs of Ascent.[17]

It might well be said that Augustine's mystical interpretation foreshadows several of the more modern proposals. That he allegorizes

---

[14]Origen, "Commentary on the Song of Songs," in Greer, *Origen,* 239.

[15]Greer, "Introduction," in *Origen,* 12.

[16]Some controversy surrounds the question of whether Augustine may be classified a mystic. The problem is surveyed in Eugene TeSelle, "Augustine," in Paul E. Szarmach, ed., *An Introduction to the Medieval Mystics of Europe* (Albany, NY: State University of New York Press, 1984) 24.

[17]Mary T. Clark, "Introductory Note," to *Homilies on the Psalms,* in *Augustine of Hippo. Selected Writings,* Trans. and Ed. Mary T. Clark (New York: Paulist, 1984) 198.

the collection as representing the soul's journey to Jerusalem may indicate that he was aware of explanations such as those of returning exiles or pilgrims to Jerusalem. For Augustine, the songs constitute the very road upon which Christ Himself ascended to God. As such, they are the steps that a Christian, as Christ's follower, must also tread. Augustine emphasizes that the ascent to which he refers is not with the bodily feet, but spiritual ascent from the "vale of misery," which he explains:

> A vale signifieth humility: a mountain signifieth loftiness. There is a mountain whither we may ascend, a kind of spiritual loftiness. And what is this mountain, whither we ascend, save our Lord Jesus Christ?...Hence therefore we must ascend, thitherward we must ascend; from His example, unto His Divinity.[18]

The spiritual pilgrimage, then, is a journey from the state in which fallen human beings exist to that of communion with Deity.[19] Augustine believes the human self to consist of three parts, flesh, soul, and spirit, in which the spirit is God-related nature and the flesh is the animal nature.

---

[18]Saint Augustine of Hippo, *Expositions of the Book of Psalms*, vol. 5, *Psalm CII-CXXV* (Oxford: John Henry Parker, 1853) 458-459.

[19]This process is clearly outlined in the *Confessions,* Book VII, Chap. 23, where he makes clear that, at least for him, even communion with God is erratic at best, and most often quite unattainable:

> And thus, by degrees, I passed from bodies to soul, which makes use of the senses of the body to perceive; and thence to its inward faculty, to which the bodily senses represent outward things, and up to which reach the capabilities of beasts; and thence, again, I passed on to the reasoning faculty, unto which whatever is received from the senses of the body is referred to be judged.... And thus, with the flash of a trembling glance, it arrived at that which is. And then I saw Thy invisible things understood by the things that are made. But I was not able to fix my gaze thereon; and my infirmity being beaten back, I was thrown again on my accustomed habits, carrying along with me naught but a loving memory thereof, and an appetite for what I had, as it were, smelt the odour of, but was not yet able to eat.

(Quote from *The Confessions and Letters of St. Augustine, with a Sketch of his Life and Work.* NPNF 1 [Grand Rapids, MI: Wm. B. Eerdmans Publishing Company, 1956], 111-112). According to TeSelle ("Augustine," 332-333, n. 24), "contact with the supreme Good is possible, and...there are those, stronger than he, who are able to fix their gaze on it 'at length' (*diu*)."

The two are mediated by the soul, which can be either fallen (tending toward the animal) or spiritual (tending toward the Divine).

> [S]ince man is most properly understood (or, if that cannot be, then, at least, *believed*) to be made in God's image, no doubt it is that part of him by which he rises above those lower parts he has in common with the beasts, which brings him nearer to the supreme.[20]

It is therefore the soul's task to ascend toward the "higher" (i.e., "spiritual") side of one's nature, rather than remaining locked into the "lower" (i.e., "animal") side of it. In doing this, the young and the mature Christian alike sing the "Songs of Ascent."

Hesychius of Jerusalem (Pseudo-Athanasius)

Similarly, the tract entitled *De Titulis Psalmorum,* traditionally attributed to Athanasius but probably actually written by Hesychius of Jerusalem,[21] interprets the superscript as the "confession of those who leave their sins in order to ascend toward faith in the Lord, and in his commandments."[22] The spiritual journey begins by coming out of idolatry, just after baptism.[23] This theme receives elaboration in the interpretations given to each of the songs, but a few examples should suffice to demonstrate the hermeneutic employed. Psalm 121 functions to encourage new believers as they begin the spiritual journey to God. The third step in the spiritual journey (Psalm 122) is to go to the house of God, confess to the priest, and thereby hear the word of God. Throughout the tract it is argued that Christ is the ascending "way" that

---

[20]Augustine, *City of God,* Book XI §2 (Trans. Marcus Dods; New York: Random House, 1950) 346. This is a common theme in Platonistic Christianity; see, e.g., Origen, *On First Principles,* Book III, Chap. 4 §2 (Trans. G. W. Butterworth; New York: Harper and Row, 1966) 233.

[21]See Quasten, *Patrology,* 3:38.

[22]ἐξομολόγησις τῶν ἐρχομένων ἀπὸ τῶν ἁμαρτιῶν ἀνιέναι εἰς τὴν τοῦ κυριόυ πίστιν, καὶ τὰς τούτου ἐντολάς. PG 27:1219.

[23]PG 27:1219.

leads to God.[24] Each "step" is another level in this Christ-enabled journey to God and heaven.[25] That this way of putting the matter has interesting parallels to Augustine's interpretation need only be pointed out here.

The idea of a mystic ascent to communion with God does not appear simply to grow out of a random interpretation of the superscript. Rather, these interpretations have in common that they presume either a one-time ascent to God, as in Origen and Hesychius—where the ascent is the life-long journey made from the fallen nature to the image of God— or an occasional "pilgrimage" in transcendental communion with God. These may be compared profitably to the historicizing "songs sung *en route* from Babylon" interpretation and the annual pilgrimage interpretation, respectively, which are discussed below.

Historicizing Interpretation

Alongside the mystical understanding of the Songs of Ascents there developed a variety of interpretations that attempted to interpret the superscript in light of historical events. This point of view has had more adherents in modern times, but its roots are ancient.

Songs Sung by Returning Exiles

For the Psalms Midrash "Songs of Ascents" means that Psalms 120-134 are songs sung by returning exiles. But it is not a matter simply of the returnees of the sixth and fifth centuries BCE. Rather it refers to that return as well as to many other possible returns.[26] The returns from exile

---

[24]This statement appears to be in contrast to Augustine's metaphor, in which the "steps" are the steps on which Christ walked to God. It is possible that Hesychius is building on the Johannine image of Jesus as "the way" (John 14:6), so that Jesus is taken here to be the ascending road itself.

[25]PG 27:1219-1258.

[26]The difference between this interpretation and that of Qimḥi seems to me to be the significance of the act. For the latter it is primarily an act of occasional ritual pilgrimage (see pp. 23-24 below), whereas for the former it has primarily to do with a

are seen as being spurred on by God: "Note that the verse does not read 'A song of going up,' but *A song of goings up*—that is to say, when the children of Israel go up, they go up not one height at a time, but will go up many heights at once." Similarly, its previous descent was not "one descent at a time," but several.[27] In a comment on Psalm 121, however, ascent seems to mean national ascendancy: "After Thou hast taken us up the last ascent, we shall not be brought down." After God has saved Israel from the "kingdom of Esau," Israel will "sing the song of the last ascent whereto Thou wilt raise us from among the kingdoms."[28] Both of these interpretations presuppose a historical meaning for the superscript. In the former it is related to the situation of exile and return (as exemplified in the returns from Egypt and Babylon); in the latter it is related to the eschatological event in which Israel becomes the cultural, religious, and legal chief of the nations.

A peculiar kind of literal historicizing interpretation is that preferred by the Syrian Athanasius (and it seems, by the Syrian church in general).[29] For him the collection begins with a song sung by exiles returning from Babylon.[30] But it does not end there. The collection progresses in a linear fashion up to his own era, so that Psalm 132 is read as a prophecy of Christ's manifestation, Psalm 133 refers to catechumens in the church, and Psalm 134 manifests the praise of the church in his

---

return as such, an actual move of the family from the diaspora back to the ancestral homeland.

[27]Quoted from William G. Braude, trans., *The Midrash on Psalms*, vol. 2 (Yale Jewish Studies 13; New Haven: Yale University Press, 1959) 289. Presumably this somewhat opaque passage is an attempt to account for the fact that מַעֲלוֹת is plural. In the context the meaning seems to be that what Israel does it does fervently, although one could also make a case that it refers to the return of diasporic Jews from many places.

[28]Braude, *Midrash on Psalms,* 2:294.

[29]Similarly, for the East Syrian church the headings point to a historical interpretation as people coming up from Babylon. Psalm 127 relates to the rebuilding of the temple after the return; Psalm 132 relates to Zerubbabel's kingship after the return. Willem Bloemendaal, *The Headings of the Psalms in the East Syrian Church* (Leiden: E. J. Brill, 1960) 29.

[30]Bede Venerabilis (PL 93:1084-1092), similarly, gives alternate interpretations of many of the psalms, which have to do with contemporaneous use of the psalms by the church. But his primary interpretations tend to be in view of Israel coming out of exile.

own day. Each song constitutes one step further in the process of the history of redemption for the people of God.[31]

The classic modern attempt to establish this interpretation was that of Heinrich Ewald, who thought it likely that the superscript—though translated "pilgrim songs" or "songs of the homeward marches"— referred more specifically to exiles returning from Babylon.[32] The argument for this interpretation is undertaken on several fronts. The real point of departure is the fact that Ezra 7:9 refers to המעלה מבבל "the returnees from Babylon."[33] The objection is often raised that the singular is used rather than the plural מעלות "ascents" (as in the superscript of Psalms 120-134),[34] but this does little damage to the argument, since the plural could be used either to intensify the meaning or to refer to the fact that there was not one return from Babylon, but actually several.[35] The argument that ascription of some of the songs to David and Solomon negates the possibility of an exilic dating[36] is more

---

[31]Robert W. Thomson, trans., *Athanasiana Syriaca, Part IV: Expositio in Psalmos* (Corpus Scriptorum Christianorum Orientalium, editum consilio: Universitatis Catholicae Americae et Universitatis Catholicae Lovaniensis, vol. 387, Scriptores Syri, Tomus 168; Louvain: Secrétariat du Corpus SCO, 1977) 80-85.

[32]Heinrich Ewald, *Allgemeines über die Hebraeische Poesie und über das Psalmenbuch* (Die Dichter des Alten Bundes, erster Theil; Göttingen: Vandenhoeck & Ruprecht, 1839) 195-196. In the second edition (1866), however, he renounces this argument in favor of the "pilgrimage songs" explanation (see below, pp. 23-25).

[33]Hengstenberg utilizes this reference as evidence *against* the idea that מעלות in the superscripts to Psalms 120-134 can mean "ascent out of Babylon," since the term must be more closely defined (מִבָּבֶל). Ernst W. Hengstenberg, *Commentary on the Psalms,* 2nd ed., vol. 3 (Trans. John Thomson and Patrick Fairbairn; Edinburgh: T. & T. Clark, 1854) 406.

[34]So Hengstenberg, *Psalms*, 3:406. So also Eerdmans: "Though the singular form מַעֲלָה designates the caravan of Ezra from Babel to Jerusalem, the plural form always means 'steps'" (B. D. Eerdmans, *The Hebrew Book of Psalms* [OTS 4; Leiden: E. J. Brill, 1947] 571).

[35]Franz Delitzsch (C. F. Keil and Franz Delitzsch, *Commentary on the Old Testament in Ten Volumes: Psalms* [trans. James Martin from German original of 1867; Grand Rapids, MI: Wm. B. Eerdmans, 1988 {Original ET 1871}] 264-265), has several lucid objections to the historical interpretation. First, Psalm 120 is prayed from the midst of exile, not after an escape. Second, Psalms 122 and 134 presume full temple service in Jerusalem. Third, מַעֲלָה is not the word one would expect, which would be in the *qal* stem and would be singular.

[36]Hengstenberg, *Psalms*, 3:406-407. He accepts Davidic and Solomonic authorship, supplemented by the work of a third author, who also collected the songs

important than is often admitted. Although one need not accept the authorship of these songs as Davidic or Solomonic, it does demonstrate that, at least, the person who ascribed these songs probably believed them to have been from a much earlier time.

There are several arguments in favor of a "historicizing" interpretation (i.e., that they are songs sung while returning from Babylon). One is in the fact that several of the songs in the collection appear indeed to be something like traveling songs. Psalm 121, for example, looks very much like a blessing upon those setting off on a journey. As many commentators have noticed (albeit with other conclusions), the brevity and simplicity of the songs, which gives them all a very memorable character, might render them useful as marching songs.[37] In addition, not only the individual songs of the collection, but also the "shape" of the whole tends to lead one in this direction.[38] The collection begins with a song that on the surface appears to refer to exile (Psalm 120). The next (Psalm 121) looks like a blessing on those setting off on a journey. The third song (Psalm 122) may tell of a recently rebuilt Jerusalem, praying for its prosperity. Psalm 126 seems to refer to the restoration of the Judean community after the exile.[39] Psalm 133 is sometimes thought to refer to temple gatherings, in which the "brothers" are all together, or to the restored community at Jerusalem. Finally, the

---

and arranged them (408). Similarly also Joseph Addison Alexander, *The Psalms: translated and explained,* vol. 3 (New York: Baker and Scribner, 1850) 200.

[37]On the likelihood of "marching songs" cf. Isa 30:29; Ps 42:5. As Seybold has remarked (Klaus Seybold, *Die Wallfahrtspsalmen: Studien zur Entstehungsgeschichte von Psalm 120-134* [Biblisch-Theologische Studien 3; Neukirchen: Neukirchener Verlag, 1978] 21), it is this repetitiveness and overall memorability that gave rise to the "step-rhythm" theory of Gesenius (see below, pp. 15-16).

[38]Karel Deurloo, "Gedächtnis des Exils—Psalm 120-134," *Theologie und Kirche* 55 (1992) 28-34.

[39]Perowne, conversely, asserts that it is the postexilic date of the songs, and not their reference to a return from Babylon, that accounts for such allusions to the exiles in Psalm 126 (J. J. Stewart Perowne, *The Book of Psalms: A New Translation, with Introductions and Notes, explanatory and critical,* 3rd ed., vol. 2 [Andover: Warren F. Draper, 1898] 69-70). Hermann Gunkel, however, emphasizes that "Uber die Zeit der Entstehung gibt die Sammlung keine Anhaltspunkte" (*Einleitung in die Psalmen: Die Gattungen der religiösen Lyrik Israels*, ed. Joachim Begrich, 3d ed. (Göttingen: Vandenhoeck & Ruprecht, 1966; original 1933] 453).

last song (Psalm 134) could be taken to refer to the re-establishment of temple worship proper.

Richard Preß has made further refinements to this argument.[40] He holds that Psalms 120-134 are obviously not pilgrim-songs sung by people going to the temple, but rather were songs sung at a specific cultic gathering. For him what must be determined is the time of that gathering. He ends up placing it (through linguistic and sociological criteria, and "historical" references) at the beginning of the postexilic period.[41]

The greatest weight of evidence resists this historical "marching songs" interpretation, however. For one thing, it appears that there is a cultus in full operation at Jerusalem (Psalms 132 and 134); and it seems evident that the city's walls were in place (Ps 122:7)—both conditions that the returned Babylonian Judeans are said to have accomplished. Moreover the poems all have as their background the land of Palestine.[42] Furthermore, an exodus *en masse* such as is imagined in this hypothesis probably never happened; at most such a return took place in a very haphazard fashion, and certainly not as a military-style march. Under such conditions march songs seem not only unnecessary, but nearly impossible.[43] It is therefore unlikely that the Songs of Ascents are so named because they actually were sung by exiles returning to Jerusalem. This is not to say, however, that some later person could not have envisioned them as being sung on such an occasion, especially given the highly stylized way such returns were envisioned in ancient Israel.

---

[40]Richard Preß, "Der zeitgeschichtliche Hintergrund der Wallfahrtspsalmen," *TZ* 14 (1958) 401.

[41]Preß, "zeitgeschichtliche Hintergrund," 414.

[42]Even in Psalm 120, which has the strongest case for having been composed in exile, the enemies mentioned are not Babylonians, but groups whose juxtaposition can only be explained as metaphorical for enemies in general.

[43]The march song serves to keep all soldiers marching in time, lends orderliness to the movements and provides entertainment during an otherwise onerous task. Such a portrayal of a military-style move from Babylon to Jerusalem is probably derived from the very similar imagery in the book of Numbers, as reinterpreted in Second Isaiah.

Other Historicizing Explanations

In apparent opposition to its more well-known linking of the Songs of Ascents with the fifteen steps of the temple (see below, pp. 18-19), the Talmud also records a curious legend explaining the superscript as a group of songs sung by David to make the waters "ascend" again after he magically made them recede. The story goes that waters rose so high around Jerusalem that it seemed they would destroy the whole world. Seeing this problem, David caused the Divine Name to be written on a shard of pottery and thrown into the deep. This made the water recede so far that there was danger of drought. So David "repeated the fifteen Psalms of Ascent, and the waters rose 15,000 cubits" (*b. Sukk.* 51*b*). This fanciful interpretation of the superscript does not necessarily displace that of the Talmud's "15-step" theory, but it does make the imprecision of that reference somewhat more apparent.

More recently, James Wilson Thirtle made an interesting, if somewhat eccentric, proposal.[44] On the supposition that superscripts in the Psalter are not liturgical notations but rather refer to historical situations, he argued that the term "degrees" does not refer to a cultic practice such as pilgrimage.[45] Nor, he says, can it refer to anything as abstract as a stylistic or poetic form. Instead, he says, the key lies in the story about God's gracious adding of fifteen years to Hezekiah's life, as narrated in Isaiah 38 (= 2 Kings 20; cf. 2 Chr 32:24-26). The sign of God's extension of Hezekiah's life given by Isaiah is that the sun's shadow will "go back the ten steps it has gone down on the stairway of Ahaz." Through a variety of circumnavigations Thirtle posits that these steps are the referent of the superscript to Psalms 120-134, so that the number of songs corresponds to the number of extra years.

---

[44]James William Thirtle, *Old Testament Problems: Critical Studies in the Psalms & Isaiah* (London: Henry Frowde, 1907) 13-19.

[45]In marshaling his argument, Thirtle (*Old Testament Problems,* 17-18) makes appeal to an erroneous conception of the construct state. For him the first element of the superscript, שִׁיר, is indefinite, whereas the second, הַמַּעֲלוֹת is definite: "To suppress the emphatic prefix (*the*) is to accommodate the words to some preconceived notion as regards their character or intention." In point of fact, the construct state makes both of these words definite, or at least one would not want to use the indefinite state of שִׁיר as a primary part of one's argument. See GKC §127a.

Formal Interpretation

The first attempt to see in the superscript a formal, rather than a cultic or historical, reference seems to be that of musical notes, either sung in a high voice or gradually rising in pitch. This interpretation was first proposed by Saadiah Gaon and accepted by Ibn Ezra,[46] and later followed by John Calvin. After vehemently rejecting the other ancient opinions rehearsed in this chapter,[47] Calvin reasons (although with some caution) that the most acceptable explanation is that the superscript denotes the way the songs were sung, namely either in a high voice or with notes "ascending" up the scale.[48] The major difficulty with this theory is that it explains the superscript's origins in a way that is essentially beyond verification insofar as it relates not to the psalms themselves but to their performance. Of course this difficulty does not preclude the possibility of its correctness, but on the other hand the theory has no explanatory power vis-à-vis the psalms themselves.

A very different attempt to see the superscript in terms of formal characteristics appeared in 1839, from the philologist Wilhelm Gesenius.[49] He proposed that מעלות in the superscript to Psalms 120-134 refers to the poetic structure of the psalm in question, namely a "climactic" parallelism: "quidem ut antecedentis sententiae pars ab initio subsequentis repeti et passim novis verborum copiis augeri et quasi *ascendere* soleat."[50] During the mid-nineteenth century this view was

---

[46]Uriel Simon, *Four Approaches to the Book of Psalms: From Saadiah Gaon to Abraham Ibn Ezra* (Albany, NY: SUNY Press, 1989) 244, 249.

[47]He disparages the fifteen-step theory—which was apparently espoused by the Talmud and therefore accepted by the medieval rabbis—as "silly conjecture," and asperses the rabbis as frivolous with such things. On the other hand, he says the explanation of the superscript as designating the "ascent out of Babylonian captivity" is "altogether forced." John Calvin, *Commentary on the Book of Psalms*, trans. James Anderson (Calvin's Commentaries, vol. 5; Grand Rapids, MI: Wm. B. Eerdmans, 1949; Original 1539) 53.

[48]The translator notes that Calvin follows Ibn Ezra (see above, n. 46). Calvin wrote, "The Hebrew word for *degrees* being derived from the verb צלה, *tsalah* [*sic*] *to ascend* or *go up*, I agree with those who are of the opinion that it denotes the different musical notes rising in succession" (Calvin, *Book of Psalms*, 53-54).

[49]Wilhelm Gesenius, *Thesaurus Philologicus Criticus Linguae Hebrae et Chaldae Veteris Testamenti*, 2nd ed., vol. 2 (Lipsiae: Fr. Chr. Wil. Vogelius, 1839) 1031-1032.

[50]Gesenius, *Thesaurus,* 1032.

accepted by some prestigious scholars, most notably Delitzsch and de Wette.[51] Later commentators, however, noted against his thesis that this "ascending structure," in which a key word or idea from one line is repeated and modified in the following line, is neither unique to the Songs of Ascents nor found throughout the collection (so Hengstenberg, Kittel, Ewald, Hitzig).[52] In fact, it has been shown by several scholars recently that repetition and modification are primary features of Hebrew poetry.[53] There is, however, a certain truth to the proposal. There is a simplicity of expression in the Songs of Ascents that lends itself to this kind of poetic structure. That the superscript is not to be explained in this way is probably correct, but that such a "stair-like" quality is common in the Songs of Ascents cannot be denied.

B. D. Eerdmans has proposed a third formal interpretation of the superscript: they are songs to be read in succession.[54] According to him,

> Trying to understand each of these little psalms [Psalms 120-125] as an independent song we do not get satisfactory results. Ps. cxx ends abruptly. In Ps. cxxi friends bid God-speed[.] Ps. cxxiii ends without saying whether a desired sign of grace is received or not. Ps. cxxiv is said by Israel. As songs of pilgrims, recited either in the temple or on their way to the holy city, the psalms are difficult to understand if they are taken separately. But the context shows that such a method should not be applied. The psalms appear to be mutually connected.[55]

---

[51]Delitzsch, *Psalms,* 266-267; Wilhelm Martin de Wette, *Kommentar über die Psalmen,* ed. Gustav Bauer, 5th ed. (Breslau: Hermann Kelsch, 1885).

[52]Hengstenberg, *Psalms,* 3:404-406; Rudolf Kittel, *Die Psalmen, übersetzt und erklärt,* 4th ed. (KAT 13; Leipzig: A. Deichertsche Verlagsbuchhandlung, 1922) 388; Ewald, *Die poetischen Bücher des Alten Bundes. Zweiter Theil. Die Psalmen* (Göttingen: Vandenhoeck & Ruprecht, 1833) 195. Hitzig admits two translations of מַעֲלוֹת, literal "steps" and figurative ones (i.e., referring to poetic structure), and against the latter he argues that such a figurative meaning is not found in the Hebrew Bible (Ferdinand Hitzig, *Die Psalmen, uebersetzt und ausgelegt* [Leipzig and Heidelburg: C. F. Winter'sche Verlagshandlung, 1863] 365-366).

[53]In Kugel's terminology, this is a variation of the "A, and what is more, B" parallelism (James L. Kugel, *The Idea of Biblical Poetry: Parallelism and its History* (New Haven: Yale University Press, 1981).

[54]Eerdmans, *Psalms,* 548-571.

[55]Eerdmans, *Psalms,* 555-556.

Thus, he regards the collection of Songs of Ascents as a "suite" of psalms, and it is this characteristic that gives its name to the collection's members. This explanation, too, makes an important contribution, which I shall address in Chap. 3, namely that the collection has a sort of narrative structure.

Two scholars have proposed that the superscript is a genre designation. The first of these is Mitchell Dahood, who, on the basis of Apostrophe to Zion 14 (11QPs^A xxii 12),[56] proposed a new translation for the superscript: "song of extolments," which he believes "fits most, though not all, of these psalms."[57] Although the text of Apostrophe to Zion 14 is clear enough at this point, his translation "May your praise, O Zion, enter into his presence, extolment from all the world," is a dubious translation of the passage.[58] Moreover, the proposed meaning is (as Dahood partially admits) largely unrelated either to the form or to the content of the songs.

A second interpretation of the superscript as referring to a genre is that proposed by Marina Mannati, who argues that the Songs of Ascents are an organic whole, not a collection of songs.[59] Each song fits into the genre of "gradual psalms," which are distinct from any genres thus far identified by biblical critics. In her view, it is not the structure of each

---

[56]The text is published in James A. Sanders, *The Dead Sea Psalms Scroll* (Ithaca, NY: Cornell University Press, 1967) 123-127. A photograph may be found in James A. Sanders, *The Psalms Scroll of Qumr'n Cave 11 (11QPs^a)* (DJD 4; Oxford: Clarendon, 1965) plate XIV.

[57]Mitchell Dahood, *Psalms,* vol. 3 (AB 17a; Garden City, NY: Doubleday, 1970) 195.

[58]Dahood first proposed this reading in a review of Sanders, *Psalms Scroll* (*Biblica* 47 [1966] 143). He bases this reading on certain Ras Shamra texts (uncited) where *ʿrbh bʾp* denotes "may it enter his presence." Thus he derives מעלה from the root *ʿillah,* which he argues means "praise." The passage reads: *ʿrbh bʾp tšbḥtk ṣywn mʿlh lkwl ṭbl,* which in my opinion is better translated, "pleasing in the nose is your praise, O Zion, ascending to [or from] all the world." Such a participial reading of מעלה is, it seems to me, more likely than "extolment," which would be a meaning otherwise unknown for this verb. The image of the offering ("pleasing in the nose") leads one to think of praise as the "smoke" that ascends through the created order. One would expect "extolment" to be derived from רום. The idiom "lifting up the hands" might be taken as evidence for "extolment," by ellipsis of ידים, but this seems to me less likely than that proposed here.

[59]Marina Mannati, "Les Psaumes Graduels consistuent-ils un genre littéraire distinct à l'intérieur du psautier biblique?," *Sem* 29 (1979) 85-100.

psalm that makes it a gradual psalm, but rather its presence in the collection, which is neatly organized by the chronological order of the events surrounding the arrival and worship of pilgrims to Jerusalem (it is important to note that she does not believe the psalms actually to have been sung, but rather that as a whole they have a kind of narrative structure that is tied to the *idea* of pilgrimage). The literary pilgrimage is the "veneer" (*revêtement*) that holds together the memory of, and the desire for, the ritual act.[60]   Mannati observes that modern scholarly identifications of genre do not necessarily correspond to how the ancients might have identified them—a point that is worth making. Nevertheless, her argument seems to me to be flawed in that as it presumes a direct relationship between the genre of each song severally and what might be called the "genre" of the collection. To confuse these two categories seems to me a fundamental misunderstanding.

Cultic Interpretation

It is mildly misleading to refer to the interpretations that I have grouped under the heading "Cultic Interpretation" as a "school" of interpretation. In reality the various proposals are quite dissimilar. Nonetheless they all have in common the idea that the songs were sung in connection with great ritual gatherings, either during those celebrations in one way or another or *en route* to them.

Songs Sung on Steps

The Talmud (*b. Sukk.* 51b; *b. Mid.* 2:5) appears for the first time to make a connection between the Songs of Ascents and the fifteen steps of the temple, as recorded in Ezek 40:26,31.[61]   The most famous is that of a

---

[60]Mannati, "Psaumes Graduels," 99.

[61]This is apparently the tradition that lies behind a saying of Didymus the Blind, as well:

Ἰστέον δὲ ὡς ὁ ἐν τῇ Ἰερουσαλὴμ νεὼς ἀναβαθμοὺς εἶχε δεκαπέντε καὶ ἐφ' ἕκαστον αὐτῶν ἐν τῷ ἀναβαίνειν εἰς αὐτὸν ἑστηκότες οἱ εἰς τὸ ὑμνεῖν τεταγμένοι ᾠδὴν ἔλεγον. διὸ καὶ

correspondence between the fifteen Songs of Ascents and the fifteen steps leading "down from the court of the Israelites to the court of women, corresponding to the fifteen songs of ascents in the Psalms. It was upon these that the Levites stood with their instruments of music and sang their songs."[62] It is true that the Songs of Ascents are not overtly said to have been the songs sung on those steps. Rather, the opposition may be between these steps and the steps of the altar. Even so, the correspondence between the fifteen songs and the fifteen steps, together with the superscript's המעלות, which properly does mean "steps," has led the early rabbis to tie the meaning of the one to the other.

Martin Luther, although rejecting the ancient theory that the fifteen songs of the Songs of Ascents corresponded to the fifteen temple steps,[63] nonetheless interpreted the superscript as meaning "Lied im höheren

---

συνέβη ἰσαρίθμους ᾠδὰς τοῖς ἀναβαθμοῖς εἶναι. κεῖται δὲ ἡ περὶ τῶν ᾠδῶν. καὶ τῶν λεγόντων αὐτὰς ἐφ᾽ ἑκάστου τῶν ἀναβαθμῶν τοῦ ναοῦ διάταξις ἐν τοῖς παραλειπομένοις.

Ekkehard Mühlenberg, *Psalmenkommentare aus der Katenüberlieferung,* vol. 2 (Patristische Texte und Studien 16; Berlin: Walter de Gruyter, 1977) 298.

[62]*b. Sukk.* 51*b.* This is seconded by *b. Mid.* 2:5. The setting portrayed in this reference is that of the water-drawing festival at the end of the first day of the Feast of Booths (cf. Gerard F. Willems, "Les psaumes dans la liturgie juive," *Bijdragen* 51 [1990] 410-411). It narrates a celebration of almost overwhelming joy, so that "He who has not seen the rejoicing at the place of the water-drawing has never seen rejoicing in his life" (*b. Sukk.* 51a). Delitzsch, *Psalms,* 266-267, rejects the fifteen-step interpretation on the grounds that the Talmudic tradition only says they are *parallel* to Ezek 40:26,31 and in fact has another tradition about the origin of the Songs of Ascents (see above, p. 14). So also Kittel, *Psalmen,* 388. Eerdmans, *Psalms,* 548, goes on to assert that, if it was specifically the Songs of Ascents that were sung on the temple steps, the Mishnaic tradition "would not have failed to report [this] further coincidence."

[63]Martin Luther, *A Commentary on the Psalms Called Psalms of Degrees; in which, among other interesting subjects, the scriptural doctrine respecting the divinely instituted and honorable estate of matrimony is explained and defended, in opposition to the Popish errors of monastic seclusion and enforced celibacy* (London: W. Simpkin and R. Marshall, 1819; original ca. 1514) 110: "But how should a man know all their [the ancient Israelites'] rites and ceremonies, especially after so long a time, whereby they are now worn clean out of the memory of all men?" Hengstenberg rejected this explanation because he thought certain of the songs (e.g. Psalms 121 and 122) could not have been sung inside the temple. Hengstenberg, *Psalms,* 3:404.

Chor." He admits much uncertainty vis-à-vis the superscript's meaning and prefers not to make frivolous conjecture. In his view it is better to

> abide in the simple and plain sense as much as I may, and judge that they are so called because the Levites or Priests were wont to sing them upon the stairs or some high place; even as with us he that beginneth the Psalms, or preacheth, standeth in a place above the rest, that he may be the better seen and heard.[64]

It is uncertain whether his translation is based on the idea of מעלה as an elevated place, or whether he was thinking of the steps on which the songs were recited, their being higher up than the rest of the congregation. In any case the interpretational crux, namely that the superscript refers to the position of the singers vis-à-vis the congregation, is not much affected.[65] In more recent times this explanation has been accepted only by Ferdinand Hitzig.[66] His opinion is that, since most of Psalms 120-129 consist of seven or eight verses, each verse corresponded to a stair on the stairway (the 7+8 steps leading from the temple to the inner sanctum). Later on this correspondence was forgotten, so that an entire psalm was thought to correspond to the ten steps for that ascent, as recorded in the LXX of Ezek 40:49. Only later, when the Songs of Ascents were correlated with the fifteen steps between the court of women and the Israelite court, were the last five songs added to the collection, in order to make the correspondence more nearly perfect. Needless to say, this all involves a fair amount of speculation on his part.

Liebreich[67] analyzed the language of the psalms in the collection and found that it corresponded closely to the wording of the priestly blessing in Num 6:24-26, specifically to its "four key words."[68] Nearly all the songs (with the exception of Psalms 124, 126, and 131, which are

---

[64]Luther, *Psalms of Degrees,* 109.

[65]It is possible that the "steps" interpretation influenced the early church, as well. It may be that the psalm known as the "gradual" (not necessarily from Psalms 120-134), which in the liturgy was sung between the first and second scripture readings and was sung on the altar steps, is related to their interpretation of this collection.

[66]Hitzig, *Psalmen,* 364-366.

[67]Leon J. Liebreich, "The Songs of Ascents and the Priestly Blessing," *JBL* 74 (1955) 33-36.

[68]Liebreich, "Songs of Ascents," 33.

"only indirectly connected with the Priestly Blessing"[69]) are directly connected with it. This blessing was pronounced (according to *t. Soṭa* 7:7) on the steps of the hall that led to the interior of the temple. Thus he renders the phrase שִׁיר הַמַּעֲלוֹת as "a Song rendered in conjunction with the Priestly Blessing which was pronounced on the מעלות האולם."[70]

The Procession to the Temple

Since Hermann Gunkel, and even more since his student Sigmund Mowinckel, the tendency in Psalms criticism has been to explain any given psalm by appeal to the presumed cultic background (*Sitz im Leben*) in which the psalm might have been performed. This program could quite easily lead (and often has led) to facile conjecture about the *Sitz im Leben* of a psalm. Gunkel argued that it was very important to offset this tendency by broad appeal to the better-known cultic services of Israel's contemporaries.[71] Mowinckel, although somewhat less well versed in the literature from the ancient Orient than was Gunkel, nonetheless took as the point of departure for much of his work in the *Sitz im Leben* of the Psalms the Babylonian *Akītu* festival.

At the *Akītu* festival, which occurred at the Babylonian new year, the cultic myth commemorated Marduk's ascendancy over all the other gods (especially over the Sumerian gods), as reflected in the so-called "creation epic."[72] It thus confirmed Babylon as the seat of governing power, and the present king as Marduk's regent over Sumero-Babylonia. Mowinckel argued that a very similar festival (the "Thronbesteigungs-fest") formed the nucleus of Israel's cultic life. In this festival YHWH was crowned as King over Israel (and, as at Babylon, over all creation) with the cultic shout יהוה מלך (Psalms 93-99), which he translated

---

[69]Liebreich ("Songs of Ascents," 36) posits that these three were added to the collection in order to make the number of songs correspond to the fifteen words of the blessing. In my opinion this is the weakest part of his thesis.

[70]Liebreich, "Songs of Ascents," 36.

[71]For example, see Gunkel, *Einleitung*, 6-7.

[72]See E. A. Speiser, "The Creation Epic," *ANET* 66-70.

"Yahwä ist König geworden."[73] This shout accompanied the festal procession of the New Year, in which the ark—symbolizing God's presence—was conveyed along the *via sacra* up to the Temple courts.

It is in this connection that Mowinckel posits that the Songs of Ascents were sung. For him they are songs to be sung during the festal procession with the ark into the temple courts.[74] This explanation is accepted by Lipiński,[75] and more tentatively by Kraus.[76] They are part of the festival itself, rather than songs sung by pilgrims *en route* to the festival. Thus Psalms 120-134 belong, along with Psalms 93-100 (and various other psalms), to the "Thronbesteigungspsalmen." Several motifs found in the Songs of Ascents attest this correlation: God as creator (Pss 121:2; 124:8; 134:3), the throne of YHWH on the hill in Jerusalem (Pss 123:1; 125:2; 134:2; 132:7), Zion as inviolable (Psalms 121; 125; 127A), and a few other minor motifs of this class of psalms.[77] Mowinckel has justly been criticized for ascribing too many psalms to

---

[73]Sigmund Mowinckel, *Psalmenstudien*, vol. 2, *Das Thronbesteigungsfest Jahwäs und der Ursprung der Eschatologie* (Oslo: Kristiana, 1921; reprinted, Amsterdam: P. Schippers, 1961) 38 and *passim*. This translation came under severe criticism, against which Mowinckel defended it in *The Psalms in Israel's Worship*, vol. 1 (Trans. D. R. Ap-Thomas from *Offersang og Sangoffer*, 1951; Nashville: Abingdon, 1962) 107-109. Mowinckel's appeal to the *Akītu* festival may be found throughout his writings, but his primary treatment of it is the second volume of *Psalmenstudien*.

[74]Mowinckel (*Psalmenstudien*, vol. 4, *Die technischen Termini in den Psalmenüberschriften* [Oslo: Kristiana, 1922; reprinted, Amsterdam: P. Schippers, 1961] 3-4) acknowledges that not all of the songs fit with this setting. For example, Psalm 134 was spoken in the temple precincts, not while on the way up to them. Similarly he thinks of Psalm 128 as a priestly blessing belonging to the temple worship. Thus he changes his position slightly, so as to include the entire festival, not only the procession, as the *Sitz im Leben* of the Songs of Ascents. Primarily, however, it is "die feierliche Festprozession" that gives its name to the Songs of Ascents. In *The Psalms in Israel's Worship* (1:3), Mowinckel specifies that the songs were "sung at the water-pouring rite on 'the great day of the festival,'" namely the eighth day of the celebration.

[75]Eduard Lipiński, *La Royauté de Yahwé dans la poésie et le culte de l'ancien Israël* (Brussels: Paleis der Academiën, 1968) 449. He relates the superscript to הַמַּעֲלוֹת in Neh 12:37, where Nehemiah and the returned Judeans ascend the stairs up from the city of David to the temple. The Songs of Ascents are "chantés lors des processions."

[76]Hans-Joachim Kraus, *Die Psalmen*, vol. 1 (BKAT 15; Neukirchen: Neukirchener Verlag, 1978) 18.

[77]Mowinckel, *Psalmenstudien*, 2:5. The references are his.

his "Thronbesteigungsfest," but even so the presence of Psalm 132 (which may envision a procession much like the one in 2 Samuel 6) in the collection, together with the many other elements leading one to think of Jerusalem, does tend to reinforce his view. It has the added advantage of being able to accommodate "steps" as a possible translation for המעלות, since it could refer to stairs leading up from the City of David to the temple, over which the pilgrims would travel on their way to the temple.[78]

Pilgrimage Songs

The more widely accepted cultic explanation of the superscript, and in fact the only theory that can be said to have approached *communis opinio,* explains the collection as a group of songs to be sung while on religious pilgrimage.[79] This view was, so far as I can determine, first proposed by Rabbi David Qimḥi. After discussing and rejecting the interpretations of the steps of the Temple and of the water that David "sang down," he proposed that they be interpreted as songs sung by people making pilgrimage to Israel from the dispersion in various

---

[78]So Kraus (*Psalmen,* 1:18), although he considers the meaning "pilgrimage" more weighty than that of "steps."

[79]Johann Gottfried Herder, *The Spirit of Hebrew Poetry* trans. James Marsh, vol. 2 (Burlington: Edward Smith, 1833 [From German *Der Geist der hebräischen Poesie,* 1782]) 261-264.   Theodoro Adriano Clarisse, *Psalmi Quindecim Hammaäloth, Philologice et Critice Illustrati* (Lugduni Batavorum: H. W. Hazenberg, 1819) 2-24. Bernhard Duhm, *Die Psalmen,* 2nd ed. (HKAT 14; Tübingen: J. C. B. Mohr [Paul Siebeck], 1922; orig. 1899) 428. Kittel, *Psalmen,* 387. Leslie C. Allen, *Psalms 101-150* (WBC 21; Waco, TX: Word Books, 1983) 220. Claus Westermann, "Formation of the Psalter," in *Praise and Lament in the Psalms,* trans. Keith R. Crim and Richard N. Soulen (Atlanta: John Knox Press, 1981) 250-258. Hans Schmidt (*Die Psalmen* [HAT 15; Tübingen: J. C. B. Mohr, 1934] 220) tentatively agrees with the "pilgrim song" hypothesis, but he emphasizes that many of the songs are not pilgrim songs, but rather pious reflections and songs from a completely different background. They were only *used* as pilgrim songs by incorporating them into the present collection. Gunkel (*Einleitung,* 453) states that since the superscript refers to the pilgrimage journey itself, none of the songs in the Songs of Ascents would have been performed in the temple. He also acknowledges that, because the superscript is itself unclear, this hypothesis is not possible to establish with certainty.

countries. He does not suggest interpreting the superscript with reference to a single historical event, such as "from Babylon." Rather, it seems that he views this pilgrimage as taking place many times, and in connection with the Jerusalem temple.[80] Qimḥi's interpretation is therefore best distinguished from the view, discussed above (pp. 9 -10), that the songs were songs sung by returnees from the diaspora who would now live in Palestine; for him it is primarily a ritual act.

Ernst Hengstenberg seems to have been the first to rehabilitate this proposal in the modern era. He took notice of the many uncommon linguistic characteristics, the simplicity of the images, and the songs' terseness and memorability. In his opinion these features were to be explained as "peculiarities of sacred popular and pilgrim song."[81] The collection, including songs that are not properly "pilgrim songs," constituted then a kind of "devotional handbook"[82] for pilgrims on their way to one of the great yearly feasts at Jerusalem.[83] More recently, Klaus Seybold has argued that Psalms 120-134 constitute a collection of songs written by pilgrims to the temple.[84] By isolating and removing additions from earlier strata and by analyzing linguistic and poetic characteristics (such as metaphorical images), he, like Hengstenberg before him, attempts to show that the songs had their origin not in "Lehrbuch-Norm" poetry of the official cultus, but in the poetry of the

---

[80]Jacob Bosniak, ed., *The Commentary of David Kimhi on the Fifth Book of the Psalms CVII-CL, edited on the basis of Manuscripts and Early Editions of the fifteenth and sixteenth centuries in the Library of Jewish Theological Seminary of America* (New York: Bloch, 1954) 153.

[81]Hengstenberg, *Psalms*, 3:407-408.

[82]Seybold (*Wallfahrtspsalmen*, 73) reckons it "wie eine Handreichung für Wallfahrer, eine Art *Vade mecum* mit Gebeten und Liedern, vielleicht ein brevier, auch mit Texten zur Meditation...." So also Duhm (*Psalmen*, 428) with the exception of Psalm 132, which he thinks is supplemental to the collection. Also Alphonse Maillot and André Lelièvre, *Les Psaumes, commentaires* (Genève: Labor et Fides, 1961) 136-137; E. J. Kissane, *The Book of Psalms*. Single volume edition (Dublin: Browne and Nolan, 1964. [orig. 1953, 1954]) xxvi.

[83]Cuthbert Cubitt Keet, *A Study of the Psalms of Ascents: A Critical and Exegetical Commentary upon Psalms CXX to CXXXIV* (London: Mitre, 1969) 15 and *passim*, preferring to make the pilgrimage occasion more general, ascribes it to the offering of first fruits, rather than purely to the yearly festivals, though he admits that the two are not mutually exclusive.

[84]Seybold, *Wallfahrtspsalmen*, 61-63.

common people.[85] Refreshingly, Seybold takes his cue not only from the superscript but also from the character of the songs themselves.[86] For him the superscript evidences the unity of the collection, but even apart from it the songs in the collection must still be treated as a unity.[87] However, he proceeds from there to edit out significant portions of nearly each of the songs, in order to fit them into his hypothesis more neatly. He then posits that the songs were votive offerings placed inside the temple, which were later edited together by cultic officials.[88] One is unwilling to agree wholeheartedly with his methods for extracting what he claims to be popular thinking as opposed to priestly thinking.[89]

Even so, the position that the collection of Songs of Ascents are "pilgrim songs," that is, a devotional collection of songs sung *en route* to the great festivals at Jerusalem, is an attractive one.[90] In the first place, most of the advantages listed for the historicizing interpretation can be applied here as well, since in many ways the return from Babylon is thought of as a pilgrimage to Jerusalem. Moreover, such an interpretation allows for the diversity of the songs[91] better than does Mowinckel's hypothesis.

---

[85]Seybold, *Wallfahrtspsalmen,* 41-42.

[86]So also Ewald, *Psalmen,* 195. He says, "Denn die Lieder sind unter einander an Geist und Leben, Sprache und Gedanken eben so eng verwandt wie sie sich von den sie umgebenden, ja auch fast allen andern Liedern scharf unterscheiden."

[87]Seybold, *Wallfahrtspsalmen,* 19-20.

[88]Seybold, *Wallfahrtspsalmen,* 60-61.

[89]Seybold's argument is circular: a given section of a psalm cannot be integral to the psalm because it is priestly in character. Therefore it must be a priestly addition. This is of course the problem faced by all attempts to separate sources from one another. But Seybold's use of this method seems to exceed normally accepted boundaries.

[90]Samuel Cox, *The Pilgrim Psalms: An Exposition of the Songs of Degrees* (London: Daldy, Ibister, 1874) 8, believes there may be a pun on the idea of the "ascending structure" of the songs, but the primary meaning is that of pilgrimage to the great feasts.

[91]W. O. E. Oesterley (*The Psalms, Translated with Text-critical and Exegetical Notes,* vol. 2 [London: SPCK, 1939] 500), for example, explains that the songs incorporated here that are not "pilgrim psalms" "may perhaps be accounted for on the supposition that they were incorporated, for one reason or another, in the course of time, in a collection of rolls which contained originally only pilgrim-psalms." Similarly also Kittel, *Psalmen,* 387-388; Mowinckel, *Psalmenstudien,* 4:3.

SUMMARY

Having rehearsed the history of the superscript's interpretation, the question remains whether any one of these has adequately explained the superscript to Psalms 120-134. The answer to this question must be No. The main reason for this is that all of the explanations outlined above had as their primary agenda (some more than others, as I have noted) precisely this concern. The function of much of this overemphasis on the superscript has been that the *Sitz im Leben* of the collection has been assumed uncritically to be that of whatever meaning the interpreter ascribes to the phrase "Songs of Ascents." It is quite preferable, as Buttenweiser hints,[92] to suspend judgment on the meaning of the superscript until one has made a thorough exegesis, with an eye to the historical and sociological milieu, of each of the songs. The basic problem with each of the attempts outlined above is that, despite the theory one espouses, at least some of the songs are problematic. The songs exhibit such apparently different *Sitze im Leben* that they could hardly be expected to fit well with any theory that posits a single background for all of them.

It is certain that מעלות, at least when in the plural and pointed in this way, means "steps" in most contexts (Isa 38:8; 2 Kgs 20:9,10,11; Neh 12:32). It seems most probable that some set of actual steps is meant by the superscript. But an examination of the theories presented above that account for the superscript will reveal that no one flight of steps comes immediately to mind. And even if it did, any of the alternatives that appeal to the meaning "steps" ultimately suffer from an inability to explain all of the songs in the collection satisfactorily.

At this point probably the most that can be said is that the precise meaning of שִׁיר הַמַּעֲלוֹת is uncertain. But the meaning must have been known at the time of its attachment to the songs in question, even if it should be impossible now to discern it. The best approach, then, is to suspend the question of the meaning of the superscript until further analysis of the individual songs in the collection, and of the collection as a whole, is made. This will help the interpreter not to ascribe characteristics and meanings to individual songs in the collection that

---

[92]Buttenweiser, *Psalms,* 375-376.

come about primarily as a result of trying to accommodate the psalm to one's idea of the superscript's meaning. It is such an analysis that the following chapters will seek to perform.

CHAPTER II

EXEGESIS OF THE SONGS OF ASCENTS

Before attempting to investigate the historical and religious background of the group of psalms in question, it is necessary to study each of them exegetically. In this chapter, the text, idiom, composition, and setting of each of the Songs of Ascents receive exegetical treatment. This investigation will provide the data with which it may be possible to hypothesize about the origin and character of the whole. Because of the nature of this study, the focus is primarily on historical and compositional issues, with other matters receiving treatment primarily in reference to those concerns. It is not my intent to try to replace or provide an alternative to the standard commentaries, but to examine primarily those aspects of the psalms that seem relevant to the question of the collection's origins and *Sitz im Leben*. The discussion is organized around two main priorities: (1) to establish the best possible textual base, and (2) insofar as possible to discuss the *Sitz im Leben* of each psalm, including any indications that there are of the date of composition and the geographical location in which it may have been composed.

I am of course aware of the difficulty of these projects, especially the latter. I am convinced, however, that some evidence may be gleaned by careful observation.

PSALM 120

1   A song of ascents:

   To YHWH, in my distress
     I call,[a] that [God][1] should answer me:

2   O YHWH, rescue my soul,[b]
     From deceiptful lip, from haughty tongue.[c]

3   What is given to you, and what is added to you,
     O haughty tongue?[d]

4   A warrior's sharp arrows
     Along with coals of broom plants!

5   Woe to me, for I have sojourned [in] Meshek,[e]
     I have dwelt among the tents of Qedar.

6   Too long has my soul settled itself[f]
     With the hater[g] of peace.

7   I am peaceful, but when I speak,[h]
     They are for war![i]

Notes to the Translation

a The perfect aspect here is probably to be read as *iterative*: that is, where the action is completed by the speaking of the words. Cf. Jonah 2:3 where almost the same exact construction appears. There it is clear that the prayer is understood as being from inside the belly of the fish, and therefore speaks in the present. So Kittel 388; cf. GKC §106i, pp. 311-312.

b In my translations I have distinguished between נֶפֶשׁ + pronominal suffix and the simple accusative pronominal suffix. Although the referents of these forms are

---

[1]The translations proffered here frequently sacrifice English idiom to clarity about the Hebrew text that lies behind the translation. They are not intended to replace the standard English translations, but rather to serve as a convenient point of reference for my readings of the psalms in question. The one exception that I have made to this general principle is that I have used inclusive language throughout. In cases where inclusive language translates the gender-specific language of the text, I have enclosed the words in question in brackets.

not usually different, their variation does seem to me poetically significant. This translation is admittedly unfelicitous because of the Platonic and Christian overtones of the word "soul," but it seems to me a greater violation to homogenize these two ways of referring to the individual.

c The phrase מִלָּשׁוֹן רְמִיָּה can be interpreted in two ways: the relationship between the two words is either genitive (with לָשׁוֹן repointed to לִלְשׁוֹן) or appositional. Gunkel's reading of רְמִיָּה as an adjective is improbable, since לָשׁוֹן is masculine in this sentence, whether read as the subject of the verbs or as the referent of the masculine pronouns.

d LXX translates πρὸς γλῶσσαν δολίαν, perhaps providing evidence that an original לִלְשׁוֹן was corrupted by haplography, as suggested by BHS (so also the Vulgate *ad linguam dolosam*; Jerome (*Iuxta Hebraeos*), however, appears to read with MT, making it likely that the Vulgate has followed the LXX). However, the principle of *lectio difficilior* would seem to argue that the MT, which still makes grammatical sense, be retained: the LXX reading clears up the ambiguity of the sentence a bit too conveniently.

e There is no preposition corresponding to the English "in," as one would expect to find. This would be the only case in the Hebrew Bible where the place of sojourning stands in the accusative case. Normally one expects a preposition such as בְּ, עַל, or עִם to precede the name of the place where one sojourns. Thus the LXX has taken מֹשֵׁךְ as a verb: οἴμμοι, ὅτι ἡ παροικία μου ἐμακρύνθη. The parallel with Qedar, however, renders unlikely the proposition that this was the original meaning.

f Taking the לָהּ as a pleonastic *dativus ethicus* (GKC §119f; also see Ronald J. Williams, *Hebrew Syntax: An Outline* [Toronto: University of Toronto Press, 1976] §272). For this idiomatic (or formulaic) construction the norm seems to be that a short form of the complaint is uttered in the last half of a sentence. This short form is then followed by the same verb with נֶפֶשׁ as the subject and לָהּ. The rest of the sentence is then often enlarged, as well. This exact construction, with a different verb, is also found in Psalm 123, but so far as I can determine, nowhere else in the Hebrew Bible.

g LXX translates with a plural τῶν μισούντων, but the Hebrew is best left in the singular, and read as a collective, despite the BHS suggestion of שׂוֹנְאַי.

h This last bicolon has puzzled nearly every translator and commentator of Psalm 120. LXX takes אֲנִי־שָׁלוֹם with the preceding verse and translates μετὰ τῶν μισούντων τὴν εἰρήνην ἤμην εἰρηνικός. But the chiasm formed by שָׁלוֹם and מִלְחָמָה argues against this. Moreover, as is often the case in the Songs of Ascents, the MT of v. 6 appears to read the verse correctly as an expansion of the ideas in both parts of v. 5. Most commentators regard 7aβ as elliptic for "I speak peace." A more accurate appraisal of the phrase אֲנִי־שָׁלוֹם may be obtained by comparing the similar construction in Ps 109:4, וַאֲנִי תְפִלָּה. The phrase makes adjectival use of a substantive (cf. JPSV, "I am all peace").

i LXX adds δωρεάν, apparently to emphasize the contrast.

Interpretation

Several difficult translational and textual problems are involved in
the interpretation of Psalm 120. These will have to be treated before any
discussion of the setting can follow.

In the first place, there is no real consensus about the tense of the
verbs in v. 1. One option is that the verb קָרָאתִי in v. 1, though in the
perfect aspect, nonetheless conveys present meaning. The main reason
for this supposition is that what follows appears not to presume an
answered prayer, but rather is a prayer *to be answered*.[2] On the other
hand, a good many scholars maintain that the prayer has already been
answered, so that the verbs communicate the past tense (more commonly
communicated by the perfect and consecutive imperfect).[3] The problem
arises from the fact that, although the perfect aspect *ought to* denote past
time in this context (most often in prayers it does just that), to view the
verbs in this way is in effect to deny the poignancy of the rest of the
psalm, in which pathos predominates. I take קָרָאתִי in the performative
or iterative sense, as in the idioms "I testify" (e.g. Deut 8:19) and "I
swear" (e.g. Jer 22:5).[4] The consecutive וַיַּעֲנֵנִי then carries the force of
"that [God] should answer me." This does justice both to the perfect
aspect of the first and to the consecutive imperfect aspect of the second,
as well as to the character of the rest of the psalm.

The second interpretational problem is that of vv. 3-4. The subject
of the verbs in v. 3 is ambiguous, as is the relationship between v. 3 and

---

[2]So de Wette, *Kommentar über die Psalmen*, 573; Kittel, *Psalmen*, 388. Kraus
(*Psalmen*, 2:1008) translates the consecutive imperfect, "Daß er mich erhöre."
Oswald Loretz (*Die Psalmen: Beitrage der Ugarit-Texte zum Verständnis von
Kolometrie und Textologie der Psalmen* [AOAT 207; Neukirchen: Neukirchener
Verlag, 1979] 238-240) simply disposes of the verse.

[3]Hermann Hupfeld (*Die Psalmen. Übersetzt und ausgelegt*, vol. 2 [Gotha:
Friedrich Andreas Perthes, 1862] 256) believes that the sentence refers to a previous
prayer, as the basis for the psalmist's hope in the present case. For Kissane (*Book of
Psalms*, 564) vv. 2-3 become an expression of confidence. Maillot and Lelièvre
(*Psaumes*, 137) posit that the pilgrim has arrived in port, and therefore can claim past
divine favors, but the fact that the pilgrim is as yet outside Judah allows the lament
that follows. Weiser (*Psalms*, 742) goes so far as to call Psalm 120 a thanksgiving
psalm, even though v. 1 is the only part that can really be adduced as such. Similarly
also Dahood, *Psalms*, 3:195.

[4]See Williams, *Hebrew Syntax*, §164.

v. 4. Because of the parallel between the verbs in v. 3 and those of the traditional oath formula (יַעֲשֶׂה...יֹסִיף), most scholars have thought that YHWH is the understood subject. The meaning attached to the verbs, then, is that YHWH would judge one called "deceitful tongue" in the same way that God would judge a violator of an oath. In this view the parallel מַה...וּמַה is thought to be an interrogatory form of the formula כֹּה...וְכֹה, so that the whole phrase becomes a mimicry of the oath formula. However, if this is the case, why is the Deity not invoked? And why not use the proper verbs? At best this sentence may be said to *imply* the wording of the oath formula. It seems to me, though, that a better way to explain this odd verbal parallel (both here and in the oath formula) lies rather in the generality of the verbs עשׂה, נתן, and יסף, all of which are used with a great variety of nuances. The meaning in the case of Psalm 120 seems to be that a deceitful tongue is only capable of doing immense harm. The metaphor of the tongue as a destructive organ that launches words as one launches arrows, or whose effects are like those of burning coals, is used often enough in Israelite lament to lead one naturally in this direction (cf. Pss 57:5; 64:4; 7:13, although the subject there could be either God or an evil man; Jer 9:2).[5] Such an interpretation receives support from the fact that the psalm continues by denouncing the poet's enemies for their "warlike" conduct. If one reads these two lines as a curse on the false-tongued one, the shift back into the lament in the verses that follow is difficult to understand. But if one reads it as a denunciation of the false tongue's primary characteristic—destructiveness—then the psalm's outline makes good sense.

The last three verses are the final indictment on the enemies, whose evil ways inspire the speaker to pray to YHWH for assistance. Whereas in the first part of the psalm the speaker describes the enemies with the metaphor of a malicious tongue (together with dependent metaphors), in this second half the metaphor is that of sojourning with hostile foreign people.[6] It is possible that the original poet indeed dwelt in regions such

---

[5]The image of God's judgment as an arrow or as fire (a theophanic image; see Ps 18:9,13,14) also occurs (cf. Pss 64:8; 140:10).

[6]It is possible that the mention of Meshek and Qedar here is only a proverbial expression for peoples that are far away. In this case the idea would be that the psalmist had sojourned afar off, and upon return to the land found his or her

as these, but the juxtaposition of the place names Meshek and Qedar, which lie at a far remove from one another,[7] tends to argue against this. This sentence seems not to refer to an actual sojourning in those lands, but rather to use them metaphorically symbolizing either the outermost reaches of the known world or the particularly bellicose people with whom the psalmist had to do (see below, pp. 35-37).

The last image to find expression in the psalm is that of war. Clearly the other images already encountered shift the focus of the image away from that of actual skirmishes and their counterparts of larger scale. Rather, this is another metaphor for the psalmist's experience of contentious enemies, to whom the psalmist refers collectively as שׂוֹנֵא שָׁלוֹם, "the one who hates peace." It is these enemies (cf. the plural הֵמָּה) who, despite the poet's peacefulness, prefer "war."

Through several distinct images, then, Psalm 120 asks for divine assistance against slanderous enemies whose intent is to deprive one of שָׁלוֹם, the state of harmonious existence with God and others, securing mutual prosperity and health. The psalmist's enemies are pictured in two distinct ways: They are slanderous, with tongues that pierce and burn; and they are foreigners, portrayed as warlike neighbors who will not listen to peaceful overtures.

Several things can be observed about the way Psalm 120 is presented. Formally the psalm is in two strophes, each consisting of three cola, plus an invocation of the Deity in the first line. After the introductory v. 1 follows a tricolon with the prayer proper, requesting Divine aid. This prayer is linked with another tricolon that probably addresses the enemy with questions about the deceitful tongue's value, although this is uncertain. Having thus addressed the slanderous person, the poet answers the rhetorical question with a bicolon about the tongue's worth, or rather, lack of it. With that said the poet moves on to the second strophe, which consists of three bicola that lament the treachery of the psalmist's enemies, through the metaphor of a sojourn among hostile people. The psalm concludes with a summary of the nature of the

---

credibility diminished, hence the lament. But such an interpretation is for the most part precluded by the parallel with "the hater of peace" (v. 6).

[7]Meshek is located in the far North (in Israelite cosmology), near the Caspian Sea; Qedar is a region of the Arabian desert.

problem, again couched in the metaphor of strife between sojourner and one's inhospitable neighbors.

Stylistically the psalm is among the best examples of the so-called step parallelism (*anadiplosis*), in which a word or idea of one line leads into a following line, providing an effective transition between parts of the poem. This linking of verses may be represented graphically as follows:

1	יהוה	
2	יהוה	לְשׁוֹן רְמִיָּה
3		לָשׁוֹן רְמִיָּה question
4		response
5	שֶׁכֶן	
6	שֹׁכֵן	שָׁלוֹם
7		שָׁלוֹם

This stylistic feature is a more subtle poetic device than first appears. It is primarily through this "step" device that the poet makes transitions between lines that at first blush have little to do with each other. For example, the transition from praying to YHWH (v. 2) to addressing the enemy is masterfully smoothed by the repetition of "treacherous tongue." Similarly, the question-answer transition provided by vv. 3-4 mediates between predominantly tricolaic lines and the longer bicola of the second stanza. The repetition of the idea of dwelling with foreigners (v. 6) mediates between vv. 5 and 7, which again appear to have little in common unless one infers in the place names a martial reference. This is a finely crafted poem.

Little can be said with certainty about the *Sitz im Leben* of the song. It is an individual lament, which, as Eerdmans observes,[8] "ends abruptly," which is to say, contains no statement of salvation. This being the case one most naturally expects it to have belonged in some sort of ritual setting. But even this much cannot be affirmed with certainty.

The names Meshek and Qedar do provide some basis on which to postulate the period in which the psalm was first uttered. The song uses these place names as proverbial for the idea, "haters of peace."[9] If a time

---

[8]Eerdmans, *Psalms*, 555-556.
[9]So Allen, *Psalms 101-150*, 146.

can be determined when people from these places were especially
notorious for their pugnaciousness, then such a time period would be
plausible for this song. Such a time does in fact seem to be in evidence
in the Hebrew Bible. In the oracles of Ezekiel against Gog of Magog
(Ezekiel 38-39), Gog is mentioned twice as the "Prince of Meshek and
Tubal," (Ezek 38:2,3; 39:1) on whom God's judgment was about to
come.[10] This prince was singled out by Ezekiel as especially worthy of
Divine judgment, since his actions of plunder were contemptible.
Ezekiel parodies Gog's attitude (Ezek 38:10-12):

> On that day ideas will enter your mind, and you will devise an evil
> plot and say, "I will go up against a land of unwalled villages; I will
> go against its quiet people who dwell securely—all of them dwelling
> without walls, and having no bars or gates—to seize spoil and carry
> off plunder; to assail the waste places that are now inhabited, against
> the people who were gathered from the nations, who have gotten
> cattle and goods, who dwell at the center of the earth."

Ezekiel also refers to Meshek as people who "spread terror in the land of
the living" (Ezek 32:26), before they go down to Sheol. Aside from
these references in Ezekiel (also Ezek 27:13, where the term seems only
to represent a people far away) there is virtually no reference to Meshek
(other than the genealogies in Gen 10:2 and 1 Chr 1:5,17) in the Hebrew
Bible. Various rebellions against Persian power took place in the two
centuries that followed the Persian conquest of Babylon in 539 BCE,
particularly the unrest at the beginning of Darius I's reign and during the
decline of Persia's power in the fourth century. It is not known whether

---

[10]In the Genesis 10 genealogy Meshek and Tubal are sons of Japheth, the son of
Noah who went North. It can safely be assumed that this is the same people group
thought of there. The Assyrian annals ("Midas [*mi-ta-a*] king of Musku [*muš-ki*]," in
the reign of Sargon II, 722-705 BCE; *ANET*, 284) and Herodotus (μοσχοι; *Hist.*
§395) place Meshek just south of the Caspian Sea. Several commentators assert that
Meshek, like Qedar, is the name of an Arabian tribe (Hitzig, *Psalmen*, 367; Hermann
Gunkel, *Die Psalmen, überseβt und erklärt* (HKAT 2; Göttingen: Vandenhoeck &
Ruprecht, 1926) 537-538; Klaus Seybold, *Die Psalmen: Eine Einführung* [Urban-
Taschenbücher 382; Stuttgart: W. Kohlhammer, 1986], 130-131), but evidence for
this seems to be lacking. For a brief summary of the place name see M. J. Mellink,
"Meshech," *IDB* 3:357-358. On the (Pseudo-?) Ezekiel pericope and its historical
referents see Walther Zimmerli, *Ezekiel* (Hermeneia; Philadelphia: Fortress, 1979)
2:302-304.

Yehud took part in these rebellions, but Egypt did, and it is quite possible that Yehud was caught in the middle.[11] The period of these rebellions would be another option for the date of the psalm.

Qedar is the tribal name of bedouin living in the Arabian Peninsula. In the Hebrew Bible the term comes to refer to almost any Arabian tribe. Primarily they were shepherds and traders; the criticism that they were warlike is somewhat unusual.[12] There are, however, two known occasions on which Qedar did fit such a description. During the reign of Ashurbanipal (668-633 BCE) the Qedarite Ammuladi rebelled against Assyria by attacking its buffer zone, Palestine. The attempt was put down by Ashurbanipal, but only after the Qedarites had succeeded in displacing large numbers of previously transjordanian Edomites, who moved onto south-Judahite territory. This seems to be the background of Jeremiah's oracle proclaiming that Nebuchadrezzar would plunder Qedar's wealth (Jer 49:28-33). A second possibility is during the time of Nehemiah, who is said to have had conflicts with a certain Geshem; according to an inscription from Tell el-Maskhutah in Egypt, Geshem is the name of a "king of Qedar," although the identification is less than certain.[13] It seems reasonable to suppose that the same antipathy might have been present during Zerubbabel's time, although there is no evidence for this. To sum up, the coupling of Meshek and Qedar provide some evidence that the psalm is postexilic, perhaps originating at the end of the sixth century, but more likely in the first half of the fifth century.

---

[11]John H. Hayes and J. Maxwell Miller, *A History of Ancient Israel and Judah* (Philadelphia: Westminster, 1986), 445-465; Lester L. Grabbe, *Judaism from Cyrus to Hadrian*, vol. 1, *The Persian and Greek Periods* (Minneapolis, MN: Fortress Press, 1992) 139-142.

[12]The phrase אָהֳלֵי קֵדָר "the tents of Qedar" is used with quite peaceful inferences (Jer 49:28-33; Cant 1:5). The name "Hazor" in the Jeremiah text should perhaps be repointed חָצֵר, an unwalled settlement, in which the Qedarites were said to live (Isa 42:11).

[13]Grabbe, *Judaism from Cyrus to Hadrian*, 1:85-86.

PSALM 121

1   A song of ascents:

    I lift up my eyes to the mountains;
      From where does my help come?[a]
2   My help is from[b] YHWH,
      The maker of heaven and earth.

3   May [God] not let[c] your foot slip,
      May your Guardian not sleep.
4   Witness![d] [God] does not sleep
      Nor does [God] slumber—the Guardian of Israel.

5   YHWH is your Guardian,
      YHWH is your Shade,[e] at[f] your Right Hand.
6   By day the sun—It shall not smite you—
      Nor the moon in the night

7   YHWH shall guard you from all harm
      [God] shall guard your life.
8   YHWH shall guard your going out and your return[g]
      From now and forever more.

Notes to the Translation

[a] *Contra* the opinion of some scholars (Alexander, *Psalms*, 205; Duhm, *Psalmen*, 429), the particle מֵאַיִן seems to me to be interrogative, not relative. I thus agree with de Wette, *Kommentar über die Psalmen*, 576-577; Julius Morgenstern, "Psalm 121," *JBL* 58 (1939) 311-323; Keet, *A Study of the Psalms of Ascents*, 27; Dahood, *Psalms*, 3:199; Kraus, *Psalmen*, 2:1012; Anderson, *Book of Psalms*, 851; and Claus Westermann, *Ausgewählte Psalmen: übersetzt und erklärt* (Göttingen: Vandenhoeck & Ruprecht, 1984), 202-203. Several scholars (T. H. Weir, "Psalm cxxi. 1," *ExpTim* 27 [1915/16] 90-91; Paul Joüon, *Grammaire de l'hébreu biblique* [Graz, Austria: Akademischen Druck, 1965] 429) interpret the particle מֵאַיִן as an indirect question. Daniel Grossberg (*Centripetal and Centrifugal Structures in Biblical Poetry*, SBLMS 39 [Atlanta, GA: Scholars Press, 1989], 30) proposes that in fact the particle functions in both ways which, using the terminology employed by

Cyrus Gordon, he calls "Janus-faced parallelism": When considered in light of what precedes it has a declarative sense; but when considered in light of what follows, it has an interrogative sense.

  b The use of a pleonastic עַם is common in the Songs of Ascents. Dahood (*Psalms*, 3:200) posits that מֵעַם means "from the home" (he compares the expression to the French *chez*), i.e. the heavenly mountain.

  c As one would expect, אַל seems to indicate here a shift into the vetitive mode (so LXX; for further arguments see below). It may be, though, that a vetitive is not necessary, but rather a strong conviction that this *cannot* happen. So GKC §107p; §109e. The rest of the verbs—which I have mostly translated with the English "shall..."—clearly have a benedictory function, even though most are not jussive.

  d The purpose of הִנֵּה here is to give the assurance of protection to the one being blessed.

  e The LXX probably rightly paraphrases צֵל with σκέπη "shelter."

  f The phrase עַל־יַד יְמִינֶךָ is translated literally, "upon your right hand." The somewhat uncertain meaning of the phrase, together with the parallel with the divine epithets "shade" and "guardian" (despite the fact that the other two cola have יהוה), has led Dahood (*Psalms*, 3:201) to interpret "right hand" as the title of a protector and עַל as a divine epithet. Most other comentators interpret it as the protector's position (Pss 16:8; 109:31; 110:5), referring to "shade" as a protector's title (Pss 17:8; 36:8; 57:2; Jer 48:45; Num 14:9; Isa 30:2,3).

  g LXX reverses the order of the two infinitive construct verbs: κύριος φυλάξει τὴν εἴσοδόν σου καὶ τὴν ἔξοδόν σου. The image in the MT is that of leaving the city in the morning to do daily work and return at night (Ewald, *Psalmen*, 250; Charles Augustus Briggs and Emilie Grace Briggs, *A Critical and Exegetical Commentary on the Book of Psalms* [ICC 15; New York: Charles Scribner and Sons, 1906] 447-448); the LXX perhaps interprets the image as that of pilgrims arriving at Jerusalem, and leaving at the end of the festival. Some authors (Kissane, *Book of Psalms*, 568; Kraus, *Psalmen*, 2:1014; Westermann, *Ausgewählte Psalmen*, 203) regard the phrase in Hebrew as a reference to leaving on pilgrimage and safe return.

Interpretation

The famous first two lines of the song have been the source of some speculation. What have the hills to do with the affirmation that help is from YHWH?[14] Are they viewed negatively, referring to the various

---

[14]Duhm (*Psalmen*, 429) sees the question as irrelevant. He interprets the phrase "to the hills" simply to mean "Nach oben." So also Westermann, *Ausgewählte Psalmen*, 202. P. H. Pollock ("Psalm 121," *JBL* 59 [1940] 411-412), perhaps with tongue in cheek, proposes that it refers to the dangers involved in mountain climbing for sport ("adventure").

"high places" from which the singer finds that help does not come;[15] are they the holy mountains as the abode of God, the place of YHWH's theophany;[16] or are they hills that separate the pilgrim, who faces severe dangers in travel, from the land to which she or he sojourns?[17] Despite the standing of scholars who support such a view, it seems to me implausible that "mountains" could represent non-Yahwistic deities. The song seems completely unconcerned with polemic against other gods. Its sole concern is that YHWH protects. At the beginning of this song, then, the idea of lifting one's eyes to the mountains means to scan the horizon, not searching out some place from which to seek help, but rather recognizing that help from YHWH comes no matter where one is. The remainder of the psalm expands on this theme.

Psalm 121 is divided into two parts. The first part (vv. 1-2) is a confession of trust in YHWH. The second part (vv. 3-8) is a response, a benediction that invokes YHWH as the one who protects the first speaker from any kind of harm during daily life.[18] This formal division is based

---

[15]Calvin, *Book of Psalms*, 62-63; Ewald, *Psalmen*, 242; Schmidt, *Psalmen*, 222; Kissane, *Book of Psalms*, 568 (with the mountains representing human help that disappoints); Drijvers, *Psalms*, 154; Otto Eissfeldt, "Psalm 121," in *Kleine Schriften*, ed. Rudolf Sellheim and Fritz Maass (Tübingen: J. C. B. Mohr [Paul Siebeck], 1966) 498; Erhard S. Gerstenberger, Konrad Jutzler and Hans Jochen Boecker, *Die Psalmen in der Sprache unserer Zeit: Der Psalter und die Klagelieder eingeleitet, übersetzt und erklärt* (Neukirchen: Neukirchener Verlag, 1972) 201; Rick Marrs, "The Šyry-Hm^{c}lwt (Psalms 120-134): A Philological and Stylistic Analysis" (Ph.D. diss., Johns Hopkins University, 1982) 24.

[16]Hengstenberg, *Psalms*, 3:417-418; Hupfeld, *Psalmen*, 2:264; Alexander, *Psalms*, 3:205; Briggs and Briggs, *Book of Psalms*, 446; Kittel, *Psalmen*, 390; Keet, *A Study of the Psalms of Ascents*, 27; Dahood, *Psalms*, 3:200.

[17]De Wette, *Kommentar über die Psalmen*, 576-577; P. Volz, "Zur Auslegung von Psalm 23 und 121," *Neue Kirchliche Zeitschrift* 36 (1925) 576-585; Morgenstern, "Psalm 121," 311-316; Albert Jan Rasker, "Psalm 121," in Georg Eichholz, ed., *Herr, tue meine Lippen auf: Eine Predigthilfe*, 2d ed. (Wuppertal-Barmen: Emil Müller Verlag, 1961) 5:78; James Limburg, "Psalm 121: A Psalm for Sojourners," *WW* 5 (1985) 184.

[18]So Dahood, *Psalms*, 3:199. The psalm is divided differently by some commentators. For Schmidt, (*Psalmen*, 221-222) vv. 1 and 3 are questions put by a pilgrim come to the temple doors and asking admittance; vv. 2 and 4 are priestly responses (he compares to Psalms 15 and 24A); the rest of the song is a priestly blessing on those entering the temple. He emends v. 2 to read the 2nd person suffix and v. 3 to read the 1st person pronominal suffix, to fit with this scheme. It is, however, unattested in the early mss and versions.

upon a number of criteria, the most important of which the repetition of two *Leitworten*, or key terms. The repetition of עֶזְרִי "my help" in the first two verses sets this unit off by itself. In vv. 3-8 the *Leitwort* is no longer "my help," but forms of the verb שׁמר "keep, watch, guard." This observation is reinforced by what appears to be a shift in speaker. The supplicant becomes a "you" rather than an "I."

Careful attention to the shifts in perspective yields fruitful results in terms of defining the nature of this poem. The first two lines are a statement of faith, in the form of an answered rhetorical question. Its rhetorical nature is reinforced by a "great pause" implied after the formulaic epithet "maker of heaven and earth," and is further underlined by the shift in person and a line of what is by all appearances a prayer in the vetitive mode (v. 3), in effect prohibiting YHWH's sleep.[19] In other words, it is a blessing over the supplicant, who has just affirmed faith in the God who created heaven and earth. Throughout vv. 4-8, as in v. 3, the supplicant is addressed in the second-person singular. Formally, then, vv. 4-8 constitute a blessing, announcing the Divine protection that was prayed for in v. 3.

The genre of Psalm 121 is that of blessing. After the supplicant's rhetorical question and answer, the second speaker (a priest?) presides over the song, which amounts to a oracle that God will "guard" (שׁמר) all of life for the worshiper. This is the meaning of the various parallel words in the song. Just as "heaven and earth" means essentially "all that exists," so the pairing of sun with moon and day with night (v. 6) means "any harm that might come to you," and carries with it the connotation that God's watchfulness never ceases, either by day or by night.[20] The two sides of this are also of course reflected in assertion that Israel's Guardian does not sleep (v. 4), and is always present to defend (v. 5bβ) and protect from "all harm" (v. 7). In the final verse the pairing of "your going out" and "your coming in" refers to the daily leaving the city to work crops outside the walls, and the return to the city at nightfall. The

---

[19]Bruce K. Waltke and Michael Patrick O'Connor, *An Introduction to Biblical Hebrew Syntax* (Winona Lake, IN: Eisenbrauns, 1990) 567, n. 6.

[20]It seems little more than speculation, given the pairing of sun and moon, to suppose that the moon symbolizes the "noxious influences operating in the night" (Alexander, *Psalms*, 206).

point of the psalm is that at all times, in all places, whatever one is doing, YHWH provides protection.

There are several important clues about the milieu of Psalm 121. The most important is perhaps the formula that has YHWH as the "creator of heaven and earth," which is almost certainly a part of Jersalemite tradition.[21] Many scholars have gone another step and identified such creation language more specifically in connection with major cultic observances, most notably that of the enthronement festival,[22] or the covenant festival.[23] Whether or not one accepts these explanations as likely, at least the overwhelming importance of the creation traditions for the Jerusalem Temple and for royal shrines in general argues for a Jerusalemite setting. This appraisal is strengthened by what appears to be another distinctively Jerusalemite formula: מֵעַתָּה וְעַד־עוֹלָם "from now, and forevermore."[24] The Divine Name is repeated enough times to cause one to think of a theophanic revelation of

---

[21]Kraus, *Psalmen*, 2:1013-1014; Norman C. Habel, "'Yahweh, Maker of heaven and Earth': A Study in Tradition Criticism," *JBL* 91 (1972) 321-337. For the phrase itself see Gen 14:19 where קנה has essentially the same meaning as עשׂה (cf. Gen 4:1, and elsewhere in the Genesis creation stories where the עשׂה is used alongside of ברא). For an examination of קנה with this meaning in both biblical and extrabiblical sources see Umberto Cassuto, *A Commentary on the Book of Genesis*, vol. 1, *From Adam to Noah*, trans. Israel Abrahams (Jerusalem: Central Press, 1961) 199ff. The formula עשֵׂה שָׁמַיִם וָאָרֶץ appears two other times in the Songs of Ascents (Pss 124:8; 134:3), and twice outside the collection (Pss 115:15; 146:6). Similar constructions (with the verb עשׂה and the same direct objects) are found in Ps 135:6 and Isa 44:24. See also the discussion in Chap. 3, pp. 137-138.

[22]The classic presentation of this view is Mowinckel, *Psalmenstudien*, 2:45-50. For him, all creation language belongs to the milieu of the *Thronbesteigungsfest*, the celebration of God's (and by extension, the temporal king's) conquering of chaos and right rulership.

[23]Weiser (*Psalms*, 34) regards the "adoption" of creation theology into Israelite belief as "a secondary phase in its [Israelite religion's] development." The covenant festival, the primary focus of which was historical rather than mythical, was prior to that phase (44).

[24]The formula appears eight times in the Hebrew Bible (Isa 9:6; 59:21; Mic 4:7; and Pss 113:2; 115:18; 121:8; 125:2; 131:3), three of which are in the Songs of Ascents, and all of which receive their impetus from the Jerusalem cultus. In Isa 9:6 it is associated with the everlasting kingship; and in Micah 4:7 it refers to YHWH's eternal rule in Zion. On the history of this "petrified" formula in the biblical and pre-biblical literature, see Samuel E. Loewenstamm, "The Formula *mē ʿattā wĕʿad ōlām*," in *Comparative Studies in Biblical and Ancient Oriental Literatures* (AOAT 204; Neukirchen-Vluyn: Neukirchener Verlag, 1980) 166-170.

the Name, as may have taken place in the Jerusalem cult.[25] In fact no extra-Jerusalemite elements (with the exception of "Israel," v. 3, which is not in any case exclusively Northern) appear in the song.

Even though the general milieu out of which Psalm 121 came is rather apparent, the date is completely enigmatic. There does not appear to be any linguistic peculiarity or historical reference of any sort that can assist in fixing a date. The language is stylized enough to be at home in almost any era of worship at Jerusalem.

Although no date can be given to Psalm 121, its genre is clear enough. It is what might be called a "responsorial blessing." The beginning of the song reads "I lift my eyes to the hills; from whence does my help come?" This question has often been taken to mean that the speaker is inside Jerusalem facing toward the hills that surround the city, and hence, that the song is a farewell blessing analogous to the entrance liturgies of Psalms 15 and 24. But the rest of the song does not support this view. What is at issue is not a safe journey for the pilgrim, but rather the protection of God in workaday life.

PSALM 122

1   A song of ascents; David's:

     I rejoiced among those who had said to me,
         "Let us go to the House of YHWH!"
2   When our feet were standing[a]
         In your gates, O Jerusalem.

3   Jerusalem is built
         As a city to which its community is bound;[b]
4   To which the tribes went up,
         The tribes of Yah,[c]
     The congregation of Israel,[d]
         To praise[e] the Name of YHWH.

---

[25]Weiser, *Psalms*, 41-42.

5   For[f] there thrones for judgment were established[g]
     The thrones of the house of David!

6   Seek the peace of Jerusalem;[h]
     May those who love you prosper!
7   Peace be inside your walls,
     Prosperity in your towers!

8   For the sake of my brothers
     And of my neighbors, I will say,
     Peace be within you!
9   For the sake of the house of YHWH our God,
     I will seek good for you.

Notes to the Translation

a   Since הָיוּ is in the perfect aspect, one is naturally inclined toward past time. The rhetorical exposure of the participle עֹמְדוֹת emphasizes the concurrent character of this verbal unit with the active verb of v. 1. The singer rejoiced (with peers) once the city gates had been reached.

b   For this substantival use of the normally adverbial יַחְדָּו; cf. Deut 33:5. The MT accentuation is probably correct in its reading כְּעִיר as part of 3b. This reading is uncertain, however, and no adequate explanation has yet been suggested for it. Somehow the idea of "built" must be taken together with the hemicolon that follows. It is not simply that the community is bound to it, but that this binding is related to "building."   Probably what is in view here is the idea that support from the community makes the city strong. Hence the translation "wohlgebaut," proposed by de Wette (*Kommentar über die Psalmen,* 579) has been widely accepted. So also Schmidt (*Die Psalmen,* 222): "לֹהּ und יַחְדָּו verstärken den im Zeitwort liegenden Begriff des festen Gefüges."   Alternatively, many interpreters translate the phrase with something like "bound firmly together" (RSV; cf. JPSV "a city knit together"), with essentially the same meaning. Dahood (*Psalms,* 3:205) vocalizes the לֹה as *lāhū* and the יַחְדּו as *yaḥīdu,* rendering the phrase "compacted by him [YHWH] alone."   Kraus (*Psalmen,* 2:1018) suggests that this verse may refer to a ritual circumambulation of the city walls, as in Ps 48:13-14.

c   The expression שִׁבְטֵי־יָהּ "the tribes of Yah" occurs only here in the HB. The normal expression is שִׁבְטֵי־יִשְׂרָאֵל "the tribes of Israel," although other tribal names occasionally replace "Israel." The best explanation for this is probably that the expression derives from a provenance other than Jerusalem (perhaps North Israel, which is probably the origin of שִׁבְטֵי־יִשְׂרָאֵל), which produced the final form of the majority of the literature in the HB.

d   11QPs[A] reads עדת ישראל (cf. Symmachus ἐκκλησία τοῦ Ισραὴλ). The *lectio difficilior* is probably that of the MT (which has been attested by another

Qumran text; see Emile Puech, "Fragments du Psaume 122 dans un manuscrit Hébreu de la grotte IV," *RevQ* 9 [1978] 547-554), but in this case the likelihood of the MT reading is somewhat diminished (in my opinion) because of the excellent parallelism produced if one follows 11QPs^A. The MT's extra *lamed* can perhaps be explained as a projection from the following two words. LXX appears to read with the consonantal MT, but goes its own way in interpretation: μαρτύριον τῷ Ισραηλ τοῦ ἐξομολογήσασθαι τῷ ὀνόματι κυρίου· The phrase עֵדָת יִשְׂרָאֵל occurs in the MT eleven times (Exod 12:3, 6, 19, 47; Lev 4:13; Num 16:9; 32:4; Josh 22:18, 20; 1 Kgs 8:5 = 2 Chr 5:6) with the meaning "congregation of Israel." These passages seem to reflect a north-Israelite tradition-historical setting.

e The MT accentuation is correct, against Kraus (*Psalmen*, 2:1016) who in order to retain the 3:2 meter takes לְהֹדוֹת together with "ordinance for Israel," rather than "the name of YHWH." The ordinance referred to is the pilgrimage, not praise.

f The כִּי probably indicates the reason for Jerusalem as the place to which pilgrimage was made, rather than the reason for the praising.

g I parse this as a hiphil perfect (possibly a hophal perfect "be inhabited"), written defectively, dividing the words שָׁם / הֵישְׁבוּ. Alternatively, the ה could be retained with שָׁמָּה as printed in BHS, and the verb could be parsed as a defectively written hiphil imperfect. It cannot be translated as an understood "they" sitting "on" the thrones. This idea is almost always conveyed by עַל (Jer 29:16 has אֶל; Pss 9:5; 132:11,12; Neh 3:7 have לְ), and is never simply in the accusative. For examples of הֵישִׁיב "be set, established" see KB 410.

h Cf. Jeremiah's exhortation that the exiles "seek the peace of the city where I have made you sojourn" (וְדִרְשׁוּ אֶת־שְׁלוֹם הָעִיר אֲשֶׁר הִגְלֵיתִי אֶתְכֶם שָׁמָּה; Jer 29:7). The question of the addressee(s) of the imperative verbs is difficult. Verses 6b-7 evidently address the city itself; but v. 6a could be taken in two ways. I have taken it, with most interpreters, as addressing the worshipers who speak the words of vv. 6b-7, but it is also possible to take Jerusalemites as the addressee, with the shift to singular verbs being understood as a shift to the collective and "Jerusalem" as vocative: "Seek peace, O Jerusalem!" Such an understanding would clear up the difficulty with the change in addressee and would make good sense, but it does not seem to me as likely as the traditional understanding (which I here accept) because the latter seems to fit better with the remainder of the psalm.

Interpretation

Alonso-Schökel and Strus have made an interesting study on the song that sees the entire song as a play on the name "Jerusalem." According to their analysis, after the opening vv. 1-2, the song consists basically of two parts, corresponding roughly to two folk etiological components of the name "Jerusalem": *yēru* (= עִיר "city") and שָׁלוֹם

"peace."[26] In the first part what is primarily in view is the city (עִיר) itself, and the things that make it glorious (although there are puns on, or at least assonances with, the *šlm* element, specifically the forms of שָׁם and שָׁם). In the second part, the primary focus is on the element *šlm*, although there too, the city is certainly closely in view. The element of assonance is indeed very important for the song; one may doubt, however, whether it plays such an important role in the form of the song as Alonso-Schökel and Strus claim.[27]

I would divide the psalm according to the apparent "dialogue" that seems to be indicated by the pronominal suffixes and verbs. The opening two verses seem to be a statement made by a pilgrim to Jerusalem, speaking for a larger group. In this section Jerusalem is addressed directly (v. 2b). There is then a kind of digression in vv. 3-5 (the identity of the speaker is unclear) on the subject of Jerusalem itself. Here Jerusalem is no longer addressed directly, but is spoken of in the third person. In fact, the city is spoken of as "there" (שָׁם), perhaps an indication of distance between the speaker and the city. These verses constitute a hymn glorifying the city on the basis of three factors: its sturdiness (v. 3), its position as the meeting place for the people of God (v. 4), and it prominence as the locus of the righteous Davidic kingship (v. 5). After this hymnic section there is a brief interlude in the masculine plural imperative (v. 6a), perhaps spoken by a priest. The clue to this lies in the immediately following direct address to Jerusalem (as in v. 2, Jerusalem is addressed in 6b by the pilgrims), which appears to be a response to the command. In the concluding verses the direct address is continued, as the worshipers pronounce the blessing on Jerusalem. That it is the pilgrims speaking is confirmed by the use of "our God" in v. 9. The alternation between the first person singular and the first person plural is artfully presented (as in vv. 1-2) in the last two lines.

---

[26]Luis Alonso-Schökel and Andrej Strus, "Salmo 122: Canto al nombre de Jerusalén [*sic*]," *Bib* 61 (1980) 239.

[27]The importance of *yērū* seems to me particularly suspect. How is it that the word שָׁלוֹם is given such meaning in terms of puns (e.g. v. 6) and other usage, where עִיר appears only in v. 3, and there are no other word that could be taken as puns on *yērū*? They posit that the first part plays with the *idea* of עִיר and the second part plays with the *sound* of שָׁלוֹם, and this seems somewhat forced.

It is almost without doubt that Psalm 122 belongs to the setting of the ascent from lower Jerusalem, the city proper, up to the temple area. Such a milieu is to be distinguished from the idea of pilgrimage from outlying areas. It could have been sung equally well by residents of the city. The song begins and ends in the city itself, and is solely concerned with Jerusalem (the same can be said of Psalm 132). The song begins with the singer's joy at Jerusalem's gates, which are also the starting-point of the ceremonial journey to the temple. Certainly it does refer to pilgrimage to the temple (v. 4), but it does so as an attribute of the city (in the same way that the throne of the Davidic line is an attribute), and does not refer to the situation in which the song was uttered. Psalm 122 belongs wholly to the milieu of the ascent from the lower areas of Jerusalem to the Temple Mount.

Several clues within the psalm point to a postexilic date. First, the references to the "tribes of Yah" and the Davidic throne have a nostalgic flavor; they are things that happened in the past, rather than as things that continue to be present. Second several linguistic clues point to the postexilic era. The use of the periphrastic genitive (v. 5) and of the *lamed* to indicate a direct object (v. 4b) are characteristics that develop fully in Middle Hebrew.[28] The relative pronoun -שֶׁ can be either northern or late; in this context the second of the two is the more likely possibility. The spelling of David's name (דָּוִיד) may also imply a late date for the psalm, since it is the standard spelling in Chronicles and is nearly absent from the Deuteronomic History. These clues are sufficient to posit a postexilic date for the psalm. The presence of gates and walls, and of "the house of YHWH," implies that one would have to date the psalm after Nehemiah's time.

---

[28]Eduard Yecheskel Kutscher, *A History of the Hebrew Language* (Leiden: E. J. Brill, 1982) 82.

PSALM 123

1   A song of ascents:

To you I lift up my eyes,
   You who are Enthroned[a] in the heavens.
2   As slaves' eyes [are lifted] to the hand of their masters,
     As a maidservant's eyes [are lifted] to the hand of her
        mistress,
     So are our eyes [lifted] to YHWH our God,
        Until have mercy on us.

3   Have mercy on us, O YHWH, have mercy on us;
        For we have had our fill of contempt!
4   Our souls are utterly filled up[b]
        With the ridicule of those at ease,[c]
        With the contempt of the haughty![d]

Notes to the Translation

a   The final *yodh* of MT הַיּשְׁבִי is probably to be explained either as an archaic case ending (Dahood, 3:209), or as an additional syllable for rhythmic reasons (So Joüon, *Grammaire de l'hébreu biblique,* §93n, p. 226-227).

b   The adverbial רַבַּת is probably not a temporal "too long" here (as in Ps 120:6; cf. JPSV, NRSV), but most naturally modifies the verb שָׂבַע, indicating the degree of satiation. As in Ps 120:6, the so-called *dativus ethicus* is used here, in agreement with נַפְשֵׁנוּ, more or less pleonastically.

c   These two nouns are in an appositional relationship. The definiteness of both nouns precludes the possibility of a bound structure, unless one emends the text. One scribe, apparently taking the phrase as a bound structure (see BHS apparatus), clarified the meaning by reading the second noun as לְשַׁאֲנַנִּים (so also Briggs and Briggs, *Book of Psalms,* 452; Kissane, *Book of Psalms,* 173; Kraus, *Psalmen,* 1021), eliminating the problem. Similarly the LXX reads τὸ ὄνειδος τοῖς εὐθηνοῦσιν, presuming a dative construction parallel to the gloss in the next line. But since apposition such as this often has the same meaning as the bound structure (see GKC §127h) it is probably unnecessary to emend the text (similarly Dahood, *Psalms,* 3:250).

d   Various proposals have been offered for the emendation of לִגְאֵיוֹנִים. The *qere* has לִגְאֵי יוֹנִים, which de Wette (*Kommentar über die Psalmen,* 582) interpreted to mean "der stoltzen Unterdrüker"; repointed to לְגֵאֵי יְוֹנִים it could also mean "the haughty Greeks" (cf. Joel 4:6). Maillot and Lelièvre (*Psaumes*, 147) state (without citation) that a medieval rabbinic commentary interprets the word as לְגְיוֹנִים, Roman legions. Keet (*A Study of the Psalms of Ascents*, 40), apparently following BHK, is quite sure that the *kethib* represents the better text.

Interpretation

Only a few translational comments need be made on this psalm, which includes no significant textual or syntactical problems. In the worshipers' comparing of their dependence on God to that of servants on their masters, one should not make too much of the alternation from the plural (servants) to the singular (maidservant).[29] This alternation probably represents poetic and stylistic concerns more than actual social realities, especially since the servants themselves are not the point of the song, but serve rather as a metaphor for the dependence of the worshiper on God. Some social reality is probably reflected, as for example the fact that feminine and masculine imagery can be applied both to God and to the worshiping community, but this should not be pressed too far.

Psalm 123 may be divided into two strophes. The song begins with an invocation of God, stating the singer's dependence upon God for rescue from a lamentable situation. Probably a spokesman for the gathered people speaks first, with the rest of the people joining the song immediately after the first verse. The verb נָשָׂא, which occurs only in v. 1 as part of this invocation, is implied by the parallelism to be the basic action of each of the three sentences that follow. Two similes indicate the relationship felt between the singer and the invoked God: it is analogous to that between servant and master, and to that between maidservant and mistress.[30] This looking to God is explicitly stated in v.

---

[29]Gunkel (*Psalmen*, 544), for example, says "daß im gewöhnlichen Hauswesen wohl mehrere Knechte zu finden sind, aber nur eine Magd: das ist etwa die Dienerin, welche die Hausfrau bei ihrer Verheiratung mitgebracht hat, wie Sara die Hagar Gen 16."

[30]Cf. the Amarna correspondence in which a supplicant addresses the king and says, "The Lord is the Sun on the hill; and as upon the 'going-out' of the sun from the hill, so [your] servants wait for the 'going-out' of the word from the mouth of their lord" (Anton Jirku, *Altorientalischer Kommentar zum Alten Testament* [Hildesheim: H. A. Gerstenberg, 1972] 232-233).

2b to have as its goal the gracious help from God that the singer expects. The first part of the psalm, then, is an extended simile on the attitude of the worshiper while waiting for God's help.

The second part is the prayer proper, together with the grounds for it. The short but fervent prayer חָנֵּנוּ יהוה חָנֵּנוּ "have mercy on us, O YHWH, have mercy on us,"[31] serves as a transition between the statement of trust in vv. 1-2 and the lament with which the song ends (v. 4).[32] The word רַב in v. 3b followed by the formula רַבַּת with נֶפֶשׁ as the subject of the verb in v. 4a is essentially the same as that found in Ps 120:5-6. It serves rhetorically to bind the request for mercy to the lament. Psalm 123 falls into the same genre as Psalm 120, in which a lament is uttered, but (in contrast to what one expects in lament psalms) is left unanswered.

Several very interesting things may be posited about the setting of this song. First, the work surely has a liturgical flavor to it. This is strongly indicated by the shift from the singular first person (v. 1) into the plural (vv. 2-4). In addition there is the liturgical cry, echoed later in Christian worship, *Miserere nostri, Domine, miserere nostri* (Jerome). A second, very illuminating signal of the milieu to which the song belongs is the pairing of masculine and feminine imagery to express the singers' relationships to God. This could well point to a setting in which both men and women partook in the cultic actions, so that the first person verbs and pronouns would include females as well as males.[33] It does

---

[31]This language is most often that of individual petition. This psalm is one of only two occasions (the other being Isa 33:2, where the request is clearly for aid in an apocalyptic battle) in which the plural חָנֵּנוּ appears. The formula חָנֵּנִי can occur in connection with a confession of guilt, as in Pss 41:5 and 51:3, becoming in effect a request for pardon; more often (indeed every time the word is repeated— חָנֵּנִי ... חָנֵּנִי) it occurs as a plea for mercy in the face of adversity. In Ps 57:2 the justification for the demand that God be merciful (חָנֵּנִי אֱלֹהִים חָנֵּנִי) is found in the soul's trust in God, a theme that closely parallels Psalm 123. This language can also be used in an non-prayer setting, as is evident from Job's cry to his friends, "Have mercy on me! Have mercy on me, O you my friends, for the hand of God has smitten me" (Job 19:21).

[32]Jean Magne ("Répétitions de mots et exégèse dans quelques psaumes et le Pater," *Bib* 39 [1958] 190) therefore thinks of v. 3 as the "centre de gravité" around which the entire psalm—in many ways only a single sentence—orbits.

[33]This fact is probably good evidence that the song derives from a setting other than Jerusalem, where women—and in particular female conceptions of divinity— appear at most in secondary roles. Unlike the state temples at Jerusalem, Bethel and Dan, local shrines seem to have had a higher degree of female participation in the

appear that women were active participants in the pilgrimages of the postexilic period,[34] but they were relegated to inferior status in temple worship; and the use of female imagery for God during that period would almost certainly be considered heterodox by Jerusalemites. Another piece of evidence for the sociological setting is in the opposition between "us" and "those who are at ease" (שַׁאֲנַנִּים). When this word is used negatively it almost always connotes rich people who oppress the poor in economic and political ways.[35] The one slim piece of evidence in favor of a Jerusalemite setting—the phrase הַיֹּשְׁבִי בַּשָּׁמָיִם, for which the only clear parallel is in Ps 2:4—is not sufficient evidence on which to posit a Jerusalemite setting. It therefore seems most likely that this prayer arose outside official Jerusalemite circles.

PSALM 124

1   A song of ascents; David's:

Let Israel say the "If it were not YHWH who was for us":

2   If it were not YHWH who was for us,
      When humanity rose up against us,
3   Then they would have swallowed us alive
      When their wrath burned against us;
4   Then would the waters have engulfed us,
      The torrent would have overflowed our necks,[a]
5   Then would have overflowed our necks
      The angry waters![b]

---

cultus, and were also more likely to have female conceptions of deity. See Phyllis Bird, "The Place of Women in the Israelite cultus," in *Ancient Israelite Religion: Essays in Honor of Frank Moore Cross*, ed. Patrick D. Miller, Jr., Paul D. Hanson, and S. Dean McBride (Philadelphia, PA: Fortress Press, 1987) 397-419, especially pp. 405-411.

[34]For a survey of the place of women and children in the second temple (specifically, in the context of pilgrimage) see Shmuel Safrai, *Die Wallfahrt im Zeitalter des zweiten Tempels* (Forschungen zum jüdisch-christlichen Dialog 3; Neukirchen-Vluyn: Neukirchener Verlag, 1981) 98-105.

[35]On one occasion (Zech 1:15) it has a nationalistic sense in addition to this meaning, but the "economic oppressiveness" meaning continues to be present.

6   Blessed be YHWH, who did not abandon us
     As prey for their teeth!
7   We have escaped like a bird from the fowlers' snare!
     The trap is broken, and we have escaped!

8   Our help is in the name of YHWH,
     Maker of heaven and earth.

Notes to the Translation

a   The noun נַחֲלָה certainly means "torrent" (usually נַחַל) here, rather than the expected "inheritance."

b   The verb does not agree with the subject. According to Joüon (*Grammaire de l'hébreu biblique,* §150j), this phenomenon is common when the verb precedes the noun, especially when the two are separated by several words.

Interpretation

Psalm 124 begins with a call to "Israel" to recite the song named in the second half of the first line. As with many ancient literary cultures, the Israelites knew their texts by the first words in the text.[36] By saying the first line the leader indicates the song to be sung.[37] The psalm proper begins in v. 2, with the repeated first line of the poem. The Hebrew לוּלֵי introduces the unreal past condition, that is, "it *was* YHWH, but if it had not been…." The three-fold corollary condition is then introduced with the element אֲזַי "then." This construction is not to be thought of as protasis and apodosis, but as an unreal condition in the past, with the *temporal* marker indicating what would "then" (i.e., at that time) have happened. It is not an "if…then" statement in the tradition of the Greek logicians, but rather a narrative about what might have occurred without

---

[36]For an excellent summary of methods by which reference was made to texts, see Wilson, *Editing of the Hebrew Psalter,* 53.

[37]In addition to the identical construction in Psalm 129, one must compare the introduction to Psalm 118. There the leader cites the song, not by its first line, but by the refrain that appears both at the beginning and at the end of the psalm (כִּי לְעוֹלָם חַסְדּוֹ). In Psalm 118 not only is "Israel" named as one who should recite the psalm, but also "The House of Aaron" (בֵית־אַהֲרֹן) and "Those who Fear YHWH" (יִרְאֵי יְהוָה).

YHWH's aid.[38]   After the narration of the situation that would have obtained without divine assistance, the song narrates the converse of the unreal past condition: God not only helped, but altogether rescued "us" from the treacherous circumstances.   For this divine beneficence, as opposed to what might have been, the Psalmist "blesses" YHWH.

The imagery of this psalm is complex: the metaphors are so thoroughly mixed and so closely knit together that it is difficult to make sense of the psalm.   However, the psalm gives several important clues as to the *Sitz im Leben* to which it belongs.   It is clear that the song celebrates some kind of victory or deliverance.   The imagery is not amenable, however, to seeing return from Babylonian exile as the setting of the psalm.   In the first place, it could hardly be said concerning Jerusalem's defeat by Babylon that vv. 3-5 narrate unreal conditions. The events of the first two decades of the sixth century would be aptly described in these lines.   The imagery of the bird in a trap appears to have been a stock metaphor in the ancient Near East for a city under siege.[39]   To follow the image, release from the trap implies a lifted siege, not simply a generic victory, and decidedly not release from Babylon, even though it is sometimes styled "captivity."   Throughout the psalm the praise is for deliverance from an *unrealized* condition that *might have been,* and not from an actual captivity.   Thematically, then, it is impossible to say more than the negative statement that the psalm does not necessarily refer to release from Babylonian "captivity."

On linguistic grounds there may be more basis for identification of the psalm as having a relatively late date, but the weight of the evidence is impossible to determine.   The use of the relative particle -שֶׁ could be

---

[38]Waltke and O'Connor (*Biblical Hebrew Syntax*, 667-668) adduce several examples of אָז (and אֲזַי) in a logical sense (including Psalm 124), but it seems to me that the force of this passage is that of narrative, rather than of argumentation.

[39]For example, an El Amarna letter (74:45-46) uses a similar metaphor probably to indicate that the speaker is besieged, but that he is safe in the city: "As birds that lie in a bird nest, so am I in Gubla."   The same imagery is used in Hittite literature: "the bird takes refuge in its nest (?), and the nest (?) saves it.   Or, if anything becomes too difficult for a servant, he makes a request to his lord, and his lord hears him and [is kind towards] him and sets right what was too difficult for him" (the quotation is from "the so-called Prayer of Mursilis II"; Walter Beyerlin, *Near Eastern Religious Texts Relating to the Old Testament* [Philadelphia, PA: Westminster Press, 1978] 173).

taken either as evidence of either late date or northern provenance (see Chap. 4, p. 160). The particle לוּלֵי, which is common in early narrative literature, occurs rarely in cultic poetry until the postexilic period. Here again, however, it is possible to see this as resulting from colloquial speech rather than as an indication of date.[40]   In fact, colloquialisms abound in this psalm (e.g., the particle אֲזַי, elsewhere unattested; the ‎הָ- affixed to נַחַל in v. 4). It therefore seems likely that these features are best explained on dialectal rather than developmental grounds.

PSALM 125

1   A song of ascents:

Those who trust in YHWH are like Mount Zion[a]
  It shall not be moved, but will remain forever.[b]
2   Jerusalem has mountains surrounding it,
    And so YHWH surrounds [God's] people
    From now and ever more.[c]

3   Indeed may the staff of the wicked not rest
    Upon the inheritance of the righteous.[d]
  So that[e] the righteous may not reach out
    Their hands wrongly.[f]

4   Do good, O YHWH, to those who are good,
    To those righteous in their hearts.
5   But those who turn aside to crooked ways[g]—
    May YHWH throw them out (the evildoers).[h]
    Peace be upon Israel.

Notes to the Translation

  a   The Syriac and a large number of mss have בְּהַר־צִיּוֹן for כְּהַר־צִיּוֹן (Johann Bernhard de Rossi, *Variae lectiones Veteris Testamenti librorum*

---

[40]Frank Crüsemann, *Studien zur Formgeschichte von Hymnus und Danklied in Israel* (Neukirchen: Neukirchener Verlag, 1969) 162-163.

(Amsterdam: Philo Press, 1970], 82). This reading is rendered less plausible (though not impossible; see note on Ps 124:5), however, by the singular verb in v. 1bβ.

b   The LXX reads יְרוּשָׁלַם with יֹשֵׁב, translating ὁ κατοικῶν Ιερουσαλημ. Walter Beyerlin (*Weisheitliche Vergewisserung mit Bezug auf den Zionskult: Studien zum 125. Psalm* [OBO 68; Göttingen: Vandenhoeck & Ruprecht, 1985], 67-68) believes יֹשֵׁב יְרוּשָׁלַם (his repointing) to be a gloss based on a misunderstanding of the meaning of the text. He sees this same misunderstanding as present in the LXX translation (see the discussion). The phrase לֹא־יִמּוֹט occurs elsewhere (Isa 40:20; 41:7; Pss 15:5; 112:6; cf. לֹא־אֶמּוֹט in Ps 62:3,7), and in Psalms 15 and 112 it occurs with לְעוֹלָם. Conversely, the phrase לְעוֹלָם יֵשֵׁב occurs in Ps 9:8 as a predicate of YHWH ("YHWH sits enthroned forever"). Because of the parallelism in v. 2, I do not think that יֵשֵׁב should be read with the following line, and I do not find sufficient warrant to strike the word.

c   The suggestion of BHS that מֵעַתָּה וְעַד־עוֹלָם is to be deleted on metrical grounds is without sufficient warrant, and must therefore be rejected (I shall argue below, however, that it is redactional). Many authors (e.g., BHS apparatus; Gunkel, *Psalmen*, 550; Schmidt, *Psalmen*, 225; Kraus, *Psalmen 60-150*, 443) have stricken it on metrical or redundancy grounds, that is, seeing that it adds an extra phrase to the basic 4:3 meter of the psalm and that, furthermore, it is outside the parallelism. Loewenstamm ("*Mē ʿattā wĕʿad ōlām*," 166-170), however, has shown that when this formula appears it is for the most part outside the normally accepted poetic structures (p. 166). Cf. Pss 113:2; 115:18; Isa 9:6; 59:21; Mic 4:7. There are important reasons for positing that this phrase is *redactional*, but this is a literary-critical argument, not a textual one.

d   The phrase probably refers to that which is gained by lot, that is, to land (so Keet, *A Study of the Psalms of Ascents*, 46; Allen 167; and most others), although the expected term would be נַחֲלָה. Lit. "the lot of the righteous."

e   The phrase לְמַעַן לֹא plus an imperfect verb indicates negative purpose (contrast the expression עַל־כֵּן לֹא plus the imperfect to indicate negative result, as in Ps 1:5: "Therefore the wicked will not stand...."). The more usual form to express this idea is לְבִלְתִּי plus an imperfect verb. The form here is characteristic of exilic and postexilic biblical Hebrew (it occurs in Ezek 14:11; 19:9; 25:10; 26:20; Zech 12:7; Ps 119:11,80). In Num 17:5 and Deut 20:18, the form לְמַעַן אֲשֶׁר לֹא occurs. This form also occurs in Ezek 31:14; 36:30; 46:18.

f   Joüon (*Grammaire de l'hébreu biblique*, §93j) believes the added הָ of בְּעוֹלָתָה is purely for rhythmical or euphonic purposes. It is better seen as a remnant of the accusative ending (so Dahood, *Psalms*, 3:195).

g   I parse מַטִּים as a *hiphil* active participle from נטה, *contra* Dahood (*Psalms*, 3:216), who suggests that it is from מוּט. The image may be that of perversion of justice (cf. מְעַקָּל in Hab 1:4); perhaps there is a pun on the word מַטֶּה which, like שֵׁבֶט in v. 3, is a symbol of rulership. The immediate context (especially לִישָׁרִים בְּלִבּוֹתָם in v. 4), however, suggests that private wickedness may be primarily in view.

h   So far as I can determine, all other commentators take the אֵת in the phrase אֵת־פֹּעֲלֵי הָאָוֶן "the evildoers" as the preposition ("with the evildoers"). Such an interpretation sees "with the evildoers" as identifying the place where YHWH will "make them go." This is awkward metrically, as well as redundant. In my opinion the phrase is an explanatory gloss, directly clarifying the referent of the accusative "them," and indirectly clarifying the unusual phrase הַמַּטִּים עֲקַלְקַלּוֹתָם "those who make their ways crooked." The particle אֵת functions deictically to signal a scribal gloss (see Michael Fishbane, *Biblical Interpretation in Ancient Israel* [Oxford: Clarendon, 1985] 48-51).

Interpretation

Psalm 125 contains several translation and textual problems, most of which are treated in the notes. One problem deserves special attention, however: the end of v. 1. The phrase לֹא־יִמּוֹט לְעוֹלָם is a formulaic phrase (cf. Ps 15:5), and one does not expect it to be supplemented with יֵשֵׁב.[41] On the other hand it is not probable that ישׁב should be read as a participle in construct with יְרוּשָׁלַם (translating "inhabitant of Jerusalem") because the image of v. 2 is that the mountains surround the city, not the city's inhabitants (cf. the feminine gender of the pronoun in v. 2aα).[42] I am not willing to go as far as Beyerlin, however, in labeling it a gloss.[43] Moreover, the use of a comparable formula in Joel 4:20 (וִיהוּדָה לְעוֹלָם תֵּשֵׁב) parallel to (וִירוּשָׁלַם לְדוֹר וָדוֹר) makes the MT reading of v. 1 quite understandable. There are two different formulae in use here: "It [Mt. Zion] shall not [ever] totter" and "It will abide [forever]"; the word לְעוֹלָם does double duty to serve both phrases.[44]

---

[41]Beyerlin, *Weisheitliche Vergewisserung*, 21-23.

[42]What is more, the parallelism of verbless clauses in v. 2, as well as the masculine gender of the verb, may argue against scanning "Jerusalem is situated with mountains around it," against Duhm, *Psalmen*, 434-435, who argues that a second comparison occurs in v. 2, and so translates,

> Wer auf Jahwe traut, ist wie der Berg Zion,
> > Der nimmer wanken wird,
> Er wird wohnen wie Jerusalem,
> Das Berge umgeben,
> > Und Jahwe ist rings um sein Volk
> > > Von jetzt an bis auf ewig....

[43]Beyerlin, *Weisheitliche Vergewisserung*, 47-48.

[44]The Masoretic accentuation, in which a disjunctive accent follows לְעוֹלָם, is in my view incorrect.

Psalm 125 offers one of the clearest examples of redactional activity in the Songs of Ascents. The formulae מֵעַתָּה וְעַד־עוֹלָם (v. 2) and שָׁלוֹם עַל־יִשְׂרָאֵל (v. 5) are characteristics of a redactional effort that pervades the collection (see Chap. 3). The first of these divides the first two verses, from vv. 3-5, a division that is reinforced by thematic differences. The primary thrust of Psalm 125 is that of vv. 3-5a. Although these lines probably do not constitute a psalm in themselves,[45] their theme is clear. It is a prayer for relief from domination by "the wicked," based upon the formula that has God doing good to those who are good, and "throwing out" those who are wicked. The vocabulary, perspective, and theme all point to a wisdom milieu for these lines.[46] Furthermore, they have nothing to say about Jerusalem (indeed, retribution seems to be completely personalized), whereas Jerusalem is a central focus in the first two lines. Furthermore, the situation of the prayer in vv. 3-5 seems clearly to imply that "the wicked" are occupying the land that properly belongs to the righteous. The prayer that "the staff of the wicked not rest on the inheritance of the righteous" (v. 3) implies this, as does the request that God "throw them out" (v. 5a). It is difficult to see how such a prayer could come from the same time as the profoundly confident statement of vv. 1-2. To summarize: we have two lines that are, at best, only somewhat related to the remainder of the psalm; and we have the formula וְעַד־עוֹלָם מֵעַתָּה, a characteristic formula for the Songs of Ascents as a whole, mediating between the two sections. It seems therefore most likely that vv. 3-5a constituted an early psalm fragment, and that this fragment was supplied with a nationalizing introduction by a redactor. I argue in Chap. 3 that the collection as a whole is characterized by a redactional reworking that converts songs of the individual and of the small community into national songs with Jerusalem as the focus. The same seems to be true, in microcosm, of Psalm 125.

Psalm 125, seen as a totality, thus belongs to two distinct tradition complexes: the local, family-oriented folk wisdom tradition of personal

---

[45]According to Seybold (*Wallfahrtspsalmen*, 52), Psalm 125 "is and remains a torso" of a poem, to which the additions only complicate things.

[46]See Beyerlin, *Weisheitliche Vergewisserung*. His book studies the wisdom elements in the psalm well, although Beyerlin assumes the integrity of the psalm.

retribution and the Jerusalemite tradition of the immovability of Zion. Because the latter is, in my view, part of a redactional effort that characterizes the collection Songs of Ascents as a whole, I shall put off treatment of that milieu until Chap. 4, where I treat it at length. The body of the psalm, vv. 3-5a, contains several clues that make it possible to delineate its milieu more closely than what is stated above. First, several linguistic elements appear to date this material to the exilic or the postexilic era. The phrase לְמַעַן לֹא to indicate negative purpose is known only in literature of these periods (Ezek 14:11; 19:9; 25:10; 26:20; Zech 12:7; Ps 119:11,80). The epithet צַדִּיקִים occurs primarily in wisdom literature, and to some extent in other literature from the exilic and postexilic periods (with the definite article it occurs only in Qoh 8:14; 9:1). Second, vv. 3 and 5 probably imply that the psalm was written at a time in which "the wicked" (probably foreigners) dominated the land that, it was felt, properly belonged to "the righteous." Third, the religion that is portrayed here is personalized; it contains no reference to corporate worship or to institutions of corporate worship. Of course this does not mean that it could not also have been prayed in groups, but there is no evidence that this was the case. Indeed, the formula שָׁלוֹם עַל־יִשְׂרָאֵל seems quite out of place at the end. The redactor supplied both this phrase and the material vv. 1-2 for a reason, however; it seems most likely the reason was to give to originally non-Jerusalemite material a Jerusalemite reinterpretation. If that is the case, then one might posit that vv. 3-5a belonged to an extra-Jerusalemite family wisdom tradition during one of the periods of Babylonian or of Persian (or Greek?) domination of the land.

PSALM 126

1   A song of ascents:

        When YHWH restored the fortune of Zion[a]
        We were like dreamers.[b]
2   Then our mouth was filled with laughter,[c]
        Our tongue with a shout of joy.

Then it was said among the nations,
"YHWH has magnified doings[d] with these!"

3   YHWH did magnify doings with us.
    We were glad.[e]

4   Restore our fortunes,[f] O YHWH,
    Like the desert's wadis!

5   May those who plant with tears
    Reap with a shout of joy![g]

6   Although[h] the one who carries the seed-bag
    Goes about weeping,
    May the one who carries the sheaves
    Come in with a shout of joy![i]

Notes to the Translation

   a   Contrary to the practice of most interpreters, I agree with Dahood (*Psalms*, 3:218) that it is best not to emend שׁיבת to read שׁבות. A precise linguistic parallel (*hšbw ʾlhn šybt b[yt ʾby]* "The gods restored the fortunes of my father's house) has been found in a Sefîre inscription (Sf III,24; see A. Dupont-Sommer and J. Starcky, "Une inscription araméenne inédite de Sfiré," *BMB* 13 [1956] 27; Joseph A. Fitzmyer, *The Aramaic Inscriptions of Sefîre* [BO 19; Rome: Pontifical Biblical Institute, 1967] 119-120; text on pp. 100-101, cf. pl. XII), where the meaning is almost certainly that of restored prosperity (in this case, land that is restored to its proper owner), and does not seem to have anything to do with return from captivity. Dahood holds, probably rightly, that the same meaning is primary also in Pss 14:7 and 85:2. The new edition of the Koehler-Baumgartner lexicon (Johann Jakob Stamm, et al., *Hebräisches und Aramäisches Lexikon zum Alten Testament von Ludwig Koehler und Walter Baumgartner*, vol. 4 [Leiden: E. J. Brill, 1990] 1369) acknowledges this meaning.
   b   The word כְּחֹלְמִים is one of the most difficult parts of the psalm. The ancient versions mostly read חלם II, "be healed", or a semantic variation of it (cf. LXX ὡς παρακεκλημένοι; Tg היך מרעיא דאיתסיין; Syr *ʾyk hnwn dḥdyn*). See the summaries by John Strugnell ("A Note on Ps. CXXVI. 1," *JTS* 7 [1956] 239-243) and Salomon Speier ("Sieben Stellen des Psalmentargums in Handschriften und Druckausgaben: 3,7 44,17 45,6 49,11 68,15.20 126,1," *Bib* 48 [1967] 506-508). Modern interpreters (de Wette, *Kommentar über die Psalmen*, 585; Briggs and Briggs, *Book of Psalms*, 456; Keet, *A Study of the Psalms of Ascents*, 50; Kraus, *Psalmen*, 1031; Beyerlin, *We Are Like Dreamers*, 15-20; Allen, *Psalms 101-150*, 171; Allan M. Harman, "The Setting and Interpretation of Psalm 126," *RefThR* 44,3 [1985] 77; Scott R. A. Starbuck, "Like Dreamers Lying in Wait, We Lament: A New Reading of Psalm 126," *Koinonia* 1/2 [1989] 128-149) have tended to translate

it "like dreamers." Some, however, have followed the ancient versions (Strugnell, "A Note on Ps. CXXVI. 1," 239-243; Alexander Reinard Hulst, "Psalm 126," in Georg Eichholz, ed., *Herr, tue meine Lippen auf*, 567-577; Marrs, "Šyry Hmᶜlwt," 76). The JPSV takes the *kaph* as an indication of identity (or perhaps an emphatic כִּי), giving a "literal" rendering of "we are veritable dreamers," and a contextual rendering of "we see it as in a dream."

Neither of these explanations satisfies completely, since neither image receives treatment later in the psalm. One is tempted to divide כְּחֹלְמִים differently from the MT. Dahood (*Psalms* 3:220) proposed the reading כְּחֹל ־ם יָם "like the sand of the sea," the *mem* of כְּחֹל ־ם being enclitic (here used in a construct chain). The standard phrase (Gen 32:13; 1 Kgs 4:20; Hos 2:1) is without the enclitic *mem*, which he thinks may explain why the ancient scribes missed the word division. On the parallelism of "sands of the sea" with v. 3 "we grew happy" he refers to 1 Kgs 4:20, where the same two ideas are juxtaposed. Another reading might be כֹּח לְמַיִם "strong [lit. "strength"] of [i.e., with respect to] water." Either of these readings might fit better with the rest of the song (especially with the wadi image of v. 4) and with the Joel parallel (see the discussion). One may object, however, that the situation thus becomes too concrete for comfort, and that the parallel between הָיִינוּ שְׂמֵחִים and הָיִינוּ כְּחֹלְמִים (v. 3) is thus destroyed. (This parallel, as well as the context of vv. 2-3, suggests that whatever the meaning of חלם here, it has to do with joy, and not with a future expectation or with disbelief of the present.) In any case, I do not agree with Beyerlin (*We are like Dreamers*, passim) that this word is a *crux interpretum* for the psalm. The meaning of the remainder of the psalm, which is a prayer for renewed prosperity, is clear enough whatever the interpretation of this word.

c   The particle אָז is often used with the imperfect to designate past time (e.g., Num 21:17; 2 Sam 2:27). It is also possible to argue for a preterit meaning the basis of the Akkadian *iqtul* pattern; so Harman, "Setting and Interpretation of Psalm 126," 78. For a good survey of recent scholarship on verb tenses see Peter C. Craigie, "Excursus II: The Translation of Tenses in Hebrew Poetry," in *Psalms 1-50*, 110-113.

d   The phrase הִגְדִּיל יהוה לַעֲשׂוֹת is very difficult adequately to render in English. The usual translation "YHWH has done greatly" reverses the Hebrew meaning, in which "make great" is the active verb and "to do" is an infinitive construct that mostly serves to modify the main verb. I have chosen this awkward translation in order to point up this difficulty.

e   The perfect verb does not here necessitate a past tense rendering; but because of what follows, such a translation seems most plausible.

f   Although I have not elected to harmonize the *text* of שִׁיבַת/שְׁבוּת in vv. 1 and 4, the words do have very similar, if not identical, meaning. For שְׁבוּת with this meaning cf. Jer 32:44 (where the reference is to returned prosperity to the land, not to returned captives); Ezek 16:53. Perhaps the variation of שִׁיבַת/שְׁבוּת in vv. 1 and 4 may be taken "as a pointer to a new beginning at v. 4 and as a means of differentiating the changes of fortune as separate events" (Allen, *Psalms 101-150*, 174). Dahood vocalizes the verb as *šābâ*, a *qatala* form, rather than an imperative. For him this eliminates the "main syntactic and semantic difficulty in this psalm"

(*Psalms* 3:220), in that it allows for his interpretation of the whole as a song of thanks for events in the immediate past. This interpretation seems strained, however.

g Allen comments that this verse "is hardly a continuation of the prayer of v. 4", and that v. 6 elaborates on v. 5b, and so should be taken as similarly indicative (Allen, *Psalms 101-150,* 171), but this seems to me quite arbitrary. Even if the verbs of vv. 5-6 are not taken as jussive, their position after such a prayer gives them jussive force.

h According to GKC §113p, "The infinitive absolute is used to give emphasis to an antithesis."

i The participial נֹשֵׂא, which is repeated in parallel in v. 6, is not verbal but substantive, in construct with the thing borne. It is thus the grammatical subject of the parallel verbal constructions "going out weeping" and "coming in with a shout". The subject appears at the end of the sentences, perhaps in order to emphasize the disjunction (hence my translation "although").

Interpretation

The most important clue to the interpretation of Psalm 126, albeit an ambiguous clue, is certainly the similarity between בְּשׁוּב יְהוָה את־שיבת ציון in v. 1 and שׁוּבה יהוה את־שבותנו in v. 4. Clearly they are set in apposition to one another; probably the words שִׁיבַת and שְׁבוּת have the same basic meaning, despite the difference in spelling (see translation notes a and f above). In the first half the phrase indicates something in the past that God has accomplished; in the second half it represents something that remains for God to do in the present. The reference is probably not to a return from captivity, but to returned fertility upon the land.[47]

A second difficulty is the meaning of the word כְּחֹלְמִים (see translation note b above). Many authorities interpret it as signifying either the unreality of the prosperity envisioned in vv. 1-3 (i.e., "we were only dreaming") or the hope for prosperity (i.e., "I have a dream!").[48]

---

[47]Even if the first part of the psalm is interpreted in terms of exiled Judeans returning from Babylon (which I do not think likely), the second part still refers to agricultural prosperity. Thus the restoration of the exiles would become a metaphor for returned prosperity, in much the same way that 2 Isaiah used the Exodus as a metaphor for return out of exile. This is the position taken by Claus Westermann, *Ausgewählte Psalmen,* 42-43. With the possible exception of the word(s) שבות/שיבת, however, nothing in the psalm points to a reference to returned exiles.

[48]So, e.g., Hulst ("Psalm 126," 572) sees it as a dream that foresees reality: "Es ist, als träume man, nicht aber einen Traum, dem eine Enttäuschung folgt, vielmehr

Beyerlin is probably correct in his judgment that these are linguistic modernisms, although his method (he examines only a modern German dictionary to determine the semantic range of "dream") is certainly suspect.[49] On the other hand, Beyerlin's proposal that "dream" here refers to a prophet's ecstatic trance[50] has little support in the rest of the psalm, into which a forecasted prosperity does not figure. A secondary meaning of the verb חלם "be healed" is often cited, and seems to be behind the LXX translation and the Targumim (see translation note b above). The analogous relationship between recovering people and a recovering Zion might fit with the rest of the psalm. The difficulty is that neither of these meanings receives elaboration in the remainder of the psalm. In addition there is the problem of the precise meaning of the preposition כ "like," which would not have much meaning in either case. Perhaps the most that can be said is that in some way the word serves to indicate the joy felt by the community at God's restoration of fertility at some point in the past.

Formally the song is rather explicit. The two main divisions are indicated by the pun on the phrase שוב...שבות, so well known from prophetic literature.[51] In the opening section (vv. 1-3) the phrase probably refers to the simple past, or perhaps to the recurring past ("whenever YHWH restored the fortunes...") in the indicative mood; in the second section it constitutes the primary prayer of the psalm, and is thus cast in the imperative mood. Within the two primary divisions several formal marks may be observed. The repetition of הגדיל יהוה לעשות עם leads one from v. 2 to v. 3 in a stair-like fashion. The two lines of v. 2 each have אז at the beginning. This gives the flavor of an inclusio between vv. 1 and 3, which flavor is emphasized by the use of היינו שמחים (echoing הָיִינוּ כְּחֹלְמִים) at the end of v. 3.

---

den Traum der göttlichen Erlösung, dem eine Freudeerregende Wirklichkeit entspricht."

[49]Walter Beyerlin, *We Are Like Dreamers: Studies in Psalm 126* (Edinburgh: T. & T. Clark, 1982) 15-18.

[50]Beyerlin, *We are like Dreamers*, 19-20. For him the phrase is parenthetic, having no direct relation to the following lines.

[51]E. L. Dietrich, שוב שבות. *Die endzeitliche Wiederstellung bei den Propheten* (BZAW 40; Gießen: Alfred Töpelmann, 1925). Cf. Psalm 85, where also a past restoration to favor becomes the basis for a plea for restoration in the present, and where the phrase שוב ... שבות also occurs.

With the nearly verbatim repetition of the opening formula, the second section begins. The phrase שׁוּב ... שְׁבוּת is here marked as referring to agricultural prosperity much more explicitly than in v. 1: the desired change is "like wadis in the desert," a clear fertility motif.[52] The fertility imagery is continued in vv. 5-6, where bounty is assured despite the hardship endured to procure it.[53] In a fine example of the "step parallelism" found often in the Songs of Ascents, v. 5 introduces the theme of weeping at seed time and rejoicing at harvest, and this theme is then expanded into two lines in v. 6. In the latter the opposition between the two cola points to the general theme of the psalm, emphasizing the idea of the reversal of the fortunes, which the singer wants God to bring about.

Psalm 126 has very strong ties—both linguistically and thematically—with the book of Joel, as has been argued (although probably too confidently) by Beyerlin.[54] Certainly the phrase הִגְדִּיל יהוה לַעֲשׂוֹת, which appears in BH only here (2bβ, 3aα) and in Joel (2:20bβ [subject understood as YHWH?[55]], 21b [subject expressed as YHWH]), as a more or less petrified formula in both places, provides evidence for a date

---

[52]Nelson Glueck, *Rivers in the Desert* (London: Weidenfeld and Nicholson, 1959) 92-94. Some scholars (Kissane, *Book of Psalms*, 579; Arnold A. Anderson, *The Book of Psalms*, vol. 2 [NCB; Grand Rapids, MI: Wm. B. Eerdmans, 1972] 865; so also Yohanan Aharoni, *Land of the Bible: A Historical Geography* [Philadelphia, PA: Westminster Press, 1979] 26) have seen the image as one of suddenness, rather than of fertility. Although this idea may well be connoted by the image, I maintain that not to see it as a fertility image is to disconnect it from the remainder of the psalm, and probably to read it too literally.

[53]Or perhaps a good harvest comes *because of* the hardship. The reference to "weeping" may well partake in the milieu of Canaanite mythology (known from the texts found at Ugarit and elsewhere), in which weeping at the time of planting accompanied the myth of a god's death, and functioned magically to insure bounty (cf. John C. L. Gibson, ed., *Canaanite Myths and Legends* [Edinburgh, UK: T. & T. Clark, 1978] Baal and Mot 6, cols. i and iii [pp. 74-78= *KTU* 1.6 VI]). It seems that weeping was part of the local, perhaps female-oriented religious traditions (cf. Judg 11:37-40; Ezek 8:14) so strongly opposed by the official Jerusalemite cultus.

[54]Beyerlin, *We are Like Dreamers*, 43-48.

[55]Hans Walter Wolff (*Joel and Amos: A Commentary on the Books of the Prophets Joel and Amos* [Hermeneia; Philadelphia: Fortress Press, 1977] 55) takes "the northerner" as the subject of the sentence.

close to that of Joel.[56] The similarity of theme (in Joel it is restoration after a plague) adds to this general conception of the two as roughly contemporary.

Beyerlin[57] argues that a prophetic background is presupposed by the language of Psalm 126. His argument hinges on several elements that he finds to be "prophetic": the idea of the prophetic dream (but see above), the motif of the nations' glorification of God (v. 2b), and the prediction of future prosperity. The motif of the nations' revilement, however, is characteristic of the communal petitions, and from there is taken up by the prophetic tradition; the reversal of this theme, in which the nations give glory to YHWH, is common in the psalms of praise (e.g., Pss 86:9; 102:16).[58] Likewise refructification is a common theme in the prophetic literature (cf. Isa 35:1-6; 41:19; 43:19-20; 51:3; Joel 4:18), but is also common in the Psalms. Even if it were possible to establish the background of Psalm 126 as prophetic or broadly Zionistic, this background still would have given way to concerns of a more mundane sort. Whereas in the prophets the restoration of Israel is a part of the greater reign of God that is about to break in on the earth, in Psalm 126 the central concern is not God's ultimate glory (although that element is present), but the fertility of the land and the resultant rejoicing of the people. Thus, although perhaps set in the context of prophetic themes and language, the psalm is primarily that of individual Israelite landowners, whose fate is almost wholly determined by whether crops will be abundant or scarce.

---

[56]Beyerlin (*We are Like Dreamers*, 46-48) argues for the literary dependence of Psalm 126 on Joel. Although he gives several arguments, the most important are this phrase and the presence of "dreamers," which he ties to Joel's oracle that the common people would have prophetic experiences. Since this psalm affirms only that the supplicants are *like* dreamers, he sees it as a reinterpretation of the Joel passage. In my opinion, however, proof of literary dependence requires both a more extensive quotation than the short one in Psalm 126, and attention to the possibility that a common milieu could explain the similarities. Beyerlin's observations are accute and very helpful, but I do not think he has proven his case.

[57]Beyerlin, *We Are Like Dreamers*, 49.

[58]The idea of the nations giving glory to YHWH is part of the royal Zion tradition complex, and I would argue makes its way from there into prophetic texts like Isa 11:10 and 25:3.

The phrase שׁוּב...שְׁבוּת is a *crux interpretum*. In the context of
this psalm the term almost certainly refers to renewed agricultural
prosperity following a time of barrenness, a meaning that differentiates
this usage from that of the prophets. Although the clear parallel between
vv. 1 and 4, together with the perfect verbs of the first three verses and
the imperfect verbs of the last three verses, has shown itself to be a
syntactical and semantic difficulty,[59] it seems to me that it may well
provide some very useful information. Verses 1-3 are best understood as
referring to a restoration of Zion's prosperity—or even to the return of
exiles—in the past, not in the future; and it is not stated that this situation
has changed. How is it, then, that prosperity is both accomplished and
prayed for? I believe that the answer is that "Zion" is *elsewhere*. This is
supported by the agrarian thrust of the prayer and perhaps by a reference
to non-Jerusalemite religious practice (weeping as a fertility practice, vv.
5-6; see above, n. 53). The force of the argument is that, although the
supplicants rejoiced at Zion's prosperity, this prosperity has had as yet no
positive impact on their own community. They felt themselves to have a
claim on Zion's prosperity—and therefore acknowledge that Zion's good
is also in some ways their own (v. 3)—but had not as yet seen the
benefits of it. The prayer in vv. 4-6 then becomes a request that Zion's
prosperity be extended to the outer reaches of Zion's sphere of influence.

Psalm 126 may perhaps be dated to some time in the postexilic era
on the basis of two facts. The phrase הִגְדִּיל יהוה לַעֲשׂוֹת is found
only here and in Joel.[60] The theme of the nations' glorification of YHWH

---

[59]For example, de Wette (*Kommentar über die Psalmen*, 584), accepting the
meaning of the nouns as "exiles," interprets the parallel to mean that God had already
brought some exiles back, and the prayer in v. 4 is therefore that more would follow.
Delitzsch (*Psalms*, 288) distinguishes between the two nouns so that the first refers to
returnees in a previous return and the second refers to the *act* of returning currently
under way. Schmidt (*Psalmen*, 227) also distinguishes between the two nouns, so
that the first part remembers a return from exile and the second refers to renewal of
prosperity. Kraus (*Psalms 60-150*, trans. Hilton C. Oswald from *Die Psalmen*
[Minneapolis, MN: Augsburg, 1989] 448-451) posits that the first part refers to a past
return from captivity that was yet incomplete: "The unique tension in which the
community found itself in reorganizing after the return consisted in the fact that
Yahweh had given his people a wonderful liberation but that the actual realization of
the prophetic promise was long in coming" (449).

[60]According to Wolff's penetrating analysis (*Joel and Amos*, 4-6), the time of
Joel is the first half of the fourth century.

is more common in postexilic writings than in earlier writings. More than this is impossible to say. The language is standardized, and the situation referred to (agricultural failure) is common enough to render any hypothesis about a specific date uncertain.

PSALM 127

1   A song of ascents; Solomon's:

> If YHWH does not build the house,
>   Its builders labor uselessly;
> If YHWH does not guard a city,
>   The guard stays awake uselessly.

2   It is useless for you who rise up early,[a]
>   Who go late to bed,
> Who eat bread much toiled for...
>   For[b] God[c] gives sleep[d] to [God's] beloved ones.[e]

3   Behold, the inheritance of YHWH is children,
>   [God's] reward is the fruit of the womb.

4   Like arrows in the hand of a warrior,
>   So are the children of one's youth.

5   Happy is the one who fills up
>   One's quiver[f] with them!
> They will not be disgraced, but will turn aside
>   The enemies from the gate.[g]

Notes to the Translation

a   The LXX reads εἰς μάτην ὑμῖν ἐστιν τοῦ ὀρθρίζειν, ἐγείρεσθαι μετὰ τὸ καθῆσθαι, thus reading קוּם with the next line, and translating מַשְׁכִּים "rise early" with the infinitive ὀρθριζειν "to appoint", perhaps reading הַשְׁכֵּם (cf. BHS), though this is not necessary (see J. A. Emerton, "The meaning of *šēnāʾ* in Psalm CXXVII 2," *VT* 24 (1974) 15-31). And μετὰ may also presuppose אַחֲרֵי for the MT מְאַחֲרֵי. Nonetheless the MT would appear to be the better reading for several reasons: the meter of v. 2a is thus consonant with the preceding two lines; the construction קוּם הַשְׁכִּים makes good sense in BH (see Joüon, *Grammaire de l'hébreu biblique*,

§124n [p. 363]); and the parallel of the participles (מַשְׁכִּימֵי and מְאַחֲרֵי, cf. also אֹכְלֵי) in construct with infinitive, is thus preserved.

b The MT כֵּן "thus" poses interpretational difficulties, since no preceding argument is discernible that may be drawn upon. The LXX ὅταν "when" seems to presume a Hebrew *Vorlage* of כִּי. If this is right, a temporal sense of the word need not be followed, since כִּי can also indicate cause. Here it would be the reason for the vanity of the three things discussed in v. 2a-bα.

c The subject of the verb יִתֵּן is clearly YHWH of v. 1, and not the human beings of v. 2, for which one would in any case expect a second person plural rather than a third person singular. Although alternation of persons is certainly not unknown in Hebrew poetry, the interpretation that sees a human being as the subject of this verb seems much too modern (see n. 63 below).

d There is a large amount of literature written on this word. The best explanation seems to be that it is שֵׁנָה "sleep" written in Aramaic style, where the *aleph* is substituted for the more normal *he* (see Joüon, *Grammaire de l'hébreu biblique*, §7b and §89k). This need not be taken as absolute evidence for a late date (see Kutscher, *History of the Hebrew Language*, 71-73; he summarizes: "the learned embellish their Hebrew style with Aramaic" [p. 73]). Dahood ("The aleph in Psalm CXXVII 2 *šēnā*," *Or* 44 [1975] 103-105) posits a root *šn* "prosperity, peace" (Syriac *šaynā* "prosperity" and Ethiopic *sene* "peace"), which would fit well with the sentence, but is based on questionable comparative data (despite his retorts, the root *šʾn* is the more likely cognate). Emerton ("The meaning of *šēnā* in Psalm CXXVII 2," 25) proposes another root *šnʾ* with the meaning "to be, or become, high, or exalted in rank" or "to shine" (his best evidence is · from *b.Šabb.* 10B, אל ישנה אדם בנו בין הבנים, which he translates "let no man exalt [show special favor to] one son above his other children" [see pp. 27-29]. But this does not fit quite so well with the psalm, which seems not to be concerned with rank so much as with prosperity. For my own proposal see below.

e The consonantal text of the MT can be read as singular, as plural, or as collective. The LXX (τοῖς ἀγαπητοῖς αὐτοῦ; cf. Syriac) apparently read a plural. The MT can be pointed as a defective plural (לִידִידָו), and since the person addressed is mostly plural in the first three verses (מַשְׁכִּימֵי, לָכֶם, עֲמָלוֹ, etc.) I think it best to do so.

f The LXX has τὴν ἐπιθυμίαν αὐτοῦ "his desire" (the only time אַשְׁפָּה is so translated). A possible explanation is that the translator misread the word as תַּאֲוָתוֹ, which is the most common equivalent of ἐπιθυμίαν and is moreover graphically similar. This may have been facilitated by the idea of "sons of one's youth," i.e., as the time when one's sexual appetites are strongest. It is possible that the translator did not know the Hebrew word (it is a *hapax legomenon* in the Psalms), but I do not regard this as likely.

g With Dahood (*Psalms*, 3:225; cf. Schmidt, *Psalmen*, 228; Maillot and Lelièvre, *Psaumes*, 162; but against Duhm, *Psalmen*, 439; Kissane, *Book of Psalms*, 581; Kraus, *Psalmen*, 1039), I parse יְדַבְּרוּ as from דבר I "destroy, drive back" (cf. KB, 199), with the preposition בְּ meaning "from." This continues the war imagery of vv. 4-5a, rather than changing it to a forensic image. Mary Cecilia Huyck ("Psalm-City: A Study of Psalm 127," *Worship* 40 [1966] 518-519) notes rightly that the images of arrows and the gate allude to the civic defense. Seeing defense

imagery here helps to clarify the difficult direct object marker in v. 5bβ, which
though it could be interpreted as a preposition, would nonetheless be a strange one in
connection with enemies in the gate (one would expect "against"). I do not accept
the argument of Allen (*Psalms 101-150,* 177) that there is no metaphor in v. 5b, and
therefore none needs to be continued. Even if this were true one would still expect
some continuity of the thought. It is rather surprising that Allen, who is generally
good at identifying literary structures, missed the obvious *inclusio* of the civic
defense imagery at the end of the psalm and YHWH's "watching" the city.

Interpretation

The psalm begins with a juxtaposition of two images that
demonstrate the futility of life without the help of YHWH. That a house
cannot be built properly without God's help has a double meaning. The
first is that of building an actual structure, such as a temple (often called
"house")—which may have been the meaning that lies behind the
ascription to Solomon—or a family dwelling.[61] This literal reading
would create a clear parallel to "city" in v. 1b.[62] But there is another,
metaphorical meaning that fits well with biblical usage and binds the
first half of the psalm with the second—that of having a family and, by
extension, of general prosperity. It appears that both meanings are not
only present but intended.

After the first two lines, there is an expansion on the theme of
YHWH's caring for people (God's "beloved," taken as plural, see
translation note e above) that takes as its starting point the vanity of
attempting to care for oneself apart from YHWH's participation in those
same activities. The first three hemicola of this section (v. 2) present a
series of three participles, which all correspond to each other and to the
participial human actors in v. 1. The verb in v. 2bβ (כן יתן לידידו
שׁנא) does not correspond to these participial phrases but rather to the
active verbs of v. 1, which have YHWH as the actor. Thus, no matter the

---

[61]Most recently see on this Hubert Irsigler, "'Umsonst ist es, dass ihr früh
aufsteht...': Psalm 127 und die Kritik der Arbeit in Israels Weisheitsliteratur,"
Biblischen Notizen 37 (1987) 52. Interestingly, the word pair *house / city* occurs
three times in Solomon's prayer at the dedication of the temple (see Daniel E.
Fleming, "'House'/'City': An Unrecognized Parallel Word Pair," *JBL* 105 [1986]
689), always with reference to the temple and its patron city, Jerusalem.

[62]See Fleming, "'House'/'City'," 689-693.

final interpretation of the word שָׁנֵא, it may at least be said that attempts to see v. 2bβ as having a human actor, and thus in some way corresponding to v. 2bα, ignore a crucial element of the composition.[63]

The second half of the psalm contains no difficult interpretive problems. Only v. 5a has occasioned significant dispute. There are really two distinct difficulties in this verse. On the one hand is that of the subject: As the MT stands, the subject of the verbs is the only available plural noun, בָּנִים "sons" (cf. JPSV "They shall not be put to shame when they contend...."). Many interpreters (e.g., NRSV) have elected to emend the verbs to singular, which would make הַגֶּבֶר "the man" the subject. The other problem is the meaning of the verbs. Are they primarily a forensic allusion or a military one?[64] The military allusion seems preferable for several reasons: 1) it makes better sense of the אֵת;[65] 2) it fits better with the context in which the sons are *"arrows* in the hand of a *warrior"*; 3) it creates an *inclusio* with v. 1, in which YHWH plays a part in the city defense—in this case by means of the gift of sons who defend it.

Many scholars have been convinced that the two "halves" of Psalm 127 (vv. 1-2; 3-5) were originally completely separate proverbial discussions—the first concerning the pointlessness of life without YHWH's help, and the second half concerning the value of progeny.[66]

---

[63]So, for example, Leo G. Perdue, *Wisdom and Cult: A Critical Analysis of the Views of Cult in the Wisdom Literatures of Israel and the Ancient Near East* (SBLDS 30; Missoula, MT: Scholars Press, 1977) 298. Perdue translates "For such a one gives to his beloved nothing" (by "nothing" Perdue means "neither sexual intercourse nor children"; 298), emending שָׁנֵא to שָׁוְא in light of a possible inclusio with v. 1 (p. 338, n. 122), and positing יְדִידוֹ as a grammatically incorrect masculine where one expects a feminine (p. 338, n. 121). Cf. F. Bussby, "A Note on שָׁנֵא in Ps. CXXVII 2," *JTS* 35 (1934) 306-307. On the other hand, attempts to see v. 2bα in a positive light fail in that they ignore the parallel of the participles; so Samuel Daiches, "Psalm 127.2. A New Explanation," *ExpTim* 45 (1933-34) 24-26.

[64]This is still something of an open question. Cf. the divergence of opinion, in fairly recent commentaries, between Maillot and Lelièvre (*Psaumes*, 162), who take דבר here as "repousser," and Kraus (*Psalmen*, 2:1039), who argues on the basis of 1 Kgs 3:22 (which is only marginally comparable) in favor of a forensic metaphor.

[65]Cf. Lam 3:12-13 for this imagery used in a very similar way.

[66]So Gustav E. Closen, "Gottvertrauen und Selbstbescheidung in der Schrift des Alten Bundes (Ps 131 [130]; 127 [126], 1-2)," *Geist und Leben* 15 (1940) 192, n. 4: "Alle Versuche, eine ursprüngliche literarische Einheit beider Proverbien

But the relationship between the two halves is much closer than first appears to be, as was first shown by Hans Schmidt.[67] An interesting parallel in Sumerian hymnody (the "Hymn to Nisiba"[68]) tends to confirm this view. The hymn begins with a very similar teaching that without the goddess no house or city, or anything else for that matter, would ever be built;[69] and it closes with a teaching that it is she who grants sons. It is clear also that in BH the phrase "build a house" often refers to the building of a family line (e.g., Deut 25:9; Ruth 4:11; Gen 16:2; 30:3; cf. also 2 Sam 7). Certainly from the standpoint of genre there are two separate proverbial statements here, but whether their collocation in this psalm is the result of its author or the work of an editor is impossible to determine. To my mind the former is more likely. The common thread between the two parts can be stated thus: Just as the source of sustenance and real protection is mysterious (i.e., belongs to the realm of the divine), so the source of children is mysterious; yet both are necessary for continued life. The verbs of the last line have the sons (not the father) as the subject. This fact is puzzling, until it becomes apparent that the poem is returning to the theme of God as the provider of a person's security: the sons, as God's gift, are the ones who are not "ashamed" in the gate, but rather are successful in providing the necessary protection for the father and for the rest of the city.

The sociological matrix in which this psalm arose is apparently that of the landed working class. They are people who stand to gain by extra hours of work, and who are protected by their sons. Thus the milieu of the small city would be primary. The psalm has thematic ties to the wisdom tradition, and can therefore be called a Wisdom psalm. But it is

---

festzuhalten, scheinen zu weniger natürlichen und geschichten Deutungen zu führen."

[67]Schmidt, *Psalmen*, 228-229; See also Patrick D. Miller, Jr., "Psalm 127—The House that Yahweh Builds," *JSOT* 22 (1982) 119-132.

[68]Adam Falkenstein and Wolfram von Soden, *Sumerische und akkadische Hymnen und Gebete* (Zurich: Artemis, 1953), 66-67. As far as I can determine, this hymn was first cited by Kraus (*Psalmen*, 2:1039).

[69]It is to be pointed out, however, that the parallel is not precise (a fact that is conspicuously neglected in many treatments; e.g., Miller's ["The House that Yahweh Builds"]), since the city in Psalm 127 is not "built" but "watched." This perhaps lends still more weight to the importance of the military reference at the end of the psalm.

not the kind of wisdom that is related to the temple and court.[70] Rather it is the popular wisdom that has its origins in family and clan tradition. The entire psalm seems to be concerned only with local, individual and family prosperity.[71] While it is true that the participles of vv. 1-2 are primarily plural, these are merely generalizations that are immediately applied to an individual (vv. 3-5).

PSALM 128

1 A song of ascents:

Fortunate is everyone who fears[a] YHWH,
   Who walks in [God's] ways.

2 The produce of your labor[b] you shall indeed eat.[c]
   May you be fortunate,[d] and have what is pleasant.
3 Your wife will be like a fruitful vine
   In the private parts[e] of your house.

---

[70]James Crenshaw (*Old Testament Wisdom: An Introduction* [Atlanta: John Knox Press, 1981] 56-57), among others, has argued against the long-standing assumption that the wisdom traditions were primarily kept alive in court schools in Israel. Certainly much of Egyptian and Mesopotamian wisdom literature belonged to such a setting, as the frequent emphasis on court manners and such concerns shows; but in Israel this seems to be less the case. Most of the sapiential material preserved in the Hebrew Bible derives from a less establishment-oriented, more family- and clan-oriented milieu. As Crenshaw puts it with respect to another genre of biblical Wisdom traditions:

> The vast majority of biblical proverbs seems to have arisen in a context other than the royal court. That setting for numerous proverbs was the family, where parental instruction was very much at home. This clan ethos saw the virtual union of law and instruction, both of which carried the full authority of the patriarch (56).

[71]I do not mean "individual prosperity" in the solipsistic sense in which this is sometimes used in the modern era. Individual prosperity has, quite naturally, important ramifications for the larger group (as can be seen in the fact that the sons defend the city), but it is nonetheless not this aspect that is primary, but the blessing of the father as the head of the family. Cf. Schmidt (*Psalmen*, 228), who views the song as the blessing on a new family: "Ein junges Ehepaar...hat einen Sohn bekommen."

Your sons will be like olive sprouts
Encircling your table.

4   Behold! Surely thus[f] is blessed the man
Who fears YHWH.

5   May YHWH bless you from Zion.
Delight in[g] Jerusalem's prosperity
All your life long!

6   Delight in your grandchildren, also!
Peace be upon Israel.

Notes to the Translation

[a] The LXX reads the participle as plural. It is possible that the plural ending
(*yodh*) has dropped out by haplography, but it is equally plausible—or more so,
because of the singular throughout the rest of the psalm—that the translator read an
extra *yodh* by dittography (whether or not this was actually present in the *Vorlage*).

[b] Most exegetes explain the phrase יְגִיעַ כַּפֶּיךָ as "the fruit of your hands'
labor." Literally the phrase designates manual, and usually strenuous, labor (as, e.g.,
in Gen 31:42). The noun יְגִיעַ on its own can mean either labor proper or the fruits
thereof (cf. Deut 28:33; Jer 20:5; Ezek 23:29; Pss 109:11; 78:46; Job 10:3). Where
the formulaic phrase יְגִיעַ כַּף is used (יְגִיעַ יַד, which would be synonymous, does
not occur in BH), the same double meaning seems also to be possible. In Gen 31:42,
for example, it clearly refers to one's hard labor, but in Hag 1:11 it is just as clearly
delineated as the fruit of that labor. Likewise in Job 10:3, the human being is the
fruit of God's labor.

[c] The particle כִּי is not directly represented in the LXX. For this reason Duhm
(*Die Psalmen* 439) regards it as a dittography from the previous pronominal suffix.
This, however, probably assumes too much literalism on the part of the LXX
translator.

[d] I have tried to retain the usual distinction between אַשְׁרֵי and בֵּרַךְ, where the
latter normally properly signifies blessing as such and the former represents a state of
being "fortunate." In this sentence, however, אַשְׁרֶיךָ functions very much like
אַתָּה בָרוּךְ. Carl Keller ("Les «béatitudes» de l'ancien testament," in Jean Cadier,
ed., *Hommage a Wilhelm Vischer* [Montpellier: Causse, Graille, Castelnau, 1960]
88-100) argues, however, that אַשְׁרֵי quite normally has the significance of blessing
in the psalms.

[e] The noun יְרְכְתַיִם refers literally to the inside of the thighs, and therefore to
the reproductive organs. It also refers to any inside corner. Grossberg (*Centripetal
and Centrifugal Structures*, 44) has recently emphasized the double-entendre here.
The wife's fruitfulness (obviously in bearing children) would take place in the
recesses of the house, but there is probably also a poetic allusion to the wife's
sexuality. I have tried to represent this double-entendre in the translation. It must be

added that the majority of scholars take this simply as representing the notion that women ought to stay out of the public eye. While this may in fact be the strict sense, I find it difficult to explain this odd turn of phrase simply on that basis.

f   The Hebrew construction הִנֵּה כִי־כֵן is so unusual that the majority of scholars have opted to drop the כִי. Kraus (*Psalmen,* 1041) may be taken as exemplary: for him the words conjoined as they are "ergeben einen kaum möglichen affirmativen Ansatz des Verses"; he therefore omits it as a dittography from כֵן. Marrs ("The *Šyry Hmᶜlwt,* 97) has noted that הִנֵּה כֵן and הִנֵּה כִי are both common expressions, the former being more common in the Songs of Ascent (Pss 123:2; 127:3-4; neither of which is quite like Ps 128:4, since both are final comparisons of extended similes, although perhaps the observation is still valid), but the latter being more common in the Psalms generally. He believes that כִי was added mistakenly for this reason. One may note that the LXX does not have a corresponding word for כִי, but this does not constitute sufficient evidence to regard it as spurious, especially since the same word is not represented in the LXX of v. 2. In the end I have opted to retain it, in spite of its linguistic difficulty, on the grounds that כִי is a very multivalent word that as such is expected to occur in a broad variety of syntactic connections. On the latter subject see James Muilenburg, "The Linguistic and Rhetorical Uses of the Particle כִי in the Old Testament," *HUCA* 32 (1961) 135-160.

g   The form of the verb is imperative. When רְאֵה is used with an indirect object בְ, as here, it often means "enjoy", as seen most clearly in Obadiah 12 or Ps 106:5a, both of which have it parallel to שָׂמַח (cf. JPSV "share the prosperity..."). I take the רְאֵה of v. 6 in this sense also (i.e., subsuming the בְ into itself for poetic purposes; cf. Ps 120:5). The meaning "live to see" might also be present, and could possibly be primary.

Interpretation

Several basic interpretational matters attach to Psalm 128. The first to be mentioned is the meaning of אַשְׁרֵי, which is one of the two typical "blessing" words. This psalm provides a good example of how the word is more than simply "happy," as it is sometimes translated. The German *glücklich* comes a little closer, but still does not do adequate justice to the word's use in this psalm. Here it seems to be used synonymously with בְרךְ "bless" (cf. v. 4).[72] It is used in the phrase אַשְׁרֶיךָ וְטוֹב לָךְ, which is almost certainly benedictory, since it uses the second person. The meaning of אַשְׁרֵי as benediction is strengthened further by the

---

[72]On אַשְׁרֵי as a benediction see Keller, "Les «béatitudes» de l'ancien testament," 92. He finds that most often the word describes a state not in the present, but hoped for in the future, and therefore posits that the semantic domain of this word is not significantly different from that of בְרךְ.

inclusio with v. 4 (see below), in which בָרך appears. In this psalm אַשְׁרֵי does not simply describe a state (as in Psalm 1, e.g.), but attempts to bring that state into being.

The second matter to be discussed is that of the conjunctions prefixed to the parallel imperative verbs of vv. 5b and 6. One normally does not expect to see such imperatives linked to other non-imperative forms in this way. Probably this is to be explained on the basis of the jussive verb יְבָרֶכְךָ which has YHWH as the subject, so that the imperatives become consequents of that blessing. The meaning of the sentence would then be, as Joüon states, "Que de Sion Jéhovah te bénisse, afin que tu contemples la beauté de Jérusalem,"[73] and likewise to the end that one's own prosperity is assured. That this is put in the imperative rather than the jussive is therefore a matter of style, which adds to the growing reservoir of stylistic irregularities found in these songs.

In its present form the psalm may be said to be composed of two parts. The first four verses begin as popular wisdom that "could be transferred into the book of Proverbs without causing havoc or alarm,"[74] but quickly modulate to direct address, lending to the section a feeling more of blessing than of exhortation. The last two verses constitute a blessing of a different sort. In this section the prosperity of the individual is bound to that of Zion and Jerusalem, and ultimately, of Israel as a whole.

Psalm 128 is among the clearest examples of redactional work in the Songs of Ascents. An *inclusio* is created by יְרֵא יְהוָה in vv. 1 and 4, and by אַשְׁרֵי (v. 1) and יְבָרך (v. 4). That these two verses surround a threefold blessing of the God-fearing man (גֶבֶר) provides a stable basis for affirming the fact of an envelope structure in vv. 1-4. Verses 5-6 lie outside this structure. Moreover they are characterized by a concern for

---

[73]Joüon, *Grammaire de l'hébreu biblique*, §99c, n. 1. So also GKC §110i: When the imperative (with *waw* copulative) depends on a jussive or cohortative, it "frequently expresses also a consequence that is to be expected with certainty, and often expresses a consequence which is intended, or in fact an intention."

[74]J. Kenneth Kuntz, "The Canonical Wisdom Psalms of Ancient Israel--Their Rhetorical, Thematic, and Formal Dimensions," in *Rhetorical Criticism: Essays in Honor of James Muilenburg*, ed. Jared J. Jackson and Martin Kessler (PTMS 1; Pittsburgh, PA: Pickwick Press, 1974) 217.

Jerusalem that does not figure into vv. 1-4. In vv. 1-4 "[n]ous sommes donc probablement en milieu rural."[75] Life revolves around the small household, food production, and human procreation.[76] The same cannot be said for vv. 5-6, which are characterized both by theme (Jerusalem as the source of individual prosperity) and by two specific phrases (יְבָרֶכְךָ יהוה מִצִּיּוֹן and שָׁלוֹם עַל־יִשְׂרָאֵל) that recur in the Songs of Ascents. In light of this evidence I believe that vv. 5-6 are added as part of a redactional program (see Chap. 3), rather than being part of the original blessing.

The vocabulary and thematic content of the first four verses belong to the Wisdom tradition. The emphasis on the individual worshiper as the "God-Fearer" (יְרֵא יְהוָה), the form אַשְׁרֵי, and the copious deployment of metaphor all point in this direction.[77] But unlike Psalm 127, the primary purpose is not that of instruction (although this element is also present in the third person of vv. 1 and 4), but that of blessing. Because the types of things blessed—the fertility of labor and family— are those found in Levitical blessings (cf. Deut 28:3-6), and, more importantly, because the latter part of the psalm applies these blessings to Israel as a whole, some scholars have seen in this psalm a priestly blessing.[78] Much of the force of such an hypothesis disappears, however, if the last two verses are part of a redactional effort. The material of the first four verses certainly has a benedictory character, but nothing there predisposes one in favor of a *priestly* benediction.

The setting of the redactional effort (vv. 5-6) is readily apparent. There the concern for the prosperity of the individual Israelite finds

---

[75]Maillot and Lelièvre, *Psaumes*, 166-167.

[76]According to Schmidt (*Psalmen*, 229), the one being blessed is not in the temple (and so is not being blessed by a priest), but is rather in the course of daily work at home. In his view, such a blessing would have been spoken by farmer visiting a friend's house.

[77]See the criteria developed by Kuntz ("Canonical Wisdom Psalms of Ancient Israel," 210), which I here adopt.

[78]Cf. Gerstenberger, Jutzler, and Boecker, *Psalmen in der Sprache unserer Zeit*, 206; Maillot and Lelièvre, *Psaumes*, 166. Allen (*Psalms 101-150*, 184) posits that the song was composed for, rather than simply used in, the processional to the temple, an interpretation that he derives both from the supposition that we have here a priestly blessing and, undoubtedly, from his beliefs about the character of the collection.

reinterpretation as being related to, perhaps even dependent upon, the prosperity of Jerusalem. The blessing pronounced in vv. 1-4 now comes from Zion, which, in other redactional materials in the Songs of Ascents, is the *omphalus mundi* from which all blessing flows. The phrase "enjoy the good of Jerusalem" does not necessarily imply that the addressee is a resident of Jerusalem; rather it refers to the general prosperity that the whole land may expect when Jerusalem as the locus of cultic life fares well (cf. Hag 1:1-11). In Chap. 3 I shall treat this text as part of what I believe is a pervasive redactional layer in the songs, and therefore omit further discussion of it here.

PSALM 129

1 A song of ascents:

Let Israel say the "Much have they oppressed me from my youth":

2 Much have they oppressed me from my youth,
But they were not too strong for me.[a]

3 Upon my back the plowers[b] plowed,
They lengthened their rows.[c]

4 YHWH the Righteous[d]
Has broken[e] the cords[f] of the wicked!

5 May all those who hate Zion
Be ashamed and turn back![g]

6 May they be like rooftop-grass[h]
Which, before it can be uprooted,[i] withers,

7 With which the reaper does not get a handful,
Nor gather it into the robe's fold.

8 So those who pass by do not say,
"The blessing of YHWH come to you;[j]
We bless you in the name of YHWH."

Notes to the Translation

a As Duhm (*Psalmen,* 440) observed, גַּם here modifies the verb rather than the negative, so that he translates the phrase "mich nicht auch überwältigt." The displacement from the normal word order, however, may help to convey the idea of asseveration, which is obvious at any rate from the content.

b The LXX has οἱ ἁμαρτωλοί (Aquila and Symmachus correct it to ἀροτριῶντες and τεκταίνοντας, respectively). The Hebrew *Vorlage* probably had רְשָׁעִים (11QPsᴬ has this reading, thus making the probability that the shift—in whichever direction the shift occurred—happened at the level of Hebrew texts quite likely), which contains four of the same five letters. Allen says that the LXX variant is "not simply a corruption based on v. 4, but an explanatory gloss in terms of v. 4, which was subsequently taken as a correction of חֹרְשִׁים 'plowmen' and replaced it" (*Psalms 101-150,* 187; so also Keet, *A Study of the Psalms of Ascents,* 70). On the side of the MT reading one notes the continuance of the plowing-metaphor; on the side of the LXX reading one notes the presence of "the wicked" in v. 4. Anderson (*The Book of Psalms,* 2:872), following the LXX and 11QPsᴬ, regards the "plowers" reading as secondary, and derived from the next line. Textually the evidence seems to me about equal. I have retained the MT reading primarily for convention's sake.

c The LXX continues its interpretation in terms of "the wicked" rather than the plow image. Here the MT has הֶאֱרִיכוּ לְמַעֲנוֹתָם (the form מַעֲנוֹת is a *hapax legomenon* in the MT; the *qere* מַעֲנִיתָם means "their furrow." The *kethib* is probably to be accepted. This word appears only in 2 Sam 14:14 [singular] in another difficult text!). The LXX translates ἐμάκρυναν τὴν ἀνομίαν αὐτῶν. It is possible that the translator read (rightly or mistakenly) עֲוֹנוֹתָם rather than לְמַעֲנוֹתָם. Given the rarity of the word in BH it is difficult to say with certainty whether this is the more correct reading. Several arguments may be put in favor of the MT's reading, however. First there is the continuance of the "plowing" metaphor was begun in v. 3 (i.e., the MT makes sense within itself); second the natural tendency with a difficult word such as this one would be to substitute a better-known word, such as עֲוֹנוֹתָם; and third, it would be a strange use of the verb הֶאֱרִיךְ "to lengthen" (often "to prolong"), with the idea of "wickedness," since "prolonging" something negative is otherwise unknown in BH (normally it is used in the sense of prolonging one's life, etc.). This latter is of course an *argumentum e silentio,* but is nonetheless important.

d I think Dahood (*Psalms,* 3:231) is correct in making צַדִּיק an epithet of God here, rather than a predicate adjective, which is the idea implied by the masoretic accentuation.

e Marrs ("The *Šyry Hmᶜlwt,*" 102) and Dahood (*Psalms,* 3:231) parse קִצֵּץ as a "precative perfect." This admittedly fits well both with the lament that precedes it and the curse that follows. As I read it, however, the perfect indicates the action that YHWH *has taken* on behalf of the people. This past action then serves as the basis for the imprecation of vv. 5-8: Since YHWH has acted in this way in the past, God ought to continue in this pattern.

f The translation of עֲבוֹת as "cords" is almost universally accepted. Equally plausible, however, would be "branch" (עֲבוֹת II, cf. Ps 118:27; KB 674). Either would fit well with the agricultural imagery of the psalm, the former with the plowing imagery of vv. 2-3 and the latter with the plant imagery of vv. 6-7. Perhaps the double-entendre is intentional.

g I understand the imperfect verbs of vv. 5-6 as precatives, rather than with the simple future tense or with the present tense. In my opinion this reading makes the best sense of the extended metaphors in vv. 6-8, which function as curses in any case. The perfect verbs of vv. 6-8 function in relationship to the precative imperfects: they describe the situation desired by the supplicant.

h Several mss (see de Rossi, *Variae lectiones*, 4:82) have the reading כַּחֲצִיר גַּנּוֹת "like grass of the gardens," which seems clearly to be a scribal error based on the similarity of the letters *nun* and *gimel*. This reading would make no sense, since grass would presumably flourish in a garden, and would therefore hardly wither before it could be uprooted.

i Reading, with the MT, שֶׁקַּדְמַת שָׁלַף יָבֵשׁ. The proposal of KB (823, 950), that it be read שֶׁקָּדִים תִּשׁדֹּף יָבֵשׁ "which the east wind scorches and dries up," is at first blush appealing because of the very close parallel in 2 Kgs 19:26, in which the "grass of the rooftops" is placed in conjunction with the root שׁדף. However, if the phrases were taken as analogous, then שְׁדֵפָה in 2 Kgs 19:26 would be the semantic equivalent of יָבֵשׁ in Ps 129:6. The analogy does suggest another fruitful line of thought, though: it could well be that in Ps 129:6 the word שׁלף would mean "grow up" rather than "uproot." This would make better sense even than the translation here given, and the parallel with 2 Kgs 19:26 might well be reckoned as decisive; but since the more normal meaning of the work is "draw forth," however I have opted tentatively to retain this translation.

j The phrase בִּרְכַּת...אֶל־ is rare. By far the most common preposition used with this noun is עַל. The LXX translated the phrase Εὐλογία κυρίου ἐφ᾽ ὑμᾶς, which would tend to argue for emending to the more common Hebrew phrase בִּרְכַּת יהוה עֲלֵיכֶם. This receives support from 11QPsᴬ and the Syriac, and is therefore argued as correct by Marrs, "The *Šyry Hmᶜlwt*," 104. However, there is one other case with the preposition אֶל: Ezek 44:30. This phrase there reads תִּתְּנוּ לַכֹּהֵן לְהָנִיחַ בְּרָכָה אֶל־בֵּיתֶךָ וְרֵאשִׁית עֲרִסוֹתֵיכֶם "The first-fruits of your barley meal (?) you shall give to the priest, so that he may set the blessing to your house." There too one expects עַל but gets אֶל, and BHS suggests emendation, but the presence of a very similar phrase in two places advises caution.

Interpretation

The interpreter of Psalm 129 must explain several salient features of the psalm. One of these is the problem of identifying the referent of "they." No non-metaphorical identification at all is made prior to v. 4, unless one reads with the LXX of v. 3, and even there only an ambiguous "the wicked" is present. Barring that, more explicit identification is found only twice in the psalm: "they" are identified as "the wicked" (v.

4) and as "haters of Zion" (v. 5).[79] The problem is exacerbated by a second difficulty: the meaning of the image of plowing on the speaker's back.[80] This image has three possible meanings: It may be intended to convey the idea of mourning;[81] or the primary meaning may be that of stripes inflicted on the back by foreign oppressors, metaphorically represented as furrows plowed in a field, and thus perhaps representing oppressive foreign domination;[82] on the other hand, because of the phrase "the cords of the wicked" (v. 4) it may be that the plowing image is primarily that of whipping a work animal while it is laboring.[83] I see it as a mixture of the latter two metaphors, beginning with the speaker as the ground upon which the furrows are being plowed and then shifting to portray the speaker as an animal forced to plow the ground.[84]

The third difficulty is the manner in which v. 8—particularly v. 8b—fits with the rest of the psalm. Two interpretational camps oppose one another. Some authors regard v. 8b as the answer to the blessing of v. 8a.[85] But since this blessing is not offered—and since a change in speaker would be thus indicated—one would expect some indication of this, such as "and they do not answer them," as the Targum supplies (cf.

---

[79]Crüsemann (*Hymnus und Danklied*, 172) argues that the phrase "haters of Zion" never indicates foreign enemies, but always "innerisraelitische Parteien," as in 2 Chr 19:2, where it refers to north Israelites. One may question this statement, however, since in the Chronicler's work north-Israelites are presented *precisely* as foreigners.

[80]Alan Cooper ("The Absurdity of Amos 6:12a," *JBL* 107 [1988] 725-727) has argued that חרש is a standardized military image, particularly in Amos 6:12a. In support of this thesis he cites Jer 26:18=Mic 3:12. In view of the other agricultural imagery in the psalm, however, I do not regard this interpretation as likely.

[81]Samuel E. Loewenstamm ("The Hebrew Root *ḥrš* in the Light of the Ugaritic Texts," in *Comparative Studies in Biblical and Ancient Oriental Literatures*, 166-170), has pointed to the Ugaritic text *CTA* 5:VI:11-22 (= *UT* 67/IV,11-22), *yḥrṯ kgn ảp lb* "he plows his breast [lit. 'the nose of his heart'] as if it were a garden," where the verb refers to the ritual cutting of oneself. So also Gibson, *Canaanite Myths and Legends*, p. 73, n. 19. The view that the mourning rite is the primary explanation for this image is accepted by Crüsemann, *Hymnus und Danklied*, 170-171.

[82]Duhm, *Psalmen*, 440; Keet, *A Study of the Psalms of Ascents*, 70.

[83]So Anderson (*Book of Psalms*, 2:872), for whom the allusion is to the taskmaster's whip; Allen, *Psalms 101-150*, 187; de Wette, *Kommentar über die Psalmen*, 589-590.

[84]Kissane, *Book of Psalms*, 585; Anderson, *Book of Psalms*, 2:873.

[85]de Wette, *Kommentar über die Psalmen*, 590; Dahood, *Psalms*, 3:223; Anderson, *Book of Psalms*, 2:874.

the responsorial indications in Ruth 2:4). The absence of this has led many interpreters, guided by their suppositions about the milieu of the Songs of Ascents, to propose an explanation on the basis of the psalm's liturgical recitation.[86] But this interpretation relies heavily on a debatable premise about the liturgical character of the Songs of Ascents as a whole, not upon the psalm itself. One line of evidence that has thus far not been adduced by scholars against this thesis is the evidence of other "liturgical blessings" in the Songs of Ascents (since proponents of this view regard the blessing as part of the milieu of the group as a whole). Should one accept such a view, the obvious comparison would be with the formulas יְבָרֶכְךָ יהוה מִצִּיּוֹן (Pss 128:5; 134:3) and שָׁלוֹם עַל־יִשְׂרָאֵל (Pss 125:5; 128:6), both of which speak of the recipients of the blessing as singular entities. By contrast, Ps 129:8b has the recipients in the plural. The latter fits, in other words, with the plurality of persons who are not blessed using the formula בִּרְכַּת יהוה אֲלֵיכֶם, who are also "the wicked" (רְשָׁעִים), but not with the hypothesized community of pilgrimage. For this reason I tentatively regard the second hypothesis, that the sentence is the answer (not) given to the (withheld) blessing, as the more likely one.

Several salient features of the form of Psalm 129 help to define both the genre of the piece and its narrative flow. The first and most obvious is the repetition of the first colon of the psalm, with the liturgical directive יֹאמַר־נָא יִשְׂרָאֵל "let Israel say." This immediately draws connections both with Psalm 124 and with Psalm 118, which are the only comparable examples of this phenomenon in the Psalms. The cultic nature of this repetition and directive is not so clear in Psalms 124 and 129 as it is in Psalm 118, where not only Israel, but also "the house of

---

[86]Weiser (*Psalms*, 770-772) believes the psalm to be a "liturgical formulary" (770), so that the psalm constitutes a "cursing of 'those who hate Zion' and a benediction upon the congregation." According to him v. 8b is therefore to be seen as the blessing upon the congregation (so also Crüsemann, *Hymnus und Danklied*, 172; Keet, *A Study of the Psalms of Ascents*, 74; Kraus, *Psalmen*, 2:1046; Marrs, "Šyry Hmᶜlwt," 104; Allen, *Psalms 101-150*, 187; A. J. O. van der Wal, "The Structure of Psalm cxxix," *VT* 38 [1988] 364-367). This explanation, however, seems somewhat forced by comparison with that given below, which is certainly the more natural reading. Duhm (*Psalmen*, 441) sees the phrase as having both the character of (un)returned blessing on the reaper and the sense of a final benediction for the psalm.

Aaron" and "those who fear YHWH" are directed to speak (although in Psalm 118 the motivation for the speaking, rather than the incipit of the psalm, is given, and the order of directive and repeated element is reversed). In both Psalms 118 and 124 this element constitutes a call to community thanksgiving for YHWH's salvific action. Conversely, Psalm 129 is a lament, the only clear elements of thanksgiving being vv. 2b and 4 (I interpret the imperfect verbs as precatives; see above). With the exception of יֹאמַר־נָא יִשְׂרָאֵל and v. 5, however, the entirety of Psalm 129 is individual in character.[87] I shall argue that the reason for this is that the song was originally the lament of an individual that was subsequently reinterpreted as corporate lament.

Structurally the psalm is divided into two parts: a narration of the oppression felt by the speaker (vv. 2-4) and a curse upon the oppressors (vv. 5-8).[88] The first bicolon introduces the psalm, but does not figure into the structure of the psalm as such. The second bicolon (which

---

[87]Crüsemann (*Hymnus und Danklied*, 168-173) argues, in my view convincingly, that the language of individual lament has been co-opted for use by the community using the formula יֹאמַר־נָא יִשְׂרָאֵל, which he regards as secondary. It is of course well known that an "I" in a psalm does not necessarily preclude community participation in it (see, among others, Mowinckel, "The I of the Psalms" in *Psalms in Israel's Worship*, vol. 1; Steven J. L. Croft, *The Identity of the Individual in the Psalms*, JSOTSup 44 [Sheffield, UK: JSOT Press, 1987]), nor is individual imagery exempt from use by the community. However, as I argue below, there are good reasons other than this to consider the two "communalizing" elements as redactional. I therefore hold that the "communalizing" tendency takes place at the redactional level, rather than at the level of the original psalm.

[88]Van der Wal ("The Structure of Psalm cxxix," 364-365) has a useful discussion of the few variants in scholarly opinion about the structure of the psalm, although he himself disagrees with this outline. For him the structure is seen clearly in the linguistic clues, with vv. 1-"8b" (i.e., v. 8aα) are one division and v. "8c" (i.e., 8aβ) is the second. He divides the first part into vv. 1-3, where the first person appears, and vv. 4a-8aα which is framed by "verbless clauses" (v. 4a, however, has a verb!). Both of these parts constitute a long "[s]ummons of the priests to sing a song to JHWH." Verse 8aβ is then the priestly response to the summons with a benediction. He posits that the entire structure is parallel to that of Psalm 134 (where vv. 1-2 are the "summons" and v. 3 is the "benediction"). In my opinion this analysis has several objectionable elements. First, such a division runs counter to the obvious content divisions in the psalm, namely the shifts in metaphor. Second there is nothing outside v. 1 to make one think of a "[s]ummons...to sing a song to JHWH." Third, the comparison to Psalm 134 seems rather forced, since in the latter case the entire psalm, not simply the first verse, is clearly a summons to worship.

repeats the first half of the first) begins the song proper and sets the tone
for the whole: From youth on, enemies have oppressed the psalmist, but
in the end they were not victorious. By presenting these two polarities
the poet introduces immediately the theme of thanksgiving to God for
preservation through opposition. One bicolon (v. 3) describes the
unfortunate situation of the speaker; the next (v. 4) narrates God's rescue
from that situation. The shift in metaphor from the poet as plowed
ground to the poet as plowing animal is not particularly bothersome,
since this psalm clearly abounds in mixed metaphors (aside from this
shift there is also a shift from the enemies as farmers to the enemies as
grass; the imagery of Psalm 129 is not steady, but rather shifts with
remarkable rapidity), and it is in any case doubtful whether ancient
Israelites had the same scruples against mixing of metaphors that western
people have.

        With the narration of God's action in the past completed, the psalm
moves on, in classic form, to pray for continued action in the future.
Here the agricultural metaphors are momentarily interrupted by a
depiction of the enemy as army. The language of "be ashamed" (בּוֹשׁ)
and "turn back" (סוֹג) is that of warfare,[89] as the phrase שֹׂנְאֵי צִיּוֹן
"haters of Zion" implies. After this short curse on the enemies of Zion
another agricultural metaphor comes to the fore, in which the enemies
are likened to grass of an especially transitory nature. The "grass on the
roof" that "withers before it can be pulled up" is obviously comparable
to the metaphor in which grass represents the transitoriness of the human
condition (cf., e.g., Isa 40:6; Pss 37:2; 103:15). It is noteworthy that in
v. 7 once again the image shifts. No longer is the grass simply an
ephemeral plant that depends upon good conditions for growth (and
therefore dies quickly when those conditions fail), serving little
purpose;[90] it has now become a plant to be reaped, but because it has

---

[89]On סוֹג: cf., e.g., Jer 46:5; Ps 35:4 (note vv. 1-3). On בּוֹשׁ (although usually
with its military meaning it is in *hiphil*) cf., e.g., Jer 2:36; Isa 42:17.

[90]In the Hebrew Bible חָצִיר refers to grasses that grow near oases or other
places where water is abundant. Thus the word can mean a leek (Num 11:5) or a
reed (e.g., Isa 44:4). In any case, however, it does not signify plants that might be
reaped, for which probably either חִטָּה or the more general דָּגָן would have been
used. By far the most common use of the word is in poetic materials, signifying the
fleeting character of existence, whether that of non-specific individuals or of the
"wicked," as here. This transitoriness is reinforced by the fact that it grows on the

died before harvest time does not achieve its destiny.[91]   Verse 8a continues this same metaphor by alluding to the custom in which passersby say a blessing on those who are reaping. Here of course it is alluded to negatively; "since there is no harvest, there is no harvest blessing."[92]   It is in this context that I believe the last line of the psalm best fits.

The language of Psalm 129, with the exceptions of vv. 1 and 5, is entirely individual. With the exception of these same verses, it is also entirely agricultural. The metaphors shift from plowing to (not) reaping, the former being metaphors for the pain imposed on the poet ("I") by "the wicked ones" and the latter being metaphorical curses on them. In the midst of this is v. 5, which applies this language of individual lament to more nationalistic concerns, utilizing both nationalized enemies ("haters of Zion") and imagery of war, rather than of agriculture. This same nationalism is what drives v. 1, which summons "Israel" to recite the psalm. Further, v. 1 uses a phrase found elsewhere in the Songs of Ascents. In Chap. 3, I argue that this phrase is part of a redactional effort to reinterpret older songs to a Jerusalemite agenda. In other words, in the same way that v. 1 stands apart from the rest of the psalm on both formal and thematic grounds, v. 5 stands apart on thematic grounds. In light of the presence of this same tendency pervading the Songs of Ascents, I think it highly likely that these two verses are redactional.[93] The remainder of this psalm is then seen as a petition, using agricultural imagery throughout, that God bring the salvific action already begun (vv. 1-4) to its completion in the utter ruin of the psalmist's enemies (vv. 6-8).

---

rooftops. The image is that of a mud-roof house, on which grass might spring up during a rainy season, but lacking depth in which plants might put forth roots and drying out more quickly than does the ground (cf. Kraus, *Psalmen*, 2:1043). That this is the type of construction in view is probably another good evidence in favor of the agrarian milieu of this language (see Victor H. Matthews, *Manners and Customs in the Bible* [Peabody, MA: Hendrickson Publishers, 1988] 44-49).

[91] An alternate reading would be that the grass is not reaped because it is not a grain, but a grass. But the point of the curse, though complex and mixed, is that the wicked should be like grass, which is here, as elsewhere, primarily a metaphor for transitoriness.

[92] Anderson, *Book of Psalms*, 2:874.

[93] So also Seybold, *Wallfahrtspsalmen*, 28-29.

The redactor reinterprets this individual lament so that it becomes a lament of "Israel" through the nationalizing elements of vv. 1 and 5.

    Several features of Psalm 129's pre-redactional form combine to point fairly clearly to the sociological milieu that serves as the background for the psalm. The evidence comes primarily from the imagery itself, which would have been somewhat out of place in an urban center. The activities referred to here are those of agrarian workers, not those of administrators and landed aristocracy. The type of house envisioned in v. 6 is the sort found in small, unwalled settlements (see n. 90 above). The method of reaping—filling one's hand, gathering into the folds of one's garment—are those of small-scale production such as that found in subsistence-farming communities. A second line of evidence is the linguistic peculiarities with which Psalm 129 (along with many of the Songs of Ascents) abounds. The use of the adverb רַבַּת (vv. 1-2); the phrase הֶאֱרִיכוּ לְמַעֲנוֹתָם, which is distinctive in several respects (see translation note c above); the use of -שֶׁ twice; and the unusual combination of בִּרְכַּת with אֶל all point to the exotic character of this psalm. None of this necessitates that the pre-redactional version of the psalm *must* have belonged to a rural, non-Jerusalemite milieu; but they, along with the redactional analysis, provide what to my mind is convincing evidence that such was indeed the case.

PSALM 130

1   A song of ascents:

     From the depths I call[a] you, O YHWH,
2   O Lord, Pay attention to my voice!
     Let your ears be attentive[b]
         To the sound of my prayer.

3   If you kept track of wrongs, O Yah,
         O Lord, who would stand?
4   But with you is forgiveness
         So that you are feared.[c]

5 I wait, O YHWH,
   My soul waits[d] for your word.[e]
6 I wait with my soul[f] for the Lord
   More than watchers for the morning,
   Watchers for the morning.[g]

7 Let Israel hope for YHWH,
   For with YHWH is faithfulness,
   And redemption is plenteous with [God].
8   [God] will redeem Israel from all its wrongs.

Notes to the Translation

ᵃ As in Ps 120:1, the perfect here probably denotes an *iterative* sense, in which the verb is seen as complete in the speaking of it. Cf. GKC §106i, pp. 311-312.

ᵇ Whereas the MT has תִּהְיֶינָה אָזְנֶיךָ קַשֻּׁבוֹת לְקוֹל תַּחֲנוּנָי ("let your ears be attentive to the sound of my prayer"), 11QPsᴬ reads תהי נא אוזנכה קשובת לי ("let your ear (please) be attentive to me"), transforming the plural "ears" to singular (the phonological value of נא תהי is very close to that of תִּהְיֶינָה), and apparently also dropping the reference to the "sound of my prayer" (there is a lacuna at this point, but it does not seem to be large enough to fit the phrase present in the MT; and in any case 11QPsᴬ of Psalm 130 appears to have variations of other kinds throughout). The MT reading is attested in the LXX and other ancient versions, but in the HB it is possible to have "attentiveness" (קֶשֶׁב) directed either to the prayer itself (cf. Pss 34:16; 78:1), as in the MT, or to the person praying (Ps 55:3), as in 11QPsᴬ. Perhaps the balance of the line is one factor that would argue for the MT reading as against the Qumran one.

ᶜ LXXᴿ reads τοῦ νόμου σου (also the Vulgate and many Hebrew mss, according to de Rossi, *Variae lectiones*, 4:82-83), and some scholars, following this reading, adopt some form of תּוֹרָה here (so Rick R. Marrs, "A Cry From the Depths (Ps 130)," *ZAW* 100 (1988) 83, and "*Šyry Hmᶜlwt*," 110-111; Kissane, *Book of Psalms*, 587) , either with or without the second person singular suffix, but most have argued for the reading of the MT (Anderson, *Book of Psalms*, 867). The LXXᴬ,ˢ read του ὀνόματος σου, which is probably to be understood as a corruption from the Greek translation cited above, perhaps also being influenced by the frequency of this phrase. Robert C. Dentan ("An Exposition of an Old Testament Passage," JBR 15 [1947] 158) calls this "the error of a sleepy translator." I do not find adequate evidence for certainty about either reading. On behalf of the reading לְמַעַן תִּוָּרֵא it may be said that God's mercy is often depicted as being primarily for the sake of God's own glory (cf. Ps 79:9; Exod 32:11-14).

ᵈ The suggestion of Marrs ("A Cry from the Depths," 84) that נַפְשִׁי in v. 5's קִוְּתָה נַפְשִׁי is a dittography (from v. 6a), yielding a "closely developed structure," seems to me to be untenable, and based primarily on a desire to see structural perfection. Collocation is necessary in order for dittography to take place. The perfect verb הוֹחַלְתִּי has, according to Joüon (*Grammaire de l'hébreu biblique*, §112a [p. 295-297]) a "quasi statif" status. Thus the perfect is best translated into the present.

ᵉ This is a change in scansion of the lines from that presented in most translations (e.g., JPSV, NRSV) and from that found, for example, in BHS. To my knowledge it was first proposed by Johannes Tromp ("The Text of Psalm cxxx 5-6," VT 39/1 [1989] 100-103). The only real problem with this scansion is the lack of agreement between הוֹחַלְתִּי and נַפְשִׁי (5b, 6a). Tromp thinks this was probably the reason for confusion in the versions (p. 102). In any case the *yodh* and the *he* are similar in all the ancient scripts, and could easily have been confused. The addition of the *waw* at the beginning of v. 5b could easily have arisen as a result of taking the verb הוֹחַלְתִּי with v. 5 or by dittography with the final *yodh* of v. 5a. (That the text is in poor shape is probably evidenced by the apparent addition of הוחילי in 11QPsᴬ , which in addition does not have the *waw*. Cf. LXX.) The text according to Tromp is as follows:

> qwyty YHWH qwth npšy ldbrw
> hwḥlty npšy ʾdny mšmrym lbqr
> šmrym lbqr yḥl yśrʾl ʾl YHWH

It should be noted, secondly, that I have emended (with the LXX but against Aquila) the third masculine singular suffix ("[God's] word") to a second masculine singular suffix ("your word"). This is required by v. 5a, which I regard as almost certainly vocative (cf. Kraus, *Psalmen*, 1047). Werner H. Schmidt ("Gott und Mensch in Ps. 130: Formgeschichtliche Erwägungen," *ThZ* 22/4 [1966] 249-250) views the shift from second person to third person as the beginning of the wisdom teacher's comment on the psalm: "Das Gebet geht in eine Lehraussage über, statt Gott anzureden."

ᶠ For this reading cf. the LXX, which probably reads a third feminine singular verb (הוֹחִילָה) with v. 6. In my view it is more likely that the MT retains the proper consonants, but misplaces them at the end of v. 5. If this is right, then נַפְשִׁי would not be the true subject of the verb (which would be "I"), but rather an appositional modifier of the subject. Although this is not good English, in Hebrew it is acceptable, since the noun נֶפֶשׁ is well known as a surrogate for the pronoun (cf. Pss 62:6; 143:6).

ᵍ Some scholars believe that the second שֹׁמְרִים לַבֹּקֶר is an addition, probably through dittography (so Claus Westermann, "Psalm 130," in Eichholz, ed., *Herr, tue meine Lippen auf*, 608). The majority, however, holds that the repetition is a poetic device intended to reinforce the impatient waiting in the image. Although it might be possible to read the phrase in connection with v. 7, translating "[Like] watchers for the morning, let Israel hope for YHWH" (so Tromp, "Text of Psalm cxxx 5-6"; see Translation note e above), it seems to me better to regard v. 7 as an editorial expansion (see below), and to interpret this phrase as a rhetorical repetition.

Interpretation

The text of Psalm 130 is by no means clear in all respects. Several problems in particular confront the interpreter, and must be solved before the psalm can be well understood. The first of these is the alternation of divine names found throughout the psalm. Beginning with the first line יהוה is juxtaposed with אדני in synonymous parallelism. This same alternation is also present in v. 3 and in vv. 5–6. Whenever יהוה is used it is balanced by אדני, which fact argues that the juxtaposition is deliberate, and not a scribal mistake in any of its instances.[94] A second textual difficulty is the famous case in v. 4 in which the consonants תורא are sometimes taken as תורה. I have treated this from a textual standpoint above. Both readings are understandable within the present context, but neither of them fits neatly. In the end I have tentatively adopted the reading of the MT as the one that fits better with the pious, almost mystical, character of the psalm. In addition, it seems more likely that a scribe would "correct" תורא to תורה than *vice versa*.

Another textual problem, and one that has been frequently discussed, is the repetition of the phrase שֹׁמְרִים לַבֹּקֶר "watchmen for the morning." Several scholars omit the second occurrence.[95] Briggs and Briggs follow the lead of Jerome and the Syriac in reading the whole of v. 6b as a single phrase, translating "from morning watch to morning watch," which they supposed fit better with the tone of the psalm.[96] The most widely accepted opinion, however, generally sees it as a repetition

---

[94]The opposite position is in fact suggested by the fact that various translations and Hebrew mss have omitted אֲדֹנָי at almost every point where it occurs. But these do not agree with each other concerning the actual point of variance. For example, the Syriac reflects neither אֲדֹנָי nor יהוה in v. 1, but the LXX seems to support the double occurrence of a divine name (of course the difference between the two is obscured). On the other hand, when a very similar juxtaposition of these two divine names occurs again in vv. 5-6 it is the Coptic that lacks it (the situation of the LXX here is the same as in v. 1). A large number of Hebrew mss also substitute יהוה for אדני; see de Rossi, *Variae lectiones*, 82-83. To make matters more complicated still, 11QPs^A puts the divine name אדני *before* the locative adverbial ממעמקים. On account of this general confusion in the ancient witnesses it is probably best (and more satisfying stylistically) to retain the MT.

[95]Kissane, *Book of Psalms*, 586; Weiser, *Psalms*, 772; Westermann, "Psalm 130," 606-612; Štefan Porúbčan, "Psalm CXXX 5-6," *VT* 9 (1959) 322-323.

[96]Briggs and Briggs, *Book of Psalms*, 464-465.

for poetic purposes, sometimes relating it to the "step parallelism" commonly seen in the Songs of Ascents.[97]

The meter of Psalm 130 is not thoroughly regular. The first line (vv. 1b-2aα) is 4:3, but the following three lines (vv. 2aβ-4) are 3:2 (though v. 3 can also be read as 3:3 or 4:3, depending on whether one counts the particles). According to my scansion of vv. 5-6 the meter would be 2:3, 3:2:2. Although the first line does not fit completely with the preceding cola, the approximate length of the whole bicolon is the same as the lengths of the preceding bicola, and for that reason does not pose a problem for reading. Perhaps the variation may be attributed to the fact that with v. 5 the poet clearly begins a new section. Verse 7 is a rather prosaic 3:3:3. I believe it to be an addition.

The main body of the psalm is divided into four stanzas. The first stanza (vv. 1b-2) is the opening appeal that the deity hear the prayer that, one assumes, is to follow (although such a prayer is not forthcoming; see below). The following stanza (vv. 3-4) is a statement of trust that God would mercifully listen to the prayer. It is a profound statement: The supplicant makes no attempt to justify his or her own right to a hearing, but rather acknowledges that the opportunity to pray and be heard by God is based solely on God's mercy. Indeed life itself (which seems to me to be the primary referent of the verb עמד; a secondary referent perhaps being the ability to stand in the temple precincts[98]) is impossible without divine forbearance. Fortunately, according to the psalm, God does not judge according to the stringent demands of retributive justice. Although this meaning is not specifically expressed, Delitzsch is right when he says that it "fills up the pause after the question."[99] On the

---

[97]E.g., de Wette, *Kommentar über die Psalmen*, 591; Robert C. Dentan, "An Exposition of an Old Testament Passage," *JBR* 15 (1947) 158-161; Kraus, *Psalmen*, 2:1047; Marrs, "A Cry From the Depths," 81-90; Marrs, *Šyry Hmᶜlwt*, 111; Anderson, *Book of Psalms*, 2:877.

[98]Schmidt ("Gott und Mensch in Ps. 130," 241-253) compares the phrase מִי יַעֲמֹד with the similar phrase (with קוּם) found in the temple entrance liturgy (Ps 24:3). He believes that perhaps the standing should be understood from this perspective.

[99]Delitzsch, *Psalms*, 303. Westermann ("Psalm 130," 606) rightly cautions, however, that this recognition of sinfulness on the part of the poet is not the primary focus of the psalm. He sees it as a kind of middle ground between the needy situation and the waiting for help.

other hand, it is precisely this mercy of God toward less-than-perfect human beings that makes human devotion to God possible. Even though the psalm implies that the supplicant needs God's forgiveness, it is not primarily a prayer for forgiveness of sin.

The third stanza (vv. 5-6) is probably an incubation formula, used by a person who "waits" for an oracle from God.[100] The words קוה and יחל, which are similar in semantic range (cf. Ps 39:8; Job 30:26), imply this, and the expectation of "morning" fortifies it. The use of an incubation formula in Psalm 130 leads one to think, not of a prayer for forgiveness, perhaps not even divine rescue from some ill, but rather of a waiting for an oracle—God's "word." Whether this would have been an "oracle of salvation" or some other kind of word is not possible to say with certainty in the absence of any explicit request.

Scholars have long noted the fact that vv. 7–8 are somewhat out of place in the psalm. In vv. 1–6 we have the beginnings of the prayer of an individual in distress (the petition itself is never stated). This stanza transforms the prayer into an example for all Israel, in the way that is common in the Psalms,[101] and that is especially frequent in the Songs of Ascents. It transforms the psalm into an example of how "Israel" ought to "hope in YHWH," and it seems to me that this transformation occurs at a time after the composition of the first part. Several observations lead to this conclusion. First the psalm, although clearly characterized by the

---

[100]So Schmidt, *Psalmen*, 232: "Man möchte glauben, daß das Gebet selbst in der Nacht, in der ja auch das Gefühl der Schuld am mächtigsten ist, seine Worte gefunden hat." On the use of יחל and semantically related words in this sense (but not for a discussion of "incubation") see Christoph Barth, "יָחַל *yāḥal*; תּוֹחֶלֶת *tôḥeleṯ*" in TDOT 6:49-54.

[101]Cf. Peter C. Craigie, "Psalm 113," *Int* 39 (1985) 70-74; Westermann, *Ausgewählte Psalmen*, 46; Crüsemann, *Hymnus und Danklied*, 166. On this subject see generally Seybold, *Einführung*, 89-92; W. H. Bellinger, *Psalms: Reading and Studying the Book of Praises* (Peabody, MA: Hendrickson, 1990) 28. Brevard S. Childs (*Introduction to the Old Testament as Scripture* [Philadelphia, PA: Fortress Press, 1979] 513) applies this understanding to the Psalter as a whole: "The original cultic role of the psalms has been subsumed under a larger category of the canon. In an analogy to Israel's wisdom collection the study of the Psalter serves as a guidebook along the path of blessing." A sentence that is very similar to the one in Ps 130:8, פְּדָה אֱלֹהִים אֶת־יִשְׂרָאֵל מִכֹּל צָרוֹתָיו, occurs at the end of the acrostic Psalm 25 after the *taw*, as Westermann (*Ausgewählte Psalmen*, 91) has noted. At the least, this raises the possibility that such sentences—especially when they occur at the end of a psalm—are redactional.

themes of individual lament, contains few *structural* elements to identify
it as such.[102] It paints no picture of the distress plaguing the individual
and makes no appeal to God for help.[103] The only depiction of an
unfortunate circumstance is that described in the opening colon, namely
that the speaker calls "from the depths." That biblical laments often
employ non-specific language is of course well known; but one expects
that such a metaphor as being in "the depths" would be expanded
somewhat (cf. Jonah 2:3-10; Ps 124:3-5). What we have in Psalm 130,
in other words, is a psalm that *alludes to* troubling circumstances but
does not say anything about them; that asks God to "be attentive to...my
prayer," but does not state one; that affirms a fervent hope that God's
word would become manifest, but does not state what that word should
concern. I find it doubtful, therefore, that this psalm would have existed
as a prayer in its own right. It seems to me more likely that this is a
fragment of an older psalm that has been taken over by an editor and
supplied with an appropriate exhortatory conclusion. Since it was this
piety that the editor wished to reinforce, to quote the entire prayer was
unnecessary. Verses 1-6, then, are in my opinion a known text taken
from an older prayer, and vv. 7-8 reapplication of that text.[104]

One difficulty such a scenario would explain is the close
relationship between the vocabulary of vv. 1-6 and vv. 7-8. In vv. 5-6
the speaker "waits" for YHWH's word, and "hopes" in YHWH. This has
obvious ties with v. 7, where the same verb, "hope" (יַחֵל) has Israel as
the subject. Moreover, the phrase כִּי־עִם־יְהוָה הַחֶסֶד "for with YHWH
is the faithfulness" forcefully recalls v. 4a's כִּי־עִמְּךָ הַסְּלִיחָה "for with
you [God] is the forgiveness." Verse 3 has the speaker trusting that God
would not "keep track of wrongs (עֲוֹנוֹת)," and v. 8 has God redeeming
Israel "from all its wrong-doings" (מִכֹּל עֲוֹנֹתָיו). It is of course quite
possible that such a reapplication of language could have taken place

---

[102]Westermann ("Psalm 130," 606-612) rightly observes that the structure of the
individual lament is almost completely gone from the psalm.

[103]Anderson (*Book of Psalms*, 2:875) believes that the place of the description of
the plight is taken by "an indirect confession of sins." Contrast this with
Westermann's view above (n. 102).

[104]Klaus Seybold ("The Asaph Psalms," Society of Biblical Literature Annual
Meeting, Book of Psalms Consultation [New Orleans, LA: 1990]) has argued that a
very similar phenomenon is present in the Asaphite psalms.

under the hand of a single poet, so that the same poet who crafted vv. 1-6 then continued by applying them to a communal understanding. I think it much more likely, however, that such application would have taken place by using a portion of a well-known prayer.

The setting of the psalm in its canonical form is therefore probably that of a teacher's proclamation, either to a group of disciples or to a larger Israelite community. Can anything be said about the historical framework in which the original psalm came to be? Historical backgrounds are of course difficult to ascertain from the psalm itself. Especially with such a multivalent psalm as this one is this statement true. Some clues, however, may perhaps be relevant.

Some scholars have attempted to date the psalm based upon linguistic clues. Westermann points out that הַסְּלִיחָה is a late word, only occurring elsewhere in Neh 9:12; Dan 9:9; and Sir 5:5 (ἐξιλασμοῦ).[105] If תּוֹרָא in v. 4 were to be read as תּוֹרָה, this might be construed as displaying a postexilic ideological framework[106] (for that matter, neither would the notion of fearing YHWH be unknown in the postexilic period). Such grounds are adequate to suggest a postexilic time frame, but it is impossible to be more specific. Apart from the very general concluding verse admonishing "Israel" to hope in YHWH as the original psalmist does, there is little in this psalm that ties it explicitly to any one social milieu as distinct from any other.

---

[105]Westermann, *Ausgewählte Psalmen*, 89. The majority of scholars agree on this point, and therefore assign the psalm a late date. Dahood (*Psalms*, 3:235), on the other hand, points out several verbal parallels to Psalm 86, which he calls a royal repentance song from the monarchical era. According to Kutscher (*History*, 128), the noun pattern *qĕṭîlā* is quite common as a verbal noun in MH.

[106]Cf. Anthony R. Ceresko ("The Sage in the Psalms," in *The Sage in Israel and the Ancient Near East*, ed. John G. Gammie and Leo G. Perdue [Winona Lake, IN: Eisenbrauns, 1990] 217-230), who posits that the majority of psalms in their present forms are creations of "the scholar-sage or scribe of the postexilic period" (230).

PSALM 131

1   A song of ascents; David's:

O YHWH, un-haughty is my heart
   And un-exalted are my eyes.
I have not walked in greatness,
   Or among things too difficult for me,
2   But rather[a] I have abased myself[b]
   And stilled my soul.[c]
Like a weaned child upon its mother—
   Like[d] the weaned child[e] upon me[f] is my soul.[g]

3   Wait, O Israel, for YHWH,
   From now and forever more.

Notes to the Translation

[a]   Godfrey Rolles Driver ("Notes on the Psalms. II. 73-150," *JTS* 44 [1943] 21) translates "but" on the basis of Aramaic *ʾillaʾ* or *ʾellaʾ*. It is possible to supply a similar translation (as here) without appeal to the Aramaic, since there are also good examples of this meaning in BH (e.g., 2 Kgs 9:26; Job 1:11), and since a simple assertion is part of the semantic domain of the "self-imprecation formula." It is well established that אִם־לֹא can mean "except" (see KB, 58), but in the present context the former meaning fits the context better.

[b]   The meaning of the stem שׁוה is uncertain. Its basic meaning seems to be that of making level, so that the *qal* stem can refer to things that are equal (as in French "au pair"), and therefore alike (e.g., Isa 40:25). In *piel* the verb normally means "to set, place; produce" (BDB, 1001 and KB, 954 treat this as a separate root, but for our purposes the separate root possibility is also relevant), but can mean "to level" (as one levels ground before planting; Isa 28:25). The dominant feature of nearly all *piel* uses of the verb is that they are transitive: only here and in Isa 38:13 (where the text should almost certainly read שִׁוִּיתִי, as MT has it, and not שִׁפּוֹתִי, as in 1QIsaA).

In fact Isa 38:13 bears some similarity to this passage, insofar as it is also the part of a prayer that supplies reasons for God to act on the petitioner's behalf. (Even though Psalm 131 contains no petition as such, the language of the psalm certainly suggests this genre.) Since these are the only intransitive uses of the verb שׁוה it is entirely possible that the traditional interpretation of this verb here is mistaken. Rather than "smooth oneself" in an inner sense (which lies behind the NRSV's "calmed" and JPSV's "contented"), it is more likely in my judgment that the meaning of שִׁוִּיתִי in both Ps 131:2 and Isa 38:13 is that of self-abasement, perhaps with standardized physical postures to indicate this. Certainly this fits better in the latter context, where the idea of "calm" does not fit well. Moreover the LXX translator's use of ἐταπεινοφρόνουν "I have humbled myself" in opposition to ὕψωσα "I have exalted myself" (reading the root רום rather than דמם and seeing the two phrases in opposition; see translation note c, below) to translate the word seems to understand the verb metaphorically as abasement. To summarize: the verb שׁוּיתי here is best understood as a contrast to the denial of pride in v. 1. The sense is that the psalmist is not prideful, but rather has abnegated herself/himself before God. More on this relationship will be included in the discussion below.

c The LXX has ἀλλὰ ὕψωσα τὴν ψυχήν μου "but I have exalted my soul" (apparently reading the Hebrew as רוֹמַמְתִּי; for a thorough discussion of this variant see Pieter Arie Hendrik de Boer, "Psalm CXXXI 2," *VT* 16/3 [1966] 289). This understands the Hebrew as half of an oath formula, in which the self-imprecation is omitted, and reads the *waw* as adversative. Although the Hebrew itself could plausibly mean this (the Hebrew דמַּמְתִּי, a *polal* form, is a *hapax legomenon*), the transition to the next bicolon would be awkward. The meaning of the word is that of "quietness," not in the sense merely of not speaking, but in the sense of awe-struck dumbness before God (in *qal,* cf. Lev 10:3; Jer 48:2; Ps 4:5; 30:13). On this see Handricus Jacobus Franken, *The Mystical Communion with YHWH in the Book of Psalms* (Leiden: E. J. Brill, 1954) 13-18.

d Many scholars believe the MT's double comparative (כִּנְמֻל...כַּנָמֻל) to be an error, and emend the second instance to תִּנְמֹל (Gunkel, *Psalmen,* 564; Schmidt, *Psalmen,* 232; Kraus, *Psalmen,* 1052). BHK suggested that the whole of 2bβ be omitted, although this suggestion was withdrawn in BHS. The attempt to read it as a verb rather than as a noun is in my view mistaken. The MT is understandable, although it does seem to convey an idea that would be unusual in the Bible (see below).

e The LXX translates each of the two instances of נמל differently: as ἀπογεγαλακτισμένον "de-milked one" and ἀνταπόδοσις "wages" (which is usually used in the negative sense of "vengeance"). Both of these meanings are possible for these consonants. In translating the two words differently it is most likely incorrect, given the juxtaposition of the two.

f It may also be possible to translate "Like a weaned child is my soul upon God." Dahood (*Psalms,* 3:239) takes the *yodh* as a third–person singular suffix akin to the Phoenician suffix and translates "with Him [God]." I, however, do not regard this explanation as likely.

g The interpretation of v. 2b has vexed every scholar who has attempted to interpret Psalm 131. There are several major difficulties here: (1) the meaning of the word נָּמֻל; (2) the sense and object of the preposition עַל; and (3) the meaning of the double comparative (if that is what is read). A fuller discussion of these problems appears below; for now perhaps it will be sufficient to note the difficulties.

Interpretation

Psalm 131 is one of the least known of all the Songs of Ascents. This is not without reason, although it is, I believe, without warrant.[107] Like Psalm 130, this psalm is probably actually a fragment of a psalm:[108] it does not fit into any of the form-critically established categories for psalms and does not seem to finish what it sets out to do (the opening lines lead one to expect a petition; see below). The translation is difficult, although not particularly problematic. The metaphors are mixed and do not follow each other without interpretational effort; consequently, the *crux interpretorum* consists in the interrelation of the metaphors of the psalm.

How may the metaphors dealing with the person's humility (v. 1) be reconciled with the image of a weaned child upon its mother? The answer may lie in the fact that a weaned child is one who no longer cries for its mother's milk, does not grasp for the breasts whenever it is near its mother.[109] Some scholars insist that the גָּמֻל "weaned child" refers not to weaning as such, but simply to the child's age.[110] This is a possibility made plausible by several passages in which the root גמל is used,[111] but unfortunately does not clear up any difficulties. I fail to see, de Boer's

---

[107]I agree with Weiser (*Psalms*, 776), who asserts that it "deserves to be classed with the most beautiful psalms of the Psalter."

[108]So Gerstenberger, Jutzler and Boecker, *Psalmen in der Sprache unserer Zeit*, 208.

[109]Anderson (*Book of Psalms*, 2:878) hypothesizes that "the older infants (before they were weaned) may have received an insufficient amount of milk, and therefore their restlessness and crying may have been proverbial. On the other hand, a weaned child could have been symbolic of contentment." This would also be the meaning if one followed Schmidt (*Psalmen*, 232) in translating "calmed child" ("gestilltes Kind") rather than "weaned child."

[110]Patrick W. Skehan, "Some Short Psalms," *American Ecclesiastical Review* 124 (1951) 107. Cf. de Boer ("Psalm CXXXI 2," 287-292), who explains גָּמֻל linguistically as "subdued child" rather than "weaned child." His final translation of v. 2 (p. 292), though not clearly related to his argument, is "But on the contrary, I have made myself without resistance or movement...just as one does with his mother, thus I have made myself content."

[111]In Gen 21:8, where Abraham makes a feast for Isaac, the meaning could be either that Isaac has been weaned or has reached adulthood (probably the latter). In 1 Sam 1:22-23 the meaning once again could be either, although from the narrative perhaps the former is more likely. But in Hos 1:8 and especially in Isa 28:9 the meaning is clearly that of privation of milk.

claims notwithstanding, how the elimination of the weaning idea from the verse solves the problem of the relation of v. 2 to v. 1.[112] And the phrase עֲלֵי אִמּוֹ "upon (or beside) its mother" at least implies some connection with the idea of weaning from milk.

The first image of the psalm is that of an exalted heart (גָּבַהּ לִבִּי, a phrase that undoubtedly betokens pride; cf. Sir 1:27; Prov 18:12) and its parallel "haughty eyes" (רָמוּ עֵינַי, which also signifies pride, as in Ps 18:28; Prov 6:17; 30:13; contrast the phrase נָשָׂא עֵנַיִם [Ps 121:1, e.g.], which connotes the proper uplifting of the eyes in dependence upon God). The psalmist denies having these attitudes. Parallel to this is the denial of improperly haughty action: "I have not walked in greatness//or among things too difficult for me." To what does this refer? The parallel pair נִפְלָאוֹת//גְדֹלוֹת is not unknown in the Psalms: it nearly always signifies God's glorious salvific acts (cf. Pss 86:10; 136:4; 145:5-6; further, in the vast majority of cases in which only one of these words is used, it also refers explicitly to the salvation history). The correct human response to these acts of God is that of "remembering" (זכר; e.g., Ps 111:4), "considering" (שׂיח II; e.g., Pss 105:2; 145:5; 1 Chr 16:9), or "recounting" (סֵפֶר; e.g., Pss 9:2; 26:7). Probably to "go about in" (-הִלֵּךְ בְּ) those normally divine activities is to arrogate divine attributes to oneself.

These images of haughtiness, denied by the psalmist, are directly and strongly contrasted with the image of "abasing oneself" and "quieting one's soul." That this latter "quieting one's soul" (if that is what it means) is perceived to be the proper posture with respect to God cannot be proven, since the *polal* of the word is used only here, is not particularly troublesome. The notion of "quieting oneself" or "being still" using other synonyms is known in the Hebrew Bible (cf., e.g., Pss 46:11a; 76:8). It fits well with the notion of "abasing oneself": both are cultic postures intended to secure the divine favor for the supplicant. The question then arises, Why are these two rather obscure words used and not some other more common words (or at least, Why is not *one* of

---

[112]De Boer ("Psalm CXXXI 2," 290) observes that when the root נמל occurs elsewhere with עַל it means "to deal with, recompense," and posits that עַל here means "against," so that the pride depicted in v. 1 manifests itself in v. 2 as rising up against one's mother.

them more well known, as usually happens with biblical parallelism[113])? It is possible that a pun is being made on another meaning of שׁוה "be like" and on the word דמה "liken," both of which are words of comparison. Perhaps this pun is a way of introducing the similes that follow.

With the relationship between the metaphors of vv. 1 and 2a clarified, it is necessary to consider the meaning of the similes in v. 2b. If the metaphors so far have contrasted pride with a proper petitionary stance, then one may expect the simile of the "weaned child upon its mother" somehow to further this same contrast. As has been asserted above, I think that the image of a weaned child upon its mother is an image of tranquillity, in contrast to what one would expect with a nursing child temporarily separated from its mother. It is the idea of quiet trust that the mother will provide that is in view here. Thus the image progresses from self-abasement, to dumb-stricken awe in the face of the holy (or perhaps "waiting" in silence for God's action), to tranquil expectation that one's need will be satisfied, despite the seemingly implausible circumstances.[114]

With this in view, the last verse, which applies what seems to be an individual's hopeful statement to the community, although not untrue to the meaning of what had gone before, is probably not originally a part of the original composition. The original material is applied to Israel by a tradent who thought that this psalm, like several others of the Songs of Ascents, held pedagogical value for the community.[115] In the same way

---

[113]Adele Berlin (*The Dynamics of Biblical Parallelism* [Bloomington, IN: Indiana University Press, 1985] 96) states that "One of the functions of the second line of a parallelism is to disambiguate the first...."

[114]Closen ("Gottvertrauen und Selbstbescheidung," 189) sermonizes, "es geht um ein 'Beschwichtigen und Zum-schweigen-bringen der Seele', das darin liegt, daß ein Mensch sein stürmisches, unbewußtes, mehr naturhaftes und instinktmäßiges Verlangen überwunden und abgelegt hat."

[115] Grossberg (*Centripetal and Centrifugal Structures*, 46-48) finds an inclusio enclosed by the vocatives of v. 1 and v. 3. For him this indicates that the psalmist has now learned something that she/he is going to teach to Israel. Moreover, he believes that the shift from perfect (v. 1) to imperfect (v. 2), and finally to jussive (v. 3) aspects of the verb indicates that "The odyssey of the soul is told by the psalmist" (p. 48). I do not find the argument convincing.

that the individual psalmist hopes in God, rather than in self, so Israel ought to do.

Psalm 131 does not fit any of the categories into which psalms usually fit. With the vocative "O YHWH" at the beginning, one naturally expects that a petition will follow. This is reinforced by the "negative confession" of v. 1, the purpose of which is normally to provide the grounds for divine action on the supplicant's behalf. The expectation of a petition goes unfulfilled, however, in the psalm. After the "confessions" (both negative and positive) one simply gets a statement of trust. This aspect of Psalm 131 is so prevalent that the psalm is usually designated a "psalm of trust."[116] Psalms of trust are really no more than developments (perhaps even "hypostases") of the regular statement of trust that is present in almost all petitions. As such, many "psalms of trust" may originally have been used as part of petitions, or they may simply have implied petitions. Whether such development occurred at the pre-literary stage or at the literary stage (that is, whether this psalm was originally composed as a "psalm of trust" or whether it was extracted from such a psalm) is at this point impossible to determine. I think that Psalm 131 is in fact a fragment extracted from a petition by the same person who added the last line (cf. my interpretation of Psalm 130). Such a redactional history would explain both the addition of the final line and the unfulfilled expectation of a prayer.

If Psalm 131 was originally part of a petition, then several things may be said about the milieu in which the psalm developed. It may be observed that the denial of *hubris* by the psalmist might best be understood as royal language.[117] If this is correct, then the king would be denying the attitude exhibited by the royal figures of foreign nations (which, to be sure, is hyperbolic) in Ezekiel and Isaiah. In contrast, the royal figure here styles himself as a weened child, whose humility and

---

[116]For a list and discussion of psalms of trust see Bernhard W. Anderson, *Out of the Depths: The Psalms Speak for Us Today* (Philadelphia, PA: Fortress Press, 1974; first printing 1970), 142-149. A few scholars (e.g., Seybold, *Wallfahrtspsalmen*, 56) understand Psalm 131 as an entrance liturgy, citing the lists of sins in Psalms 15 and 24 as illustrations of negative confessions before the temple gates. This seems to me to be a misunderstanding of the genre of entrance liturgies, which involves the form of question and answer more than that of negative confession.

[117]So Dahood, *Psalms*, 3:238.

quiet dependence are self-evident. Even if the speaker is not royal, the
rhetoric implies that s/he is a person of station, not a peasant.[118] This
means that interpretations that see a reference to an Israelite mother
carrying her child on pilgrimage are tenuous at best,[119] based as they are
more on the general interpretation of the collection than on the psalm
itself. It may well be that the psalm (or only v. 2b) would have been
spoken by a woman, but this does not then necessarily imply pilgrimage.
It seems to me more likely that the metaphor is used *as a metaphor,* with
no factual connection to the speaker. If this is the case, then it is not
necessary to see a woman as the speaker, even though this is not ruled
out.

PSALM 132

1   A song of ascents:

     Remember, O YHWH, to David's credit[a]
         All his efforts[b]
2   When he swore to YHWH,
         Vowed to the Bull of Jacob:[c]
3   "I will not enter into the tent of my house,
         I will not go up upon the couch of my bed,
4   I will not give sleep to my eyes,
         Nor to my eyelids slumber,[d]
5   Until I find a place for YHWH,
         A dwelling[e] for the Bull of Jacob."

6   Behold, we heard it in Ephratha,
         We happened across it in the fields[f] of Jaar:[g]

---

[118]Grossberg (*Centripetal and Centrifugal Structures*, 46) rightly perceives that
the rhetoric, strong as it is, implies this: "The fourfold disavowal of any pride
indicates, by its abundant denials, a familiarity with pride.   The next
verse...intimates that once the psalmist was indeed intimate with the loftiness that is
now controlled and tempered."

[119]So, e.g., Quell, "Struktur und Sinn des Psalms 131," 173-185; Seybold,
Wallfahrtspsalmen, 37-38.

7   Let us enter into [God's] dwellings,
       Let us worship toward the footstool of [the divine] feet.

8   Arise, O YHWH, for the sake of your resting place—[h]
       You and the ark of your might.

9   May your priests put on righteousness,
       And your faithful ones shout.

10   For the sake of David your servant,
       Do not turn the face of your anointed one.[i]

11   YHWH swore to David a sure thing;[j] [God] will not turn
           from it:
       "Someone of your offspring[k] I will place on your
           throne.

12   If your sons keep my covenant,
       And my testimonies, which[l] I shall teach them,
       Then their sons also forever
           Shall sit upon your throne."

13   For YHWH has chosen Zion,
       [God] desired it as a dwelling for [God]self.

14   "This is my resting place for ever,
       Here I shall dwell, for I have desired it.

15   Its food production[m] I will surely bless.
       Its poor ones I will satisfy with food.

16   Its priests I shall clothe with salvation,
       And its pious ones will rejoice greatly.

17   There I shall make a horn to sprout for David.[n]
       I have prepared a lamp[o] for my anointed one.

18   His enemies I will clothe with shame,
       But upon him his[p] diadem will shine.

Notes to the Translation

a The verb זכר plus a *lamed* preposition indicating "to the credit of" is a standard phrase in BH asking God to remember one kindly on specified grounds (cf. the confessions of Nehemiah, e.g. Neh 13:14). Heinz Kruse ("Psalm cxxxii and the Royal Zion Festival," *VT* 33 [1983] 281) brings the present phrase into line with the standard formula—and balances out the colon—by adding לְטוֹבָה at the end of v.

1a, but this seems unnecessary. The opposite meaning, that of remembering *against* someone, is also found, however (cf. Ps 137:7).

ᵇ Keet (*A Study of the Psalms of Ascents*, 86) rightly points out that in 1 Chr 22:14 the word עֲנִי denotes David's effort in assembling the materials with which Solomon would build and supply the temple. This—not "hardships" (cf. NRSV)—seems to be the meaning implied in these verses. JPSV attempts to include both the idea of "hardships" and the idea of "efforts" with its translation, "his extreme self-denial."

ᶜ The pointing of "bull" is different from what one expects for this word: normally it is אַבִּיר rather than אֲבִיר. In the words of KB (p. 5), the uses in which the word refers to God are "artificially differentiated" from the normal uses. The Masoretes understood "strong one" (rather than a metaphorical reference to an animal) to be the primary meaning in this expression, and tried to guard against this theriomorphism in description of God. However, in light of Jeroboam's revival of the calf as a symbol of YHWH (1 Kgs 12:28-32; cf. Exodus 32), it seems likely that this archaic symbol continued to be used in north Israel while it was seen as apostate in the south.

ᵈ This is evidently a stock formula to express diligence (cf. Prov 6:4). The LXX has the plus καὶ ἀνάπαυσιν τοῖς κροτάφοις μου. Probably this is simply a matter of having alternative translations of the same Hebrew line. One of the two may originally have been marginal (James Barr, private communication of 20 August 1990; so also Sidney Jellicoe [*The Septuagint and Modern Study* {Oxford, UK: Oxford University Press, 1968} 322], who regards it as an example of the "Haggadic touches" that the LXX occasionally adds).

ᵉ The feminine plural is used of the "dwelling place" of YHWH also in Pss 43:3 and 84:2. Similarly, the masculine plural (מִשְׁכְּנֵי עֶלְיוֹן) appears in Ps 46:5. The plurals probably connote the grandeur or superlativity of God's dwelling.

ᶠ A large number of Hebrew mss have בשׂדה rather than בשׂדי, and this is supported by several versional witnesses, including Aquila, Symmachus, and Jerome (de Rossi, *Variae lectiones*, 4:82).

ᵍ Two important translational difficulties occur in this verse. The first is the referent of the third-person feminine suffixes; the second is the meanings of the words אֶפְרָתָה and שְׂדֵי־יַעַר. Because I shall treat these difficulties in detail below (see the discussion), I omit to discuss them further here.

ʰ The preposition לְ has three possible meanings in this context. It is usually taken in the directive sense "to," which implies a processional of the ark to its "resting place" in the temple (J. R. Porter, "Interpretation of 2 Samuel vi and Psalm 132," *JTS* 5 [1954] 161-173; Terence E. Fretheim, "Psalm 132: A Form-Critical Study," *JBL* 86 [1967] 293-295; Dahood, *Psalms*, 3:245; Anderson, *Book of Psalms*, 882; Kraus, *Psalms 60-150*, 475-479; Allen, *Psalms 101-150*, 202-203, 204-205). Hillers, arguing from the Ugaritic preposition, takes it in the directive sense "from" (Delbert R. Hillers, "Ritual Procession of the Ark and Ps 132," *CBQ* 30 [1968] 50) but, as Allen (*Psalms 101-150*, 204-205) points out, this would be the only instance of this meaning with the verb קוּם in the BH. I am convinced by Huwiler (Elizabeth F. Huwiler, "Patterns and Problems in Psalm 132," in *The Listening Heart: Essays in Wisdom and the Psalms in Honor of Roland E. Murphy, O. Carm.*, ed. Kenneth G.

Hoglund [Sheffield, UK: JSOT Press, 1987] 203-204), who presents a good case that the meaning of the *lamed* is "for the sake of" in this context.

ⁱ Verses 8-10 are similar to the end of Solomon's prayer at the dedication of the temple in 2 Chr 6:41-42. The latter verses cannot be said, however, to be a quotation from this psalm; at best they are a paraphrase of it. The expression "turn the face" undoubtedly means "reject" (JPSV).

ʲ Although it is possible that אֱמֶת functions adverbially here (Joüon, *Grammaire de l'hébreu biblique*, §102d [p. 269]), it seems to me that this use is substantive, and that it is the referent of the feminine pronominal suffix on מִמֶּנָּה.

ᵏ Literally "from the fruit of your womb." The use of this clearly female language to describe a male's production of offspring is striking. The *mem* is partitive. Anderson (*Book of Psalms*, 883) believes that a word, perhaps "kings," is missing at the beginning of this line.

ˡ Joüon (*Grammaire de l'hébreu biblique*, §145c [p. 448]) is quite certain that the correct way to read this word is as a relative, rather than as a demonstrative, pronoun. For a thorough discussion of this, see Waltke and O'Connor, *Biblical Hebrew Syntax*, §19.5 (pp. 336-338).

ᵐ Lit. "its hunting." This noun could also be translated "food supply," from צֵיד II. Driver ("Notes on the Psalms," 21) has proposed that צֵידָהּ be read צְרֵיהָ or צְרִיֶּיהָ "her destitute ones", citing evidence of LXXᴬ and the "Jud.-Aram." root צְרִי "was laid waste." Although this seems possible, it would be rather a rare word, and moreover is not really needed, since the theme of filling the hungry is present in the second strophe of v. 15, and therefore fits well with the context.

ⁿ The expression "I shall make a horn to sprout" (אַצְמִיחַ קֶרֶן) is found elsewhere only in Ezek 29:21, an editorial addition to one of Ezekiel's oracles against Egypt in which the defeat of that nation is seen as equivalent to renewed strength for "Israel" (see Walther Zimmerli, *Ezekiel*, vol. 2 [Hermeneia; Philadelphia: Fortress, 1979] 120-121). The symbol of the horn, which appears nine times in the Psalms, primarily signifies strength in the face of, or deliverance from, opposition (cf. Pss 18:3; 89:18,25; 112:9). In Psalm 132 the meaning is tied specifically to the renewal of prosperity and security for the Davidic king and for Jerusalem.

ᵒ In connection with a royal dynasty, the image of a lamp symbolizes the continuity of that dynasty. Cf. 2 Sam 21:17; 1 Kgs 11:36; 2 Kgs 8:19 (=2 Chr 21:7).

ᵖ The LXX reads ἐπὶ δὲ αὐτὸν ἐξανθήσει τὸ ἁγίασμά μου, apparently understanding נֵזֶר in its more usual sense, "consecration" and therefore interpreting it as the "consecrated place" or "temple" (ἁγίασμα), which of course properly belongs to God rather than to David (hence the first person possessive pronoun).

Interpretation

Psalm 132 has generated more scholarly treatment than any other of the Songs of Ascents. Several interpretational matters require treatment beyond that given in the textual and translation notes. The first of these, as mentioned above, is the antecedent of the feminine suffixes in v. 6.

Scholars have explored several different possibilities, none of which is satisfying.[120] Most authors regard them as referring to the ark,[121] to David's oath,[122] to his "efforts,"[123] or to God.[124] The primary problem with all of these is that they suffer from the lack of any clear nominal antecedent and from ambiguity about how each of these interpretations relates to the rest of the psalm. Because of the parallelism, it is most probable that the antecedent is the same for both pronouns. The parallelism also means that the "finding" should be taken as an instance of "disambiguation" (to use Berlin's term[125]) vis-à-vis "hearing," providing to the hearing a feeling of happenstance, as opposed to giving both verbs full referential weight. If these observations are correct, then the possibility that it is the ark, heard about and now found after its sojourning in Philistia, is eliminated. Such an interpretation puts too much weight on the verb מָצָא and would in any case involve an unusual meaning of the verb שָׁמַע (with the accusative it normally refers to hearing a sound). Rather the sentence would refer to happening to hear some sound. The sound could be either that of David's uttering an oath (vv. 3-5) or the call to worship (v. 7); of these two I favor the latter, although it is possible that both are in view.

A related question is the meaning of בְאֶפְרָתָה and בִשְׂדֵי־יָעַר. Many scholars hold that these refer to places in the story of David's bringing the ark to Jerusalem after its sojourn in Philistia, either David's

---

[120]In the words of Aubrey Robinson ("Do Ephratha and Jaar Really Appear in Psalm 132:6?," *ZAW* 86 [1974] 221), all of these possibilities "strain either the Hebrew or the imagination."

[121]Fretheim, "Psalm 132," 291; Robinson, "Ephratha and Jaar," 222. This analysis of the scholarly opinion is derived from Robinson (221).

[122]Dahood (*Psalms*, 3:244) believes that the referent is an unstated שְׁבוּעָה "oath."

[123]Kruse, "Psalm cxxxii," 293; Huwiler, "Patterns and Problems," 206.

[124]Gunkel (*Psalmen*, 566) interprets the "we" as referring to "David und seine Männer" (in a literary, rather than a historical, sense) so that what "we" have heard is the salvation history, and more precisely the one of whom that history speaks, namely God. So also Otto Eissfeldt ("Psalm 132," in *Kleine Schriften*, 483), pointing the suffixes *hū*, makes God the direct referent, as opposed to Gunkel's rather indirect approach. Despite the stature of these interpreters, this position has not attracted great numbers of adherents.

[125]Berlin, *Dynamics of Biblical Parallelism*, 96.

ancestral home,[126] or the region in Ephraim in which the ark is said to have had its home before this episode.[127] A few have held that they are not place names, but rather general hendyadic descriptions of geographical zones ("in Wald und Flur"), connoting that "we" heard echoes throughout the whole land.[128]de Wette, n. 128   Robinson rearranges the consonants for the entire sentence, to read *hen hăšamă'nû habe' parot* // *hămĕṣa'nûha biśĕdê ja'ăd* "Surely, we heard the oxen leading on? Surely we found the ark in the field he appointed?"[129] All of these interpretations see this entire strophe as referring to the ark in some way. Kruse, on the other hand, doubts that any hearer would think of the ark, since the words are hardly unambiguous and since the ark is yet to be mentioned.[130] He posits that they would have thought of Micah 3:12 (= Jer 26:18), which uses similar language to describe Jerusalem. According to him, these words refer to the disappointment felt by persons who "had heard it would be a 'Fruitland', but...found it in 'Woodland and Wilderness'."[131] It does not seem likely that any solution to this problem will achieve a consensus. At the very best perhaps it may be said that, even if these words did not originally refer to the ark narrative, at least they may be taken as puns when subsequently connected to the ark.

These difficulties are indeed complex, and are not likely to be solved here. I would posit, with Allen,[132] that the structure of the psalm is more likely to reveal its meaning than is further exploration of

---

[126]Aubrey R. Johnson, *Sacral Kingship in Ancient Israel* (Cardiff: University of Wales, 1967) 21; Kraus, *Psalmen*, 2:1063.

[127]De Wette, *Kommentar über die Psalmen*, 596-597 (however, Gustav Bauer, who edited the commentary, saw them as referring to David's ancestral home); Weiser, *Psalms*, 780; Fretheim, "Psalm 132," 297; Carol Meyers, "David as Temple Builder," in *Ancient Israelite Religion: Essays in Honor of Frank Moore Cross,* ed. Jr. Patrick D. Miller, Paul D. Hanson, and S. Dean McBride (Philadelphia, PA: Fortress Press, 1987), 358.

[128]de Wette, *Kommentar über die Psalmen*, 596-597.

[129]Robinson, "Ephratha and Jaar," 221.

[130]"Nobody listening to the psalm could take such an abbreviation to be the name of the ark's accidental and temporary domicile before the ark had been mentioned" (Kruse, "Psalm cxxxii," 294). One may observe, however, that the vocalization of the words would clear up a considerable amount of the ambiguity.

[131]Kruse, "Psalm cxxxii," 296.

[132]Allen, *Psalms 101-150*, 204.

individual cruxes. As I see it, the psalm is a petition divided into two
parts, the first (vv. 1-10) being properly a petition, and the second (vv.
11-18) being a prophetic oracle of salvation. The idea that it is a song
used for the ritual "ascent" of the ark to the Jerusalem Temple derives
primarily from the mention of the ark, although influence from the
superscript may also have had a part in it.[133] Fretheim has argued, on the
basis of repeated words, that the break actually occurs between vv. 1-9
and vv. 10-18.[134] His proposal has the advantage of relating the two
parts to one another (through the parallel petitions in vv. 1 and 10) into a
single unit, and also points to the important connections between ideas in
the first half of the psalm and in the second half.[135] I am convinced by
Huwiler's study,[136] however, that this division is in error. Huwiler
believes that the key to understanding Psalm 132's structure is to see new
strophes as occurring chiefly where the structure *inflected verb + YHWH
+ preposition + noun* appears. This structure occurs four times in the
psalm (vv. 1,8,11, and 13). She proceeds to analyze the four strophes as
two sets of parallel strophic pairs, with the pattern A (1-7) // B (8-10); A₁

---

[133]This position was proposed by Mowinckel (e.g., *Psalms in Israel's Worship*,
1:129) and defended by Porter ("Interpretation of 2 Samuel vi and Psalm 132," 161-
173). The following quotation from Taylor and McCullough (William R. Taylor and
W. Stewart McCullough, *Psalms: Introduction and Exegesis* [IB4; New York, NY:
Abingdon Press, 1955] 684) provides a convenient example of what could be quoted
from many commentaries.

> This psalm is a liturgical processional hymn by the rendition of
> which...the events connected with David's bringing of the ark to Zion
> are dramatically presented. The purpose of the re-enactment of that
> historical occasion was to impress on all who witnessed or
> participated in it how the fortunes of the city...and those of the house
> of David...are intertwined.

Hillers ("Ritual Procession," 48-55) argues forcefully against this position. His own
proposal, which relies heavily on the first verse, is that the psalm belongs to the
genre of building dedications.

[134]Fretheim, "Psalm 132," 291-293.

[135]For example, the parallel swearing of David and of God (vv. 2 and 11); God's
מְנוּחָה in vv. 8 and 14; and priests and pious ones in vv. 9 and 16 (interestingly,
although the petition includes no prayer for the food supply or for the poor, the
promise includes them). The parallel of vv. 6-8 and 13-14 in this reconstruction may
help to clarify the meaning of the former and argue, as Fretheim ("Psalm 132," 293)
states, in favor of a "processional" reading of the psalm.

[136]Huwiler, "Patterns and Problems in Psalm 132."

(11-12) // B₁ (13-18). This patterning retains the majority of parallels found by Fretheim, while at the same making sense of the obvious formal difference between YHWH as "Thou" (vv. 1-10), and David as "thou" (vv. 11-12) with YHWH as "I" (vv. 11-18, less third-person oracular introductions in vv. 11 and 13).

It is my opinion, then, that the first strophe (vv. 1-7), however one construes the difficult passages, must be considered an introduction to the petition of which it is a part. What we have here may well be a fragment of a *hieros logos* for a yearly ascension ritual;[137] but the context into which it is placed subordinates that feature to the prayer in v. 1. In this context one must take the entire strophe as a recounting of past events that serve as the basis for a present petition. Similarly, the second strophe, often taken as a cultic shout upon the occasion of the ark's ascension itself, should be taken as part of a petition, with the prayer that God arise being parallel to God's acts of salvation. The imagery of God's rising up is holy war imagery, which is probably the reason for the ark's presence. The third and fourth strophes are God's response to the prayer, answering the specific petitions, and concluding with a promise not only to aid the city of Jerusalem but also to ensure the prosperity and longevity of David's progeny.

Psalm 132 is a carefully crafted prayer, with important connections between its two "halves."[138] To my mind, these considerations make it highly unlikely that the psalm is a compilation of various originally separate songs (the exception being vv. 7-9, which resemble 2 Chr 6:41-42 and may be a fragment of an earlier song).[139]

Two elements of north-Israelite religious identity occur in Psalm 132. The ark was originally an item of the cult at Shiloh, in Ephraim.[140]

---

[137]Philip Nel, "Psalm 132 and Covenant Theology," in W. Classen, ed., *Text and Context: Old Testament and Semitic Studies for F. C. Fensham* (Sheffield, UK: JSOT Press, 1988): 183-191. Robinson ("Ephratha and Jaar," 222) asserts that "It may be that v. 6-7 are a quotation from an older song about the ark."

[138]I concur with the analysis of Philip Nel ("Psalm 132 and Covenant Theology," 183), who finds the psalm to be "a perfect example of a symmetrically constructed poem."

[139]Against Seybold, *Wallfahrtspsalmen*, 32; Cornelius B. Houk, "Psalm 132, Literary Integrity, and Syllable-Word Structures," *JSOT* 6 (1978) 41-48.

[140]Interestingly, Psalm 132 is the only psalm in which the ark is mentioned directly, although "cherubim" are mentioned in Psalms 80 and 99.

David's bringing of the ark to Jerusalem was a maneuver to lend northern religious sanction to his capitol. Similarly, the epithet of YHWH as "bull of Jacob" is a tradition that, especially in light of "Jeroboam's sin" narrated in the book of Kings, probably belongs to the sanctuaries of north Israel.[141] The epithet occurs in the tribal blessing of Genesis 49 in connection with Joseph (Gen 49:24,26). It also occurs in Deutero- and Trito-Isaiah (Isa 49:26; 60:16; cf. אביר ישראל in Isa 1:24), but not in a context that controverts its use primarily as a northern image. These northern images are woven into Psalm 132 in a way that emphasizes very strongly that it is Zion that God has chosen as a dwelling; vv. 13-14 are emphatic on that point. It seems to me likely, then, that the use of these northern symbols—i.e., the ark and the "bull of Jacob," neither of which occurs anywhere else in the Psalms—is precisely to emphasize the importance of Zion for north Israelites.

There is inadequate evidence for a judgment concerning the date of the psalm. Opinions on the psalm's date range from the time of David or Solomon[142] to the exilic period.[143] The psalm does seem to presuppose the existence of a temple in Jerusalem, and of the monarchy; but the language at the end of the psalm could be a promise of the monarchy's return as easily as it could be a promise of prosperity for an existing monarchy. Neither is the "messianic" language of vv. 10 and 17 necessarily either postexilic or preexilic. If my judgment that the psalm uses northern imagery in order to argue for the primacy of Zion is correct, then the psalm would fit with what I see as the primary program of the Songs of Ascents (see Chap. 4). Whether it was composed by the

---

[141]In treating the epithet "Bull of Jacob," Arvid S. Kapelrud ("אביר *ʾābhîr*; אביר *ʾabbîr*," *TDOT* 1:44) notes its use in Psalm 132, "where David and his successors are closely connected with the ark of the covenant, and where statements from the realm of the ancient North Israelite cult are preserved. This psalm bears witness to the amalgamation of the North Israelite and Judean cult traditions which David undertook."

[142]De Wette, *Kommentar über die Psalmen*, 593; Eissfeldt, "Psalm 132," 484-485; Dahood, *Psalms*, 3:241;

[143]Briggs and Briggs, *Book of Psalms*, 468-469; Kissane, *Book of Psalms*, 590; Kruse, "Psalm cxxxii," 285. For a survey of the various positions on dating the psalm, see Antti Laato, "Psalm 132 and the Development of the Jerusalemite/Israelite Royal Ideology," *CBQ* 54 (1992) 49-66.

person who redacted the collection, or whether it existed prior to that redaction, is probably impossible to determine.

PSALM 133

1   A song of ascents; David's:

      O[a] how good, how pleasant
         Is the dwelling of brothers together![b]

2   Like the "sweet oil" upon the head,
         Which flows down[c] upon the beard—
      The beard of Aaron,
         Which used to flow down over his whole body[d]—

3   Like the dew of Hermon,
         Which flows down upon the Mountains of Zion![e]

      There has YHWH commanded the blessing,[f]
         Life, forever![g]

Notes to the Translation

a The particle הִנֵּה functions to emphasize the exclamatory nature of the sentence, rather than to draw attention to anything in particular.

b The phrase גַּם־יָחַד occurs only here in the HB, and is moreover an unusual usage of the particle גַּם. The particle seems to be somewhat pleonastic, perhaps connoting emphatic coordination (Waltke and O'Connor, *Biblical Hebrew Syntax*, 663-664). In any case the additive meaning of the particle is almost certainly not what is intended. For further discussion see below.

c I have supplied a -שׁ, which I believe was omitted by haplography. This brings the יֹרֵד in v. 2a into conformity with the other two instances of יֹרֵד in the psalm. A cautionary note is in order, however: the more difficult reading is certainly that found in the MT, and there is no ms evidence to support my reading. So also Kraus, *Psalms 60-150*, 484.

d Lit. "according to his stature." 11QPs[A] reads מדיו for the MT's מִדּוֹתָיו. This could be a mere stylistic or vocabulary variation (cf. 2 Sam 10:4 = 1 Chr 19:4), but more probably it shows that the scribes at Qumran understood the phrase as referring to Aaron's robes (cf. LXX ἐπὶ τὴν ᾧαν τοῦ ἐνδύματος αὐτοῦ). The precise meaning of the word (and its accompanying phrase) is uncertain. Assuming the correctness of the MT, Othmar Keel ("Kultische Brüderlichkeit — Ps 133," *Freiburger Zeitschrift* 23 [1976] 71-72) has made a convincing case that the phrase does not refer to Aaron's robes, but rather to his whole height. The form מִדּוֹת appears to be a plural of מִדָּה "measure," rather than a plural of מַד "garment" (which normally uses the masculine ending for the plural; but note the Ugaritic example of *mdt* "attire" cited by Dahood [*Psalms*, 3:252]). In this case עַל־פִּי has the meaning "according to" (cf. Mic 3:5; Prov 22:6; Waltke and O'Connor, *Biblical Hebrew Syntax*, §11.3.1a, p. 221).

Schmidt (*Psalmen*, 236), followed by Kraus (*Psalms 60-150*, 484), regards the whole of v. 2b as "handgreiflich" a religious gloss adding reference to the beard of an historical person, destroying the parallelism of oil and dew, and giving a religious flavor to an otherwise secular wisdom saying ("Es ist nach dem ganzen Sinn des kleinen Gedichtes völlig ungereimt an einen bestimmten Bart, noch dazu an den Bart einer Gestalt der Geschichte zu denken. Ein klerikal gestimmter Leser hat dem weltlichen Gedicht eine Beziehung zum Gottesdienst gegeben, die aber 'an den Haaren herbeigezogen ist'"). Keel ("Kultische Brüderlichkeit," 68-75) has shown that this is almost certainly not the case.

ᵉ The 11QPsᴬ reading הר ציון is probably a substitution of the more familiar expression for a less familiar one. Joüon (*Grammaire de l'hébreu biblique*, §136j [pp. 418-419]) posited that the morphological plural here is a "pluriel de généralisation," but this does not seem to fit this case. Aubrey Robinson ("The Meaning of *rî* and the Dubiety of the Form *harrê* and its variants," *VT* 24 [1974] 500-504) suggests that the MT הררי actually represents two separate words, הר רי, with the meaning "mountain valley." His evidence from the HB is substantial, but does not fit as well in all contexts as he implies. It seems more likely, after the suggestion of Stig Norin ("Ps. 133. Zusammenhang und Datierung," *ASTI* 9 [1978] 91-92), that the word should be vocalized הַרְרִי, in which the final *yodh* would be a *hireq compaginis*. Scholars have made various proposals for emending the text to harmonize the problem of the "dew of Hermon" falling on the "mountains of Zion." The most well known is probably that of A. Jirku (Cited by Gunkel, *Psalmen*, 571), who proposed עִיּוֹן (misprinted in the BHS apparatus as עִיּוֹ, according to Allen, *Psalms 101-150*, 213, n. 3c; cf. 1 Kgs 15:20 [= 2 Chr 16:4]; 2 Kgs 15:29). Taylor and McCullough (*Psalms*, 690) omit the whole line as a gloss, so that the "psalmist...uses only one simile."

ᶠ The כִּי is probably emphatic (Allen, *Psalms 101-150*, 213). See Waltke and O'Connor, *Biblical Hebrew Syntax*, §39.3.1d (p. 657).

ᵍ The text of 11QPsᴬ lacks חַיִּים, yielding "YHWH has commanded the blessing forever." There is also a plus of שָׁלוֹם עַל־יִשְׂרָאֵל, which rounds out the line. Marrs ("*Šyry Hmᶜlwt*," 139) notes the absence of חַיִּים but apparently does not notice the plus of שָׁלוֹם עַל־יִשְׂרָאֵל. Anderson (*Book of Psalms*, 887) believes that the plus might have been "derived from" Psalm 128. I think a liturgical reason for the plus would be more likely, especially in view of the several repeated formulae in the Songs of Ascents. The text of 11QPsᴬ makes sense within the contexts both of the Songs of Ascents and of this psalm. With the weight of the versional evidence strongly in favor of the MT, however, it is probably best to regard the Qumran reading as secondary.

Interpretation

Psalm 133 begins with what seems to be a proverbial saying about the value of "dwelling of brothers together." The axiomatic character of the saying seems to find support in the phrase "how good!" which occurs often in the wisdom literature.[144] This has led many scholars to conclude that Psalm 133 is primarily proverbial in character, and only cultic because of later additions.[145] But the parallel pair טוֹב // נָעִים is, so far as I can determine, found in the wisdom literature only in Job 36:11 (נְעִימִים // טוֹב).[146] I do not find sufficient evidence that this pair constitutes distinctive wisdom vocabulary, nor am I convinced of such for either of the two words separately.

Another argument for the sapiential character of Psalm 133 is the theme of "fraternal harmony."[147] This interpretation of the first line is, however, coming under increasing criticism. Keel has seen in the psalm a cultic sense in which the "brothers" are the gathered community of worshiping Israelite males.[148] Berlin, on the other hand, has found the

---

[144]Gershon Brin, "The Significance of the Form *mah-ṭṭob*," *VT* 38 (1988) 462-465. As he acknowledges, however, it normally occurs in "better than" sayings, and is therefore not particularly relevant to this case, which is a "superlative" use (463).

[145]Hermann Gunkel, "Psalm 133," in *Festschrift für Karl Budde*, ed. Karl Marti (BZAW 34; Giessen: Alfred Töpelmann, 1920) 69-74; Schmidt, *Psalmen*, 236; Gunkel, *Psalmen*, 571; Gerstenberger, Jutzler, and Boecker, *Psalmen in der Sprache unserer Zeit*, 210; Kraus, *Psalmen*, 2:1067-1068; Seybold, *Wallfahrtspsalmen*, 25-26.

[146]The root נעם occurs twelve times in the wisdom literature; but this does not qualify it as a distinctive feature of wisdom vocabulary, since it occurs also ten times in the Psalms. The only other instances in the HB in which this pair occurs are in Pss 135:3 and 147:1.

[147]Schmidt, *Psalmen*, 236; Gunkel, *Psalmen*, 571; Gerstenberger, Jutzler, and Boecker, *Psalmen in der Sprache unserer Zeit*, 210; Kraus, *Psalms 60-150*, 485-486; Dahood (*Psalms*, 3:250) believes that the psalm teaches that "the reward of fraternal harmony will be everlasting life." So also de Wette, *Kommentar über die Psalmen*, 598-599.

[148]Keel, "Kultische Brüderlichkeit," 68-80. The blessing in v. 3b comes "nicht auf das bloße Zusammensein der Brüder als solchem, nicht auf den Zion als Ort, sondern auf die brüderliche Versammlung an der von Jahwe erwählten Stätte" (p. 80). So also Anderson, *Book of Psalms*, 2:885; Allen, *Psalms 101-150*, 214-215. Commentators before Gunkel (e.g., Delitzsch, *Psalms*, 320; Briggs and Briggs, *Book of Psalms*, 475) had already taken this position, but it was largely abandoned after Gunkel's determination that the psalm was a "wisdom psalm" (Gunkel, *Psalmen*, 570-571).

image of "brothers dwelling together" to be primarily nationalistic in character. She sees the image as a symbol for the (re)united monarchy.[149] The former position receives some support from Sir 50:12, where the Aaronite priests are a "crown of brothers" (στέφανος ἀδελφῶν) for the High Priest Simon I as he stands before the altar. In light of the psalm's conclusion (which may be secondary, but is not necessarily so) I do not think it indispensable to choose either of these interpretations to the exclusion of the other. It does seem that the cultic sense is primary (see below), but the "flowing" of northern Israelites to Zion would certainly also have political ramifications.

Two possibilities exist for the interpretation of the phrase גַּם־יָחַד. The phrase probably means "all together" or "together indeed," rather than "also together." The construction is comparable to the several instances of גַּם־שָׁנִים, where the meaning is similarly "all the years."[150] But does it describe *where* the "brothers" dwell (i.e., "all together"),[151] or the climate of the dwelling (i.e., "in unity")? The latter interpretation, so that the incipit of Psalm 133 speaks about "fraternal harmony," is common.[152] As Berlin has shown, however, a careful examination of the biblical evidence gives a different picture.[153] In Gen 13:6 and 36:7 the

---

[149]Adele Berlin, "On the Interpretation of Psalm 133," in *Directions in Biblical Hebrew Poetry*, ed. Elaine R. Follis (JSOTSup 40; Sheffield, UK: Sheffield Academic Press, 1987) 142-143.

[150]Gen 27:45; Deut 22:22; 23:19; 1 Sam 4:17; Prov 17:15; 20:10; 20:12; Ruth 1:5. Kittel, *Psalmen*, 407; Keet, *A Study of the Psalms of Ascents*, 102. Friedrich Baethgen (*Die Psalmen, übersetzt und erklärt* [HAT II, 2; Göttingen: Vandenhoeck & Ruprecht, 1904] 347) says simply that "גַּם verstärkt יָחַד." Waltke and O'Connor (*Biblical Hebrew Syntax*, 663) rightly acknowledge the multivalency of this and other similar adverbs: "Hebrew grammars tend to assign well-defined roles to these words, but as the lexicons usually recognize, such assignments do not describe the usages adequately. All these terms have quite broad emphatic uses as well as the specific senses to be discussed." Waltke and O'Connor do not, however, discuss Ps 133:1 as an example.

[151]So Skehan, "Some Short Psalms," 108.

[152]The quote is from Dahood, *Psalms*, 3:250. So also Keet, *A Study of the Psalms of Ascents*, 102. NRSV translates "when kindred live together in unity." Many interpreters refer to "family solidarity" (Weiser, *Psalms*, 784. So also Schmidt, *Psalmen*, 236; Taylor and McCullough, *Psalms*, 688; Allen, *Psalms 101-150*, 212), but they derive this more from the literal meaning of families that remain together even after the brothers are married.

[153]Berlin, "On the Interpretation of Psalm 133," 141-143.

phrase שֶׁבֶת...יַחְדָּו indicates patrilocal residency together as an extended family. In these two narratives "the land was not able to bear" the whole family's making a living on the same estate. The levirite law in Deut 25:5 states that

> when brothers dwell together (כִּי־יֵשְׁבוּ אַחִים יַחְדָּו), and one of them dies without a son, the wife of the deceased shall not marry a man who is not kin; rather, her husband's-brother shall go in to her, take her as his wife, and serve her in her husband's stead....

This law refers not necessarily to dwelling in the same house, but on the same patrimony.[154] It protects the wife's right to continue living with her deceased husband's family, as well as the latter's right to an heir of the household. The need for an heir is, of course, intimately bound up with the family's ownership of an estate. Another use of the phrase denotes simply sitting down together for a meal (Judg 19:6; וַיֵּשְׁבוּ וַיֹּאכְלוּ שְׁנֵיהֶם יַחְדָּו). This might at first blush seem to be an insignificant case, but upon examination it reveals another possible meaning for the phrase: It can refer generally to "fellowship," that is, to sharing things in a common enterprise for mutual benefit.[155]

To these texts should be added Jeremiah's vision of a future in which YHWH would restore the exilic community to the land: "Judah and all its cities shall dwell in it [the land] together—both tenant-farmers and those who drive herds" (Jer 31:24). In this stunning portrait of future blessing for Jerusalem and Judah the phrase יֵשֵׁב...יַחְדָּו depicts a situation that I think is close to that envisioned in Psalm 133, namely the restoration of the Judahites to their own land in prosperity. In Jeremiah's oracle this naturally implies both living in the land and worshiping at the

---

[154]Many commentators, following Sigismund Rauh (*Hebräisches Familienrecht in vorprophetischer Zeit* [Berlin: Gustav Schade, 1907] 35ff; cited in Kittel, *Psalmen*, 407), have noted this verbal similarity. A few (e.g., Ehrlich, *Psalmen*, 347) focus on this passage almost to the exclusion of other relevant passages. For a good overview of the social relationships within the family, see Victor H. Matthews and Don C. Benjamin, *The Social World of Ancient Israel, 1250-587 BCE*, (Peabody, MA: Hendrickson, 1993) .

[155]Kissane (*Book of Psalms*, 594) takes the phrase in Psalm 133 to mean sitting down at a sacrificial banquet. This is probably putting too heavy, and too literal, an emphasis on Judg 19:6.

"holy mountain."[156] Berlin's analysis of the phrase therefore points in the right direction. The phrase refers to the benefit of having the country together (again). It is necessary, however, to go beyond this. In light of the rest of the psalm, this (re)unification of the country is more important than simple "political" matters; it is concerned with the very blessing that comes down from God on the living and worshiping community. I therefore do not find it necessary to make a sharp distinction between the "nationalistic" interpretation and the "cultic" one. They are aspects of the same reality.

The phrase "sweet oil" (שֶׁמֶן הַטּוֹב) reminds one of the special perfumed oil with which high priests were anointed (שֶׁמֶן הַקֹּדֶשׁ in Num 35:25), especially in connection with Aaron.[157] The term שֶׁמֶן הַטּוֹב is used only one other time in the HB, where it is one of the treasures of the coffers which Hezekiah "showed" to the Assyrian emissaries.[158] The phrase שֶׁמֶן טוֹב, without the definite article, occurs in Qoh 7:1: "A [good] reputation is better than sweet oil." Both of these cases seem to denote non-sacral oil, having the everyday uses of making the house smell sweet—and driving away insects—when burned in a lamp or incense burner, or sweetening the fragrance of a person when used as a cosmetic.[159] If this profane sense is primary in Psalm 133, then

---

[156]John Bright (*Jeremiah* [AB 21; Garden City, New York: Doubleday, 1965], 282, n. 24) rightly points to the fact that the antecedent of the feminine pronominal suffix is the "land," not the "holy hill." However, this does not exclude a double-*entendre* referring also to the latter.

[157]Anderson, *Book of Psalms*, 2:886; Keet, *A Study of the Psalms of Ascents*, 103. Delitzsch (*Psalms*, 317) asserts that "שֶׁמֶן הַטּוֹב is the oil for anointing described in Ex. 22-23, which consisted of a mixture of oil and aromatic spices strictly forbidden to be used in common life."

[158]2 Kgs 20:13 = Isa 39:2. Ronald E. Clements (*Isaiah 1-39* [NCB; Grand Rapids, MI: Wm. B. Eerdmans, 1980], 295) states that Hezekiah's action receives its negative overtone only from the later history, not from the text at hand. His actions are only the customary polite boasting of a king.

[159]Ehrlich, *Psalmen*, 347; Briggs and Briggs, *Book of Psalms*, 475-476; Weiser, *Psalms*, 784. For a discussion of this practice see Matthews, *Manners and Customs*, 122. Kraus (*Psalms 60-150*, 486) states: "There is no thought here of holy oil but of soothing cosmetic that brings refreshment." He probably bases this, however, upon his exegesis which eliminates Aaron (and all culticity) altogether. It is possible that כַּשֶּׁמֶן should be read כְּשֶׁמֶן, with הַטּוֹב being then the noun signifying "perfume," as Baethgen (*Psalmen*, 396) suggested.

the connection with Aaron is strange.[160] It is possible that the use of this mundane vocabulary rather than the technical priestly term שֶׁמֶן הַקֹּדֶשׁ in the image implies a lay author for the poem.[161] The connection with Aaron, together with the overall purpose of the psalm, almost mandates that the oil be the sacred oil with which high priests were anointed. In this case the substitution of הַטּוֹב for the expected הַקֹּדֶשׁ could be due either to the author's desire to produce a word-play between טוֹב in v. 1 and in v. 2 or to a lay author's non-use of priestly vocabulary.

What place does the "beard of Aaron" have in this emerging vision? As an element of the poem, Watson believes the line to be a separate metaphor.[162] Two observations follow from his analysis of the structure, according to him: (1) that *ᶜal-hārōʾš* is not part of the "underlying pattern but forms part of the unit preceding *šeyyōrēd*," and (2) that "Aaron's beard" ought to be taken as a simile, despite the ellipsis of the comparative particle. The first is clearly enough true, and I have adopted this structure for my translation rather than the one in BHS, which is based upon metrical considerations. The second assertion, however, has been challenged by Tsumura,[163] who argues that v. 2b is an example of "sorites" (climax or gradation), a poetic device that builds on, rather than parallels, what has gone before. Tsumura points (as Dahood before him

---

[160]For arguments about the psalm's thrust and the place of the Aaron-saying within it see below. On the practice of anointing the high priest with oil cf. Exod 29:21 and Leviticus 8. So also Keet, *A Study of the Psalms of Ascents*, 103; Anderson, *Book of Psalms*, 2:886.

[161]Keel ("Kultische Brüderlichkeit," 73, n. 17) takes this position on the basis of Leonard Rost's study of the sacrificial vocabulary in the Psalter (Leonard Rost, "Ein Psalmenproblem," *TLZ* 93/4 [1968] 241-246). Rost concludes that very few of the psalms derive from priestly circles, but rather from pious lay persons. In his words, "Die Psalmenverfasser sind...keine Priester" (p. 246).

[162]Wilfred G. E. Watson, "The Hidden Simile in Psalm 133," *Bib* 60 (1979) 108-109. He observes a parallel structure for vv. 2a, 2b, and 3, which he identifies in the following way:

kaššemen haṭṭôb ᶜal-hārōʾš	*šeyyōrēd ᶜal-hazzāken*
zᵉkan-ʾahᵃrōn	*šeyyōrēd ᶜal-pî middôtāyw*
kᵉtal-ḥermôn	*šeyyōrēd ᶜal-harᵉrê ṣiyyôn*

[163]David T. Tsumura, "Sorites in Psalm 133,2-3a," *Bib* 61 (1980) 416-417. He points out that "dew of Hermon" means "the dew on Mt. Hermon," and so the parallel with "oil upon the head" is precise.

had done[164]) to the known word pair שֶׁמֶן // טַל. This pair occurs in Gen 27:28,39 and in the Ugaritic Anat cycle (*UT* ʿnt:IV:87), which reads *ṭl . šmm . šmn . ảrṣ*.[165] The existence of this known pair makes a third simile on the beard of Aaron (v. 2b) somewhat awkward. This does not mean, however, that it cannot be the subject of the verb יֹרֵד.[166] The extended sorites includes the whole line. Thus there is no reason either to strike the line or to regard it as a separate simile. As I will try to demonstrate below, the long beard of Aaron foreshadows the last words of the psalm: "life forever."

One of the interpretational cruxes of Psalm 133 is the simile of "Like the dew of Hermon, // which flows down upon the Mountains of Zion!" (v. 3a). Literally speaking, this is a geographical impossibility. The region of Mt Hermon is located in the lush Anti-Lebanon range to the northwest of the region known as Bashan and northeast of Dan. Its summit reaches to about 9,100 feet, and receives more than 60 inches of annual precipitation.[167] The expression "dew of Hermon," therefore, is easily enough understood: During the dry summer a wind brings moisture from the Mediterranean, giving moisture to the hill country when the ground cools during the night. "So abundant is the moisture of the night-mist on Hermon that those who encamp there during a summer night will find their tent as completely saturated as if a heavy rain had fallen."[168] But how does one explain the fact that the poem has dew

---

[164]Dahood, *Psalms*, 3:251.

[165]The context in which this occurs is also helpful: it depicts Anat bathing herself before Baal's approach. The line constitutes two metaphors for the water with which she cleanses herself. Gibson, *Canaanite Myths and Legends*, 3D, 86-90; p. 52.

[166]So Kissane, *Book of Psalms*, 594-595; Keet, *A Study of the Psalms of Ascents*, 104; Dahood, *Psalms*, 3:252. For "beard" as the subject see Anderson, *Book of Psalms*, 2:886; Berlin, "On the Interpretation of Psalm 133," 144.

[167]Herbert G. May, G. N. S. Hunt and R. W. Hamilton, *Oxford Bible Atlas* (New York, NY: Oxford University Press, 1984) 51; Alfred Haldar, "Hermon, Mount," in *IDB* 2:585; Rami Arav, "Hermon, Mount," ABD 3:158-160.

[168]T. K. Cheyne, "Hermon" and "Dew," in T. K. Cheyne, and J. Sutherland Black, eds., *Encyclopædia Biblica* (New York, NY: MacMillan Company, 1914) 2021-2023; 1094-1096. Gustaf Hermann Dalman (*Arbeit und Sitte in Palästina*, vol. 1, pt. 1, *Herbst und Winter* [Gütersloh: C. Bertelsman, 1928; reprinted, Hildesheim: Georg Olms Verlagsbuchhandlung, 1964] 89-96), however, says that the dew actually becomes more common in the fall than in the summer. He believes the "dew of Hermon" refers not specifically to this dew but to the mythological dew that drips

from a mountain almost 100 miles away descending upon Zion?[169] Many commentators, following Gunkel, elect to emend the text so that it does not read "Zion."[170] Several different interpretations are possible if one retains "Zion": the saying (1) reflects ancient meteorological speculation;[171] (2) is a metaphor for God's blessing coming down on Jerusalem;[172] (3) is a frozen proverbial expression meaning "copious dew" that refreshes and invigorates, and therefore is an appropriate metaphor for the abundant life-giving presence of God at Zion.[173]   A

---

on mountains. It is an image for God's blessing. Nonetheless the image could not exist without the actual summer dew (95-96).

[169]For a good discussion of the exegetical problems involved see Keet, *A Study of the Psalms of Ascents*, 105-106.

[170]Seybold, *Wallfahrtspsalmen*, 39. Schmidt (*Psalmen*, 236) and Kraus (*Psalms 60-150*, 484) read צִיָּה "parched"; E. Power ("Sion or Si'on in Psalm 133 (Vulg 132)?," *Bib* 49 [1922] 346-347) reads שִׂיאֹן/שִׂיאִיֹן (alternate spellings), the mountain range in which Hermon is located; Gunkel (*Psalmen*, 571-572), following Jirku (who is mentioned but not cited), reads עִיֹּון (the shift to צִיֹּון is a result of a "fanatisch-jüdische Bearbeitung"). Keel ("Kultische Brüderlichkeit," 79) argues that a word-play exists on צִיֹּון and צָוָה (v. 3), but this argument in favor of retaining the MT reading is hardly compelling. As I shall try to show, however, there are other reasons for retaining צִיֹּון.

[171]Ludwing Köhler, "Zur Weiterfuehrung des alttestamentlichen Wörterbuches," *ZAW* 32 (1912) 13-14 (cited in Gunkel, *Psalmen*, 572); Keet, *A Study of the Psalms of Ascents*, 106. Delitzsch (*Psalms*, 319-320) asserts that "an abundant dew, when warm days have preceded, might very well be diverted to Jerusalem by the operation of the cold current of air sweeping down from the north over Hermon. We know, indeed, from our own experience how far off a cold air coming from the Alps is perceptible and produces its effects. The figure of the poet is therefore as true to nature as it is beautiful."

[172]Dalman, *Arbeit und Sitte in Palästina*, 1,1:95-96; Keel, "Kultische Brüderlichkeit," 70.

[173]Baethgen, *Psalmen*, 396; Ehrlich, *Psalmen*, 348; Kittel, *Psalmen*, 2:407; Dahood, *Psalms*, 3:252; Skehan, "Some Short Psalms," 109; Kissane, *Book of Psalms*, 595; Anderson, *Book of Psalms*, 2:886; Briggs and Briggs, *Book of Psalms*, 476; Weiser, *Psalms*, 784; Gerstenberger (Gerstenberger, Jutzler, and Boecker, *Psalmen in der Sprache unserer Zeit*, 210) says that both the oil and the dew are images of quickening energy, and for this reason the geographical remove of Hermon and Sinai is simply "nicht beachtet." Walter Brueggemann (*The Message of the Psalms, A Theological Commentary* [Augsburg Old Testament Studies; Minneapolis, MN: Augsburg Publishing House, 1984], 48) sees the dew as a metaphor for the unity of the brothers "which is given miraculously and which gives life in an otherwise parched context." Allen (*Psalms 101-150*, 215) thinks it may be simply "the amount of dew which befits a sacred mountain."

comparable phenomenon occurs in Ps 48:3, which locates Zion "in the far north" (NRSV) or identifies it with sacred Mt. Zaphon, depending on how one translates יַרְכְּתֵי צָפוֹן. It does not seem to me, however, that the mythological North (the place of the North Star, the *omphalus mundi*) is what is in view in Psalm 133 (צָפוֹן does not appear); rather it is a use of North-Israelite language and symbology to communicate Jerusalemite meaning. Hermon does not represent the mythological abode of God; rather the expression "dew of Hermon" must have been a fixed expression, and is now put to new Jerusalemite use.

The mention of both of these sacred mountains identifies one of the major rhetorical purposes of this poem: the unification of north and south in Jerusalem, the place where YHWH dwells,[174] which is also the quintessential place of YHWH's presence and the place where gifts of life and unity are expected. Additional support for seeing north-south unity as a major theme in this psalm lies in the fact that Aaron is primarily a northern personage, at least in the early period.[175] On the basis of linguistic evidence, Rendsburg finds Psalm 133 to be almost certainly from a north-Israelite provenance.[176] Even if one does agree with the degree of certainty that he claims, a major theme of the psalm seems to be binding the north with the south in the experience of the blessing that YHWH gives at Zion.

---

[174]Norin, "Ps. 133," 93. Berlin ("On the Interpretation of Psalm 133," 142-143) has shown quite lucidly that the use of this imagery serves such a rhetorical purpose. Of course, this rhetorical purpose does not explain the meaning of the imagery, it only describes its function within the psalm.

[175]Aelred Cody, *A History of Old Testament Priesthood* (AnBib 35; Rome: Pontifical Biblical Institute, 1969).

[176]Gary A. Rendsburg (*Linguistic Evidence for the Northern Origin of Selected Psalms* [SBLMS 43; Atlanta, GA: Scholars Press, 1990] 91-93) gives several converging lines of evidence that point to the psalm's northern origin: the word נעם, the relative particle -שׁ, the form מדות, which is also used at Ugarit (or, if it is from מדד, is a characteristic northern form), the presence of Mt. Hermon (interestingly, he does not mention Aaron), and the form הררי. He concludes that these factors "represent a significant bunching of IH [Israelian Hebrew] traits to justify our labeling this chapter an Israelian poem" (p. 93). As he points out at several points in the book, the presence of "Zion" does not disprove its northern provenance, since it could have been written by "a northern poet who accepted the centrality of Zion in Israelite theology" (p. 90).

The last line of Psalm 133 also presents several problems. The phrase "command the blessing" is an unusual one in the HB. It occurs in only two other places: Lev 25:21 and Deut 28:8 (cf. also Ps 42:9, יוֹמָם יְצַוֶּה יהוה חַסְדּוֹ[177]). It is important to realize that both of these passages denote the special fertility that YHWH gives in response to faithfulness. Lev 25:1-24 deals with the question of the sabbatical and jubilee years. According to the priestly author, who speaks as God's mouthpiece, every seven years Israel was to observe a fallow year in which all the land's crops would lie un-harvested. The author was aware that this might create a problem for people, since they relied on their crops for subsistence. The author addressed this potential problem thus (Lev 25:20-22):

> Should you ask, "What shall we eat in the seventh year, since we may not sow nor reap our crop?" I will command my blessing for you (וְצִוִּיתִי אֶת־בִּרְכָתִי לָכֶם) in the sixth year, and it will yield three years' produce. When you sow in the eighth year, you will eat from the preserved product; until the ninth year, when its produce comes in, you shall eat stored food.

In this passage it is clear that "command my blessing" refers to extraordinary fertility that YHWH provides in special circumstances and as a reward for faithfulness to God's commandment. The same is true in Deut 28:1-14, which describes the blessings that YHWH provides for people who are faithful to the commandments. It is not ordinary fertile life that is depicted here, but rather an idyllic abundance that allows for no harm to come upon the righteous. This fertility is in sharp distinction to the "curses" (הַקְּלָלוֹת) that would "come upon" (בָאוּ עָלֶיךָ) the one who does not keep the commandments. Curse is the antithesis of the blessing, and YHWH is the ultimate source of both.[178] The book of Deuteronomy probably derives from north-Israelite Levitical circles,[179]

---

[177]Anderson, *Book of Psalms*, 2:887.

[178]*Contra* Klaus Koch, "Is There a Doctrine of Retribution in the Old Testament?," in *Theodicy in the Old Testament*, ed. James L. Crenshaw, trans. Thomas H. Trapp (IRT 4; Philadelphia, PA: Fortress Press, 1983; reprinted from *ZTK* 52 [1955] 1-42.) 57-87.

[179]For a balanced discussion of the possibilities for the authorship of Deuteronomy see Andrew David Hastings Mayes, *Deuteronomy* (NCB; Grand Rapids, MI: Wm. B. Eerdmans, 1979) 103-108. He concludes that, despite

and there are good reasons to regard the Holiness Code (Leviticus 17-26) similarly. It is probable, then, that the phrase "YHWH commanded the blessing" in Ps 133:3b has a priestly character. Moreover, it ties the technical phrase for superabundant blessing to Zion ("*there*") in a way that is quite similar to the argument being made by the redactor of the Songs of Ascents (see Chap. 4, pp. 184-185).

The last phrase of the psalm is extremely difficult to interpret. A possible word play with the opening line of the psalm (חַיִּים/אַחִים)[180] and the play on the length of Aaron's beard argue (though admittedly not too forcefully) that the word probably has a place in the psalm's purpose, and is not simply a gloss. Is this, as Dahood believes, a reference to eternal life?[181] I do not think this is the intention of the author. Normally the various combinations of the words חיה and עוֹלָם refer only to God (the point of Gen 3:22 is that such "eternal life" would be contrary to the primeval parents' nature, making them God-like; Dan 12:2 is a late text, contrasting "everlasting life" with "everlasting contempt"). In Psalm 133, however, "eternal life" is a counterpart, even the result, of the blessing discussed above. Even if one accepts the presence of the idea of "eternal life," one must express a qualification. The emphasis is not on the idea of eternality but on the idea of life. To introduce the notion of "eternal life" in an abstract sense is to stray from the direction in which the rest of the psalm moves. But to emphasize "life" is to carry the idea of blessing to its logical end. The phrase עַד־הָעוֹלָם therefore may be seen as referring to the duration of God's fructifying activity rather than to the length of life as such. Alternatively, if עַד־הָעוֹלָם modifies "life," then it would probably mean "long life" rather than "eternal life" in the modern sense. If one accepts this interpretation then "long life" would provide an interesting anamnesis with the "beard of Aaron." The end of God's blessing is venerability, in the sense both of old age and of nobility. This

---

difficulties of the theory of Levitical authorship for the book, it still explains the data more completely than would authorship by court scribes or prophets.

[180]Allen, *Psalms 101-150*, 214.

[181]Dahood, *Psalms*, 3:253.

combination of meanings is intimately bound up in the symbolism of the beard.[182]

In addition to employing vivid and beautiful imagery, Psalm 133 is artfully constructed. It is arranged on a concentric pattern. What may have originally been a proverb about the glories of a (re)united family (although this is far from certain) is immediately transformed into an image of the abundance that God provides at Zion. This transformation is accomplished through the use of similes that compare the joy of family togetherness with two traditional symbols of divine bounty: oil and dew. An extension of the first simile, the image of Aaron's long beard, focuses the point of the psalm still more sharply: the blessing that comes down from God correlates with the hoary beard of venerability. Brueggemann identifies the general movement of the psalm: "The opening line celebrates an experience. The conclusion identifies that experience as blessing."[183] Between these affirmations the repetition of the verb ירד emphasizes the idea that the blessing from God comes down.

To where does it descend? Ultimately it descends upon Zion. With this allusion to "brothers" in v. 1 shifts meaning. What at first seems wholly general, applying to any family gathered together, becomes an image of the community, gathered at Zion, that receives God's extraordinary blessing. It is not simply a proverb that has been reinterpreted in a cultic light; it is a turning of imagery from the common life of the family to the community entire. As Brueggemann goes on to say, "the reasoning is 'from below.'"[184]

The comprehensibility of Psalm 133 is perhaps due more to its rich and vivid imagery than to clarity in the usual sense. Like the "tone poems" of Franz Liszt or Richard Strauss, this psalm aims to convey a mood rather than to communicate specific ideas. This is why the psalm is able to move freely from one idea to the next while maintaining unity. Strictly speaking, the psalm is not "about" the (re)united monarchy,[185]

---

[182]Cf. the beard as a sign of venerability for El; e.g., *šbt.ilm.lḥkmt // šbt.dqnk.ltsrk* "You are great, O El, You are truly wise // The greyness of your beard truly instructs you" (*UT* 51:5:65-66).

[183]Brueggemann, *Message of the Psalms*, 47.

[184]Brueggemann, *Message of the Psalms*, 48.

[185]Taylor and McCullough, *Psalms*, 688; Berlin, "On the Interpretation of Psalm 133," 141-147.

the assembled pilgrims in Jerusalem,[186] or proverbially "fraternal harmony,"[187] although any of these may have been the occasion for the psalm's composition. What it is about is found in the notion implied by the constant reference to the descent of blessing. This culminates in the last line, which depicts YHWH's blessing as "commanded" upon Zion, to the end of a long and full life.

Two hypotheses about the milieu in which Psalm 133 was composed seem plausible; either the north-Israelite images are there because the psalm is north-Israelite in origin, or they are there because a Judean author deliberately used northern language. The first of these has difficulty with the last verse, which not only names Zion but insists on its essentiality for the desired blessing. Although it is quite plausible that the reference to Zion and the final verse are redactional additions, it seems to me more likely, in view of the themes of "brothers dwelling together" and of the descent of blessing, that the use of northern imagery is purposeful. If one were to accept the redactional explanation, one would have to grant that the themes of the two parts of the psalm certainly complement one another very well—so well, in fact, that the line between original and redaction becomes very fuzzy. If, on the other hand, the author of Psalm 133 deliberately uses northern imagery in order to argue that Zion is the source of fructification, the psalm would naturally be placed at a period in which an effort to gain northern support for the Jerusalem temple is under way. Such an effort would also fit with the priestly terminology discussed above. Because such an effort also seems to be presumed by the redactional materials in the Songs of Ascents, I believe that the *Sitz im Leben* of this psalm is identical to the historical matrix in which the collection was produced. I shall treat this historical matrix in depth in Chap. 4.

---

[186]Briggs and Briggs, *Book of Psalms*, 475; Keet, *A Study of the Psalms of Ascents*, 104; Anderson, *Book of Psalms*, 2:885; Seybold, *Wallfahrtspsalmen*, 26; Allen, *Psalms 101-150*, 214.

[187]Schmidt, *Psalmen*, 236; Gunkel, *Psalmen*, 571; Gerstenberger, Jutzler, and Boecker, *Psalmen in der Sprache unserer Zeit*, 210; Kraus, *Psalms 60-150*, 485-486; Dahood (*Psalms*, 3:250); de Wette, *Kommentar über die Psalmen*, 598-599.

PSALM 134

1   A song of ascents:

O bless YHWH,[a]
   All you servants of YHWH,
   Who "stand" in the house of YHWH
       All night long!
2   Lift your hands to the sanctuary
   And bless YHWH![b]

3   May YHWH bless you[c] from Zion,
   The one who made heaven and earth!

Notes to the Translation

a "O" is an attempt to render the "attention-getting" function of הִנֵּה. The combination of הִנֵּה with an imperative verb is otherwise unattested in the Hebrew Bible. Gunkel (*Psalmen*, 573) believed הִנֵּה to have been transposed from the incipit of Psalm 133, but in view of the otherwise broad range of meanings possible with this particle, this is probably not wise. The primary function of הִנֵּה is that of calling "special attention either to a certain statement as a whole or to a single word out of a statement" (Waltke and O'Connor, *Biblical Hebrew Syntax*, §16.3.5b; 300). Perhaps it is possible to state that the particle emphasizes the imperative force of the verb.

b The LXX has an important plus that may provide evidence of an alternate textual tradition. It adds an extra line—in many ways what one would expect from the standard practices of Hebrew parallelism—and reads בַּלֵּילוֹת with v. 2. The LXX reading is as follows:

οἱ ἑστῶτες ἐν οἴκῳ κυρίου,
   ἐν αὐλαῖς οἴκου θεοῦ ἡμῶν
ἐν ταῖς νυξὶν ἐπάρατε τὰς χεῖρας ὑμῶν εἰς τὰ ἅγια
   καὶ εὐλογεῖτε τὸν κύριον.

A retrojection into Hebrew yields the following:

בחצרות בית אלהינו   העמדים בבית יהוה
 וברכו את־יהוה   בלילות שאו־ידכם קדש

The plus in the LXX corresponds precisely to the wording of LXX Ps 134:2 (MT 135:2). The reasonable inference is that the LXX translator, or a copyist at some point in the process, probably imported his knowledge of this latter text into his translation of the present psalm. However, other verbal parallels exist between Psalms 134 and 135 in the Hebrew (cf. the use of שֵׁם יהוה "the name of YHWH" in

Ps 134:2 of the 11QPs^A text, which seems to tie with , even though the two are not juxtaposed in that ms). Since this is so, the judgment that the plus in the LXX results from an anamnesis (whether on the part of the translator or of a copyist) of Ps 135:2 must remain tentative.

   c The addressee in vv. 1-2 is plural; in v. 3 it is singular.

Interpretation

The identity of the group of people commanded to "bless YHWH" is not clear. One possibility is that it refers to temple personnel.[188] On the basis of the chiasm with v. 3, Dahood repoints the word to עָבְדִי "works."[189] This proposal does not fit well with the context, however, which clearly refers to people praying. Allen believes that any reference to cultic personnel is "less likely," since עֲבָדִים "nowhere else refers to priests and/or Levites."[190] This assertion must be qualified, at least. The singular "servant of YHWH" appears 22 times in the HB. In all but one of these the reference is certainly to a person who has special connections to the cultus.[191] The one uncertain example appears in the notoriously difficult "servant songs" of Isaiah (Isa 42:19), and probably refers there to a special person, whether the prophet, Moses, or the Messiah.[192] The cases of the phrase "servant of YHWH" (in the singular) in the HB call Allen's assertion into question. References to the plural "servants of YHWH" are mostly ambiguous in their referent.[193] Deutero-Isaiah (54:17) uses the term in a way that seems to be synonymous with the worshiping community. Psalm 135 uses it similarly. Its beginning

---

[188]Weiser, *Psalms*, 786; Taylor and McCullough, *Psalms*, 692.

[189]Dahood, *Psalms*, 3:254.

[190]Allen, *Psalms 101-150*, 216. He admits, however, that the verbal form and the noun עֲבֹדָה do.

[191]Moses: Deut 34:5; Josh 1:1,13,15; 8:31,33; 11:12; 12:6; 13:8; 14:7; 18:7; 22:2,4,5; 2 Kgs 18:12; 2 Chr 1:3; 24:6. Joshua: Josh 24:29; Judg 2:8. David: Pss 18:1; 36:1.

[192]Claus Westermann (*Isaiah 40-66: A Commentary* [OTL; Philadelphia: Westminster, 1965], 20-21) judiciously pronounces that the "veiled allusions, now to one now to another of these, forbid the adoption of any one to the exclusion of the rest."

[193]In later literature one finds a clearer meaning for the term: the "servants of YHWH" are any persons who are faithful to YHWH (Azar 63; 1 Esd 6:13; 2 Esd 16:35).

mirrors that of Psalm 134, but vv. 19-20 probably clarify the expression, making it refer to the whole assembly, including priests, Levites, and "You who fear YHWH."[194]   Also instructive is 2 Kings 9-10, which refers both to "servants of YHWH" and "servants of Baal." The NRSV and JPSV translate these expressions using "servants" and "worshipers" synonymously.   But the usage seems to connote a more specifically priestly function. Jehu provides the prophets of Baal with "vestments" (לְבוּשׁ; the clothes' cultic character is probably implied by the fact that they don them on the premises; 10:22), and they proceed to make sacrifices (2 Kgs 10:24). None of these plural usages is specific enough to warrant certainty that "servants of YHWH" refers to temple officials, but in my opinion the singular usage makes this meaning more probable than the general one.

Some sort of dialogue is probably presumed by the change in addressee from plural to singular. One would be hard pressed to support a conclusion that the worshipers are addressed in the plural in vv. 1-2, and then in the singular in v. 3. Such a conclusion depends more on a supposition about the character of the collection than upon the character of this psalm in particular; as Allen puts it, "If the collection of Pss 120-134 comprises processional songs, it would be appropriate for worshipers to be called to praise in this final psalm."[195]   Moreover, this interpretation must posit a situation in which the gathered community spends the night in the temple courts—a situation that is otherwise unknown and certainly finds no further warrant in the psalm itself.

Furthermore, the verb עמד has the technical meaning of one who ministers before the altar. So, for example, 1 Kgs 8:11 says that the priests "were not able to *stand* to minister" (וְלֹא־יָכְלוּ הַכֹּהֲנִים

---

[194]The group referred to here as "those who fear YHWH" (cf. also Pss 115:9-13; 118:1-4) could be "the eschatological community remaining faithful to the Lord, and standing in readiness to serve as Yahweh's agent in restoring true worship, righteousness, and compassion in the land" (Paul D. Hanson, *The People Called: The Growth of Community in the Bible* [San Francisco, CA: Harper and Row, 1986] 284), as it is in Malachi 3. However, I see no reason to define the group so sharply in Psalm 135. For a review of the expression and its analogs elsewhere in the ancient Near East see R. H. Pfeiffer, "The Fear of God," *IEJ* 5 (1955) 41-48.

[195]Allen, *Psalms 101-150*, 217.

לַעֲמֹד לְשָׁרֵת) since God's glory filled the temple.[196] It does not always mean this; it can refer simply to someone who "stands" to give a speech. But in connection with the "house of YHWH" it is most natural to see priestly functionaries as the addressees.[197]

That this "standing" in the temple is בַּלֵּילוֹת "by night" (lit. "in the nights") has occasioned a large amount of speculation.[198] Many scholars posit a service in which the assembled pilgrims would worship at the temple (interpreting קֹדֶשׁ locatively[199]) on the night prior to the beginning of a festival.[200] Some, conversely, have taken the accusative קֹדֶשׁ directionally, implying a devotional prayer "toward the holy place," which could happen almost anywhere and at any time.[201] Assuming the hypothesis to be true that the עֹמְדִים are cultic officials, it is possible that "those who stand by night" refers to the Levitical temple guards, who "spent the night near the house of God" (1 Chr 9:23-27). The prepositional phrase בַּלֵּילוֹת probably means "throughout the night," rather than "every night." This receives support from the only other occurrence of בַּלֵּילוֹת in the Psalter, Ps 92:3, where it parallels בַּבֹּקֶר. In Isa 21:8 the prophet puts a speech into the mouth of a

---

[196]Cf. 1 Kgs 13:1; Zech 3:7 (of Joshua the high priest); 1 Chr 6:17; 23:18. In the latter two עמד stands parallel to עבד (a pun?). In Jer 28:5, however, הָעֹמְדִים בְּבֵית־יהוה seems to refer to the worshiping community in contradistinction to the priests.

[197]So de Wette, *Kommentar über die Psalmen*, 600; Keet, *A Study of the Psalms of Ascents*, 107.

[198]A few scholars, following the LXX, read בַּלֵּילוֹת with v. 2a: Kissane, *Book of Psalms*, 596; Keet, *A Study of the Psalms of Ascents*, 108. This proposal needs to be taken more seriously than it sometimes is. As far as I can see there is warrant for neither to the exclusion of the other (see textual note b). Perhaps this is a case of "ambiguity" in the sense that it can apply to both lines at the same time, a phenomenon that Paul R. Rabbe has recently discussed ("Deliberate Ambiguity in the Psalter," *JBL* 110/2 [1991] 213-227).

[199]Waltke and O'Connor, *Biblical Hebrew Syntax*, 169-170.

[200]Gunkel, *Einleitung*, 18; Kittel, *Psalmen*, 408;

[201]Kissane (*Book of Psalms*, 596), for example, takes בַּלֵּילוֹת to mean "every night" and conjoins it to the beginning of v. 2. He attributes this scansion of the lines to Gunkel, but in fact Gunkel only cites the LXX's reading, and takes בַּלֵּילוֹת with v. 1b (Gunkel, *Psalmen*, 573).

Babylonian "lookout"[202] (an image of the prophet himself) who is watching from the watchtower to see the first signs of that city's destruction:

On the watchtower, O Lord, I stand (אָנֹכִי עֹמֵד) all day (תָּמִיד יוֹמָם);
At my post I am stationed (אָנֹכִי נִצָּב) all night long
(כָּל־הַלֵּילוֹת).

Once again "all the nights" (plural) means "throughout the night," as the parallel with תָּמִיד יוֹמָם shows (the clear meaning is that the guard has been on watch continually, as opposed to watching for a long time; cf. Isa 60:11). These parallels do not, however, prove that בַּלֵּילוֹת in Ps 134:1 must mean "during the night," precisely because in those places it is parallel to "by day" whereas in Psalm 134 it is not. They do, however, make it somewhat more likely than the alternative. The phrase "stand by night" therefore probably refers to the vocation of a group of cultic functionaries in the temple. Beyond this any identification of those personnel would consist in mere speculation.

The phrase "to lift the hand" can refer to a variety of actions. Most commonly it is an idiom for taking an oath, especially with God as the subject (e.g., Num 14:30; Deut 32:40; Ezekiel uses it frequently with this meaning). Another common usage is the equivalent of "to fight" (e.g., 2 Sam 18:28; 20:21). When used with the plural "hands," however, it normally depicts a posture of supplication. In Lam 2:19 and 3:41 (in both of which כַּף replaces the more standard יָד) it is a gesture of entreaty. In Ps 28:2 (cf. Isa 1:15, where the lifting of hands clearly implies entreaty of favor, albeit in vain) there is a very interesting parallel to Ps 134:1. There the supplicant asks God to hear the prayer "when I lift my hands to your most holy place" (קָדְשֶׁךָ אֶל־דְּבִיר). But Psalm 134 does not entreat God; rather it merely exhorts the addressees to "bless" God. Only in Lev 9:22, where Aaron lifts his "hands"[203] to bless the assembled people during a sacrifice, do we have a similar positive usage. Despite the close similarity of Ps 28:2 to Ps 134:1, the

---

[202]The MT reads אַרְיֵה, which "is obviously a textual corruption of "the lookout" (Heb. *hārô'eh*)" (Clements, *Isaiah 1-39*, 179). The latter is the reading that occurs in 1QIsa^A.

[203]The Kethib is the singular יָד, which the Masoretes read as the plural יָדָיו. It is possible that the tradition based the Qere on an observation such as I have made above.

Leviticus usage implies that "lifting the hands" can be used as a posture of blessing, thus fitting well with the rest of Psalm 134.

Psalm 134 concludes with two formulae that pull together both this psalm and the collection as a whole. The formulaic benediction "YHWH bless you from Zion" (יְבָרֶכְךָ יהוה מִצִּיּוֹן) is especially interesting. The same phrase occurs in Ps 128:5 (it is one of several repeated phrases in the Songs of Ascents), and a very similar one (יהוה מִצִּיּוֹן בָּרוּךְ) occurs in Ps 135:21 (further evidence that Psalms 134 and 135 are closely related). It implies a well-developed Zion theology that sees the Jerusalem temple as the center from which God's blessing flows (cf. Isa 2:3; Micah 4:2; see also Chap. 3, pp. 155-157). In the context of Psalm 134 it serves another purpose: it creates an *inclusio* with v. 1. Other echoes also exist in the psalm, giving the impression that its overall framework is a chiasm.[204]

This final blessing recalls the wording of the "Aaronic blessing" in Num 6:24, יְבָרֶכְךָ יהוה וְיִשְׁמְרֶךָ "YHWH bless you and keep you." But the added element מִצִּיּוֹן "from Zion" occurs elsewhere only in Ps 128:5. A parallel to the formula "YHWH bless you from Zion" occurs in an Aramaic document (in Demotic script) from the Achaemenid period, which is precisely the same as Ps 134:3a; only Baal and Zaphon are substituted for YHWH and Zion.[205] The phrase "the maker of heaven and earth" also occurs in non-Israelite literature, but is more archaic, going

---

[204]Pierre Auffret ("Note on the Literary Structure of Psalm 134," *JSOT* 45 [1989] 87-89) has gone so far as to see the entire psalm as organized on a chiastic principle with two collated chiasms. Although his analysis is insightful at points, it stretches the boundaries of reason in its attempt to make the chiasm perfect. So, for example, he argues for the lifting of the servants' hands as parallel to "maker of heaven and earth" with pseudo-logic:

> According to the stereotyped expression…it is characteristic of the hands "to make" something. Since we can say that just as the blessing of Yahweh responds to that of his servants, the gesture of the hands of the servants makes a fitting echo of his characteristic work of having made heaven and earth. A perfect mirror effect (ABC/C'B'A') exists between vv. 2 and 3. (p. 89)

[205]William Foxwell Albright, "Notes on Psalms 68 and 134," in *Land Ogkirke*, ed., *Interpretationes ad Vetus Testamentum pertinentes Sigmund Mowinckel, septuagenario missae* (Oslo: Fabritius & Sonner, 1955) 6-9.

back to the Ugaritic epics.[206] Both of these phrases seem to be integral to Zion theology. One may compare, for example, Isa 2:3 (= Mic 4:2), where Torah goes forth "from Zion" to refresh the whole world. It is the idea of Zion as the *omphalus mundi* from which all blessing comes. In this context the formulaic epithet of God "maker of heaven and earth" is quite at home.[207]

Several data figure into any identification of the form of Psalm 134. The imperative formula in v. 1aα (בָּרְכוּ אֶת־יהוה) is repeated in v. 2b, forming an *inclusio* that sets the first two verses off from the last. This is corroborated by the shift in addressee between vv. 1-2 and v. 3: in the former the addressee is a plurality of persons, whereas in the latter it is a singular (or collective) person. But the last verse is not unconnected with what has gone before. Indeed the repetition of ברך and יהוה (although with YHWH as the subject rather than the object of the verb) creates another *inclusio* that ties the whole psalm together. "Zion" recalls the "sanctuary" of v. 2 and the "house of YHWH" in v. 1b. What emerges is a tightly woven piece that focuses on the imperative בָּרְכוּ and the answering יְבָרֶכְךָ יהוה. The two are a kind of mirror image of each other: God's action of blessing the worshiper is reciprocal to the human action of blessing God.

A precise milieu for Psalm 134 is probably impossible to determine. Certainly one may affirm that it centers around the temple in Jerusalem, in view of the three times the psalm refers to it. Most probably the psalm is an extended summons to worship, whether one sees this as happening at the beginning or the end of a period of worship. Whenever the phrase בָּרְכוּ אֶת־יהוה (plural imperative, with or without the direct object

---

[206]On the tradition history of the phrase see Habel, "'Yahweh, Maker of heaven and Earth'," 321-337. Also see above, translation note on Ps 121:8, and Chap. 3, pp. 137-138. Albright ("Notes on Psalms 68 and 134," 6-9) believed that this occurrence was an archaeization that no longer remembered the original usage ("the substitution of the synonym ʿôśêh [for the earlier qônêh]...suggests that the phrase had lost any significance as a sacral formula and had become an edifying expression, which could be modified in wording with impunity"), but Habel concludes the opposite: that this formula (either with קנה or with עשה) occurs always in connection with blessing, and therefore is probably correctly used by the writers. With respect to the the Songs of Ascents, at least, Habel seems to have the better argument.

[207]Habel, "'Yahweh, Maker of heaven and Earth'," 332.

indicator) is used it functions in this way.[208] The speaker of this "call to worship" is indeterminate, although the dialogical character of the psalm perhaps identifies the speaker as a lay worshiper or group of worshipers. The addressees are probably temple functionaries, perhaps the Levites who, in the Second Temple period, not only had charge of guarding the temple at night but also were the primary "temple singers" (see Chap. 4, pp. 179-180). The blessing of v. 3 looks very much like an "Aaronic blessing," addressing the gathered community in the singular as occurs commonly in Deuteronomic usage. Beyond this very general statement little about the milieu of the psalm is possible to know. Albright's argument that the use of archaism and the formula "YHWH bless you from Zion" places the psalm squarely in the fifth century BCE[209] is difficult to uphold solely on these grounds. If one can assign such a date to the psalm one will have to do so on the basis of other criteria. In the following chapters I will attempt to place the collection Songs of Ascents into a concrete setting. It is possible that Psalm 134 derives from this same environment.

---

[208]The phrase occurs fewer times than one would expect: twice in Judges 5 (vv. 2,9), three times in Psalm 103 (vv. 21,22,23), twice in Psalm 135 (vv. 19,20) and once on the lips of the Levites in Neh 9:5. The comparable בָּרְכִי נַפְשִׁי אֶת־יהוה (cf. Pss 103:1-2,22; 104:1,35) is used as an opening and closing formula similar to the use of הַלְלוּ־יָהּ. It is possible that, like the closing formulae of Psalm 103, this entire psalm serves as a concluding "bless YHWH" for the collection of Songs of Ascents. Whether or not it was composed for this purpose is at this point probably impossible to determine.

[209]Albright, "Notes on Psalms 68 and 134," 6-8.

CHAPTER III

THE SONGS OF ASCENTS AS A
COLLECTION

Psalms 120-134 seem well unified. Several factors contribute to this feeling of unity. Not least important is the length of the poems. The average length of a psalm in the Psalter is 16.9 verses. The average length of a psalm in the Songs of Ascents is 6.7 verses (bracketing out Psalm 132, the figure is 5.9 verses).[1] The shortness of the Songs of Ascents is still more striking in light of their location immediately after the 176 verses of Psalm 119. Another unifying factor is the language of the songs, which seems to be a dialect significantly different from that of most other psalms.[2] Finally, several recurring motifs heighten the sense of unity.

On the other hand, the diversity of the Songs of Ascents is remarkable. The songs are self-evidently diverse in respect to genre, meter and other poetic devices, theme, and presumed world. The purpose of this chapter is to answer the question, How does the collection of Songs of Ascents achieve unity despite its diversity? After

---

[1]The average length of psalms in Book Five of the Psalter (less Psalm 119) is 12.3 verses, significantly lower than that of the rest of the Psalter, but still nearly double that of the Songs of Ascents. Seybold (*Wallfahrtspsalmen*, 20), apparently rounding up the number, figures the average length of a psalm in the Psalter at 17 verses.

[2]For example, the particle -שֶׁ appears ten times in the Songs of Ascents, and only eleven times in the entire remainder of the Psalter (all of which are after the Songs of Ascents in Book V of the Psalter). The Songs of Ascents contain an abundance of Aramaisms and North Israelite Hebrew elements. As Dahood (*Psalms*, 3:196) states, "Pss cxx-cxxxiv teem with dialectal elements...." See also Kutscher, *History*, 30-31.

a review of several possible explanations, I shall take the position that a theory of redaction best explains both the unity and the diversity of the collection.

THE REDACTION OF THE SONGS

The exegetical treatment in Chap. 2 revealed a number of discrete cases of redactional activity among the Songs of Ascents. In the discussion that follows, I will make the case that there are discernible redactional *layers* present in the collection as a whole. The broad outlines of my argument are as follows. First, a group of repeated formulae frames and pervades the collection. These formulae are best explained as resulting from redactional activity. Second, exegetical observations make it possible to isolate several additional cases of redaction, most of which find treatment in Chap. 2. Third, the coherence of the redactional elements identified using the previous two means makes it reasonable to posit a thematic basis for isolating still more instances.

Six Formulaic Phrases

There are six phrases scattered throughout the collection that are repeated verbatim. Numerous other (not verbatim) "correspondences" may be found within the collection, some of which also bear on this discussion, but many of which are at best uncertain.[3] For methodological reasons the soundest policy at this point is to treat only those formulae (by which I mean meaningful, self-contained units of

---

[3]Pierre Auffret ("La collection des Psaumes des montées comme ensemble structure," in *La Sagesse a bâti sa maison: Etudes de structures littéraires dans l'Ancien Testament et spécialment dans les Psaumes* [OBO 49; Göttingen: Vandenhoeck & Ruprecht, 1982] 439-531) has argued that the entire collection is arranged on an elaborate chiastic structure. Based on this analysis he posits that the "cantiques des Montées constituent donc un ensemble particulièrement bien structuré et unifié" (531). Many of the "correspondences" he finds seem to me, however, to be spurious.

more than one word) that are repeated verbatim in separate contexts.[4] This is not to deny that poets and redactors had a much broader view of their artistry; it is only to impose a defensible standard by which to discuss the question of artistry. The six phrases that meet this standard are listed in Table 1 below.

Table 1.—Repeated Formulae in the Songs of Ascents

Phrase	Instances in the Songs of Ascents
עֹשֵׂה שָׁמַיִם וָאָרֶץ	121:2; 124:8; 134:3
מֵעַתָּה וְעַד־עוֹלָם	121:8; 125:2; 131:3
יֹאמַר־נָא יִשְׂרָאֵל	124:1; 129:1
שָׁלוֹם עַל־יִשְׂרָאֵל	125:5; 128:6; 133:3, according to 11QPs[A]
יְבָרֶכְךָ יהוה מִצִּיּוֹן	128:5; 134:3
יַחֵל יִשְׂרָאֵל אֶל־יהוה	130:7; 131:3

The phenomenon of the repeated formulae (RFs) can be explained in five different ways. (1) It could be simple coincidence. (2) It could arise from the use of the Songs of Ascents at a common liturgical occasion, such as that of pilgrimage. (3) It could be that the collection was compiled *on the basis of* these formulae (and other considerations). (4) The Songs of Ascents could have been written as a single piece, not collected from an existing stock of songs, in which case the RFs would

---

[4]I do not count the repetition of the same line in Pss 124:1-2 and 129:1-2 among this number, since the repetition there is clearly a liturgical device that finds its place in the psalm, not in the collection. The repetition occurs in a titular sense rather than in a formulaic sense. I treat the formula that ties the repetition together (יֹאמַר־נָא יִשְׂרָאֵל), however, as one of the repeated formulae, since it occurs in both of those contexts.

be more like literary motifs than ritual formulae.[5] (5) The RFs could be a product of a redactional program, in which case the RFs would be primary clues about its character. In the following paragraphs I shall address each of these possibilities separately.

(1) There is of course a possibility, however slight, that the RFs recur in the Songs of Ascents purely as a matter of chance. In any grouping of literary pieces in the same language there would likely be some degree of repetition that occurs without either forethought or subconscious influence. This results simply from the finite number of possible expressions, and the even more finite number of actual expressions. Random chance does not, however, adequately explain the RFs in the Songs of Ascents. There are too many repeated phrases, and they do not belong to the frequently used linguistic stock (i.e., they occur at least twice here, and several of them occur seldom or never in the rest of the HB). The probability of this occurring is low enough that it is not really a viable explanation.

(2) A higher degree of phrase recurrence could be expected in a situation in which all of the poems arose from a common milieu, such as that of pilgrimage to Jerusalem. If the RFs were to be explained on this basis one would expect that several correlates would be true. First, each of the Songs of Ascents that contains an RF would fit with the milieu in which the whole is thought to have fit. This need not require that they be formally identical (although that would be one possibility), since any given ritual or liturgy might include several topoi that make use of different genres. It does mean that the group would make sense as a whole, since rituals and similar phenomena are by definition meaningful. A review of the exegetical discussion in Chap. 2 shows that the Songs of Ascents do not belong to a single genre. It also shows that, for those songs that are possible to locate temporally or spatially, a common

---

[5]Robert C. Culley (*Oral Formulaic Language in the Biblical Psalms* [Toronto: University of Toronto Press, 1967] 18) takes an approach to formulae that is influenced by the study of classical Greek poetry, in which metrical uniformity was a primary concern. For him, formulae are the building blocks with which poems are constructed: "Poets use formulas to build lines, lines are added to one another to fill out the frameworks of themes, and themes are added one to another to tell the story of the particular poem being narrated." Such a view would be most consonant with this explanation of the RFs in the Songs of Ascents.

spatio-temporal location is improbable.[6] Second, the RFs themselves would be primary units of meaning (by virtue of their repetition and formulaic character), and so should fit into a unified system of meaning that correlates with the practice. (Unfortunately, because of the small sample, the degree to which all the RFs fit together is difficult to assess.) Third, the RFs would be integral to the psalms in which they occur, since it is the common milieu of these psalms that is thought to have given rise to the presence of the RFs. This is the major difficulty with the theory that the RFs result from a common milieu. In several cases the formulae are strikingly unnecessary—even interruptive—in the songs in which they occur. This is the case in Psalm 125, where two RFs occur seemingly unconnected with the intent of the psalm as a whole. The first is מֵעַתָּה וְעַד־עוֹלָם in v. 2b, and the second is שָׁלוֹם עַל־יִשְׂרָאֵל in v. 5b. As I have argued in Chap. 2 (pp. 57-57), both of these phrases are best regarded as additions. The same is true of Ps 128:5-6, which contain two more RFs (שָׁלוֹם עַל־יִשְׂרָאֵל and יְבָרֶכְךָ יהוה מִצִּיּוֹן) surrounding two lines that change the meaning from a blessing on an individual's house to that of a *de facto* blessing on Jerusalem. These are only the most striking cases. They render unlikely the hypothesis that the RFs appear as a result of the psalms' use in a single liturgical setting.

(3) The third possibility to be examined is whether the collection might have been collected *on the basis of* the RFs. If this were true one would expect that most, if not all, of the psalms that include the RFs would be present in the Songs of Ascents. Conversely, one would also expect that all of the Songs of Ascents would contain such elements. The first of these is certainly not the case. Psalm 113 would seem to be a primary candidate for inclusion in the Songs of Ascents. Not only is its length approximately the same as most of the Songs of Ascents (9 verses), but it also includes the RF מֵעַתָּה וְעַד־עוֹלָם. Moreover, the incipit is quite comparable to the beginning of Psalm 134. Psalm 115

---

[6]I have argued, for example, that Psalm 120 was composed early in the sixth century, based on the parallel uses of Meshek and Qedar as symbols of "haters of peace." Psalm 132 almost certainly presumes the existence of the monarchy in Jerusalem. Furthermore, Psalm 122 presumes the existence of both walls and a fully functional temple in Jerusalem, a datum that places the psalm either prior to the destruction of the city in 587/6 BCE or after the rebuilding of the walls in 445 BCE (See Hayes and Miller, *A History of Ancient Israel and Judah*, 447-472).

would be another excellent candidate for the collection, if the latter were compiled on the basis of the RFs. The psalm contains two RFs: עֹשֵׂה שָׁמַיִם וָאָרֶץ in v. 15 and מֵעַתָּה וְעַד־עוֹלָם in v. 18. It is 18 verses long, longer than the majority of the Songs of Ascents, but the same length as Psalm 132. A similar case might be made for Psalm 146, which has עֹשֵׂה שָׁמַיִם וָאָרֶץ in v. 6. The other point, that not all of the Songs of Ascents include RFs, is equally important. RFs are lacking in half of the songs in the collection (Psalms 120, 122, 123, 126, 127, 132, and 133). It is possible, of course, that factors other than the RFs influenced the compiler in the decision to include a psalm in the collection. Nevertheless, when one considers (1) that there are other psalms that could perhaps easily have been included but were not, and (2) that half of the Songs of Ascents do not contain RFs, the most reasonable conclusion is that the collection was not compiled on the basis of the RFs.

(4) Several proposals have been made to consider the Songs of Ascents as a single composition, rather than as a collection of songs. This is implied in the treatment by Eerdmans, who argues that each of the songs builds on the last. In his opinion, none of the songs is complete within itself, but rather needs the songs that follow as complements.[7] Beaucamp has defended the unity of the Songs of Ascents on the basis of a thematic pattern.[8] He groups the collection into three movements: "montée vers Jérusalem" (Psalms 120-122), "Certitudes à l'intérieur de Jérusalem" (Psalms 123-128), and "Guaranties d'avenir" (Psalms 129-134).[9] Auffret has found an elaborate chiasm (containing three smaller chiasms that correspond to the three movements stated above) that draws the whole of the Songs of Ascents together into a very tightly knit composition. According to Auffret, the chiastic structure is so complex that it could only have been the work of a single—and highly gifted—author.[10] There are, however, important

---

[7]Eerdmans, *Psalms*, 571. So also Mannati ("Psaumes Graduels," 85-86), who views the songs as the literary production of a single author *reminiscing about* pilgrimage, not actually involved in it.

[8]Evode Beaucamp, *Le Psautier* (SB; Paris: Gabalda, 1979).

[9]Beaucamp, *Psautier*, 252-255.

[10]Pierre Auffret, *La sagesse a bâti sa maison*. Similarly, Evode Beaucamp, "L'unité du recueil des montées: Psaumes 120-134," *Studium Biblicum*

difficulties with this proposal that Auffret's painstaking analysis seems to miss. First, it suffers from one of the problems encountered in the above discussion: several of the RFs occur in contexts that make their secondary nature rather clear. One might counter that those incongruities that lead one to suspect interpolation are merely evidence that the poet has had to struggle to make the pattern fit. Although I admit that such an explanation is possible, it does not seem to me entirely plausible. A poet has a high degree of control over the words of a poem. It follows that, if the Songs of Ascents were composed as a single piece using the RFs and other elements in a pattern, they would display a very low level of discontinuity between the RFs and the remainder of the psalms in which they appear. This is not the case. Second, Auffret's chiastic structure is too neat. Some of the parallels he finds are clear and obvious, on the level of the RFs considered in this study. A good many, however, are so obscure as to require long leaps of the imagination, many of which are actually counterintuitive.[11] One gets

---

Franciscanum 29 (1979) 73-90. Grossberg (*Centripetal and Centrifugal Structures*, 49-50) is convinced by Beaucamp's argument for the unity of the collection. He provides further support by citing strange collocations of ideas. For example, Pss 132:17, "grow" with "horn"; 132:18 "shine" with "crown"; 130:3 "keep" 130:8 "redeem" with "wickedness"; 125:1 "dwell" related to Jerusalem; 132:13 "desire" related to Jerusalem with YHWH as subject; 122:4 "tribes of Yah." He also notes that linguistically the collection is strange. Both הִנֵּה and כֵּן occur much more frequently than elsewhere in the psalter. The adverb רַבַּת occurs four times in the Songs of Ascents out of seven in the entire HB. Likewise, the particle -שֶׁ occurs 10 times of the 140 instances in the HB. In spite of the usefulness of his observations, however, none of them proves that the group is an organic unity. These features can be explained on dialectal grounds equally well.

[11]The method by which he arrives at these parallels is also suspect. In some cases the parallels are on the level of assonance. For example, he believes Psalm 120, which juxtaposes מִלְשׁוֹן, שָׁלוֹם שָׂנֵא שָׁלוֹם, אֲנִי שָׁלוֹם, and שְׁנוּנִים, to have strong ties with Psalm 122, which includes the similar-sounding לְשֵׁם, שֶׁשָּׁם, יְרוּשָׁלָ͏ם, שַׁאֲלוּ שְׁלוֹם יְרוּשָׁלָ͏ם, שָׁמָּה, and יִשְׁלָיוּ (Auffret, *La sagesse a bâti sa maison*, 446-462) On the other hand, some of his parallels are thematic, so that the "house" that cannot be built apart from YHWH's assistance (Psalm 127) has strong ties to the "house" which David swears to YHWH (pp. 514-515), despite the fact that the only time בַּיִת occurs in Psalm 132 (v. 3) refers only to David's house. There is no need to go into more detail than this, although numerous other similar examples are quite apparent. It suffices to point out that Auffret's conclusions appear to be based more on his preconceptions than on the evidence itself. A humorous critique of Auffret's approach, specifically as applied to Psalms 1-37, was recently offered by William J.

the impression that he pursued parallels assiduously until he arrived at a tidy chiasm, and then simply decided to quit. Third, the songs themselves give evidence against their having been written at the same time. In most cases it is not possible to determine precisely when a song was written, but the presumed world is so different from psalm to psalm as to make any single author and time unlikely.[12] Although the RFs, together with the linguistic peculiarities and other common elements, impart to the collection a feeling of essential unity, this feeling cannot be regarded as adequate evidence that the RFs are present as a result of the songs' composition as a single integral whole.

(5) A theory that posits a redactional process as the source of the RFs deals more adequately with the circumstances discussed above. It is no longer necessary to show that all of the songs derive from the same hand, because a redactional theory does not depend upon it. A common original liturgical setting for each of the songs severally is not necessary, because it is the redactor who supplies the essential unity. Incongruities between the original material and the redactional material now become meaningful precisely because the latter tries to reinterpret the former. In short, it becomes possible to posit the unity of the collection based upon the redactor's work, while allowing that the individual psalms come from various places and times.

The RFs are best explained, then, as arising from the efforts of a redactor. In addition to the general purpose of providing unity, the redactor probably also had other purposes, which can to some extent be discerned by studying the redactions themselves. The RFs are a good point of entry for studying the redactional materials, but are not necessarily the only redactional activity that took place.

Urbrock ("Psalms 1-37 as a Chiastic Arrangement," Psalms Group, Society of Biblical Literature Annual Meeting [Washington, DC: 1993]). In his paper he demonstrated that a random ordering of Psalms 1-37 resulted in a chiastic structure that was equally plausible and orderly as the one offered by Auffret.

[12]In Psalms 120 and 123, foreigners are the cause of the supplicant's distress; but in Psalm 126 they glorify YHWH. Likewise, the famine presupposed in Psalm 126 bears little resemblance to the fertility presupposed in Psalm 128. The admission of guilt in Psalm 130 is difficult to reconcile with the statements of innocence in Psalms 120 and 131. Psalm 132 asks for (and predicts) a renewal of divine favor, which seems to contradict the presupposed presence of divine favor in Psalms 128 and 133.

The Coherence of the Redactional Layers

In the pages that follow I shall argue that these RFs provide a point of entry into a discernible, consistent redactional reworking of a group of psalms. For the sake of simplicity, I refer to the latter materials with the adjective "nucleus" and to the former with the adjective "redactional." I start by attempting to demonstrate that the RFs fit into a common thematic and social milieu. I then attempt to show that other demonstrably redactional materials belong to this same milieu. Finally, I examine several whole psalms that seem to fit into the same background.

The Provenance of the Repeated Formulae

The RF that is most easily identified with Jerusalem is the one that mentions Zion. The benediction יְבָרֶכְךָ יהוה מִצִּיּוֹן occurs only in the Songs of Ascents (Pss 128:5aα; 134:3a), although one might expect that it would occur elsewhere. The *idea* that God blesses "from Zion" does occur elsewhere, even though the precise formula does not. In the vision of the future glory of Zion envisioned in Isa 2:1-4 (=Mic 4:1-4), "many peoples" make pilgrimage to Zion "for from Zion Torah goes forth, and the Word of YHWH from Jerusalem." Similarly, in Ps 14:7 (=53:7) the "salvation of Israel" (יְשׁוּעַת יִשְׂרָאֵל) comes "from Zion" (the verse seems to me quite clearly redactional). In Isaiah 2 it goes forth to "many peoples," and in Psalm 14/53 it goes forth to Israel/Jacob.[13] In both of these cases the point seems to be the spreading of God's blessing to non-Jerusalemites. This usage becomes important if the hypothesis (which I argue below) is correct that the Songs of Ascents are songs of non-Jerusalemites that are reinterpreted with Jerusalemite interests in mind.

The phrase עֹשֵׂה שָׁמַיִם וָאָרֶץ also has a clear Jerusalemite tradition history.[14] The earliest form of this tradition is preserved in

---

[13]In Psalm 14/53, this does not seem necessarily to be a reference to North Israel, but rather is a formulaic pair designating the entire people of God. Cf. H. -J. Zobel, "יִשְׂרָאֵל *yiśrāʾēl*," *TDOT* 6:419.

[14]Habel ("'Yahweh, Maker of heaven and Earth'," 321-337) has studied this epithet and the narrative expansions of it, and has concluded that it is almost certainly Jerusalemite. According to his findings it belongs to the Canaanite tradition

Genesis 14, where Melchizedek the king of Salem blesses Abram by the god El-Elyon. He (and later, Abram) calls El-Elyon by what appears to be a characteristically Jerusalemite epithet: קֹנֵה שָׁמַיִם וָאָרֶץ (Gen 14:19, 22).[15] It seems that the root קנה was replaced with the root עשה after the former lost the meaning "create" from its semantic field.[16] In the psalms the epithet always uses the root עשה. When the phrase עשה שָׁמַיִם וָאָרֶץ is embedded in narrative it is less reliably Jerusalemite, but even there seems to be primarily localized in literature in which Jerusalem figures prominently. The epithet עֹשֵׂה שָׁמַיִם וָאָרֶץ occurs only in Psalms 115, 121, 124, 134, and 146, that is, all in the last "book" of the Psalter. As is the case with Psalm 134, Psalm 115 ties the epithet עֹשֵׂה שָׁמַיִם וָאָרֶץ to the divine blessing. One presumes that the blessing comes from Jerusalem, although this is not explicit.[17] Psalm 146 makes the connection of this blessing with Zion explicit (v. 10), but uses the phrase עֹשֵׂה שָׁמַיִם וָאָרֶץ as both an epithet for YHWH and the point of departure for a discussion of God's creative activity (v. 6a). Narrativizations of this phrase are common in exilic and postexilic writers.[18] The metaphor of God as "maker of heaven and earth" occupied an important position in the religion of postexilic Judea, which centered around the Jerusalem temple.

---

complex in which blessing comes from the sanctuary of El. So also Kraus, *Psalmen*, 2:1013-1014.

[15]There is little doubt that the Salem over which Melchizedek reigns is thought by the tradents to be the city later called Jerusalem. Whether this is right is immaterial, since it is also presumably these tradents who used the formula in question.

[16]This meaning is clearly present in texts other than Genesis 14, such as Genesis 4, where it provides a popular etiology for Cain's name.

[17]The fact that another apparently Jerusalemite RF, מֵעַתָּה וְעַד־עוֹלָם, occurs in Ps 115:18 (see below) may perhaps be seen as evidence in favor of a Jerusalemite provenance for this psalm.

[18]Cf. Isa 42:5; 44:24; 45:18; 51:13,16; 65:17; 66:22; Zech 12:1; Ps 135:6; Neh 9:6; 2 Chr 2:11. This is not to say that it is unknown in preexilic literature (Cf. Exod 20:11; 31:17; 2 Kgs 19:15 [=Isa 37:16]; Jer 32:17), but the relative frequency of postexilic uses is significant. One should also consider the three occurrences of this phrase in the Apocrypha, although one cannot be sure that the exact Hebrew phrase lies behind them: Add Esth 4:17c (ὅτι σὺ ἐποίησας τὸν οὐρανὸν καὶ τὴν γῆν); Bel 5 (τὸν κτίσαντα τὸν οὐρανὸν καὶ τὴν γῆν); Pr Man 2 (ὁ ποιήσας τὸν οὐρανὸν καὶ τὴν γῆν). These lend some weight to the argument that the formula is probably late postexilic.

Another RF that seems to lie within the sphere of Jerusalemite tradition history is the formula מֵעַתָּה וְעַד־עוֹלָם.[19] The formula occurs three times outside the Psalter, two of which are in the sayings of preexilic prophets at Jerusalem. Isaiah 9:6 and Micah 4:7 are both clearly oracles of salvation for Zion. In the former it is the divine son (i.e., the Davidic king) who establishes a prosperous reign. In the latter it is God's own self who establishes and maintains the welfare of Zion. Trito-Isaiah (Isa 59:21) also uses the formula in connection with the restoration of Zion to its place as chief of the nations. The two occurrences of מֵעַתָּה וְעַד־עוֹלָם in the Psalms (apart from the Songs of Ascents) are in Psalms 113 and 115. Neither of these explicitly names Jerusalem or Zion. The fact that this formula occurs in Psalm 115 along with עֹשֵׂה שָׁמַיִם וָאָרֶץ does lend some weight to the hypothesis of a Jerusalemite provenance for that psalm. Psalm 113 is understandable in the context of worship in postexilic Jerusalem, but nothing in the psalm limits it to that time or place—in fact, it is reapplicable to a variety of contexts.[20] In light of the above evidence, however, it does seem most likely that the phrase had its home in the worship at Jerusalem.

The other three RFs all include reference to Israel, a term which, although not exclusive of Jerusalemite ideas, is certainly no indicator of a specifically Jerusalemite provenance. The formula שָׁלוֹם עַל־יִשְׂרָאֵל occurs commonly in later Rabbinic literature as a blessing, but apart from the Songs of Ascents is unattested in the biblical literature.[21] This may well be an important factor in dating the Songs of Ascents as a unit

---

[19]Similar formulae are known in Ugaritic and Aramaic (Elephantine) texts, and so one should not press the notion of Jerusalemite provenance too strongly. The Ugaritic equivalent, *ᶜnt...pᶜlmh* (e.g., 1 Aqht:154,161), is similarly a formula of blessing, although its roots lie in legal practice. The precise phrase מֵעַתָּה וְעַד־עוֹלָם occurs in relatively few biblical texts. The formula's absence from all but the last "book" of the Psalter is, I think, significant. For a detailed discussion of the history of this phrase, including the evidence from Ugaritic and Elephantine texts, see Loewenstamm, "*mē ᶜattā wěᶜad ōlām*," 166-170.

[20]Craigie, "Psalm 113," 70-74.

[21]Avi Hurvitz, "אימתי נטבע בעברית הצירוף שלום על ישראל," *Leš* 27/28 (1964) 297-302. According to Elisha Qimron (*The Hebrew of the Dead Sea Scrolls* [HSS 29; Atlanta, GA: Scholars Press, 1986] 96), the blessing also occurs in Qumran literature (4Q503:56-58). One may also compare Paul's blessing in Galatians (6:16): καὶ ὅσοι τῷ κανόνι τούτῳ στοιχήσουσιν, εἰρήνη ἐπ᾽ αὐτοὺς καὶ ἔλεος, καὶ ἐπὶ τὸν Ἰσραὴλ τοῦ θεοῦ.

to the late postexilic era.[22] Two other times in the HB the noun שָׁלוֹם is conjoined with the preposition עַל. In both 1 Chr 22:9 and Isa 9:6 (less certainly), the blessing that comes *upon* Israel is mediated by the messianic king. This would seem to fit very well with the first three RFs discussed (especially יְבָרֶכְךָ יהוה מִצִּיּוֹן). I would thus conclude tentatively that the RF שָׁלוֹם עַל־יִשְׂרָאֵל has its place in Jerusalemite worship.

Likewise, the RF יַחֵל יִשְׂרָאֵל אֶל־יהוה has no direct link to the traditions of Zion. The formula occurs only in Psalms 130 and 131. In both cases the body of the psalm is an individual's statement of trust in the mercy of YHWH. The RF יַחֵל יִשְׂרָאֵל אֶל־יהוה is appended to reinterpret those personal statements as examples for "Israel" to follow. There are other cases in the Psalter of this type of reapplication (most notably Pss 27:14; 31:23-24; 64:10), but nothing that would lead one to suspect a specifically Jerusalemite provenance for either the formula or the tendency to "democratize" in this way.

Finally, Psalms 124 and 129 begin in the same way. Both of them begin with a one-colon incipit of the song to be sung, and then have what seems to be a liturgical directive, יֹאמַר־נָא יִשְׂרָאֵל. The implication is that "Israel" is present and ready to "say" the song. The song proper then begins with the incipit named in the first line. Psalm 118 begins similarly. The first line of Psalm 118 is an extended introduction: "Give thanks to YHWH for [God] is good, for [the divine] loyalty is eternal [כִּי לְעוֹלָם חַסְדּוֹ]." Then each of three groups—the house of Israel,[23] the house of Aaron, and those who fear YHWH—is directed to "say" (using a formula identical to the one in Psalms 124 and 129) the formula כִּי לְעוֹלָם חַסְדּוֹ. This formula is well known in the last "book" of the Psalter.[24] The psalm concludes with a repetition of the first line. It is noteworthy that in Psalm 118 (cf. Psalms 115 and 135) the gathered

---

[22]Shemaryahu Talmon, "Songs of Ascents" (lecture to the class "Postexilic Literature," Vanderbilt University: Fall 1989).

[23]The LXX adds οἶκος, which would fit well with the usage in Pss 115:12 (but not in v. 9, as Kraus suggests, unless emended) and 135:19. So Kraus, *Psalms 60-150*, 393.

[24]The phrase belongs very clearly to the liturgical life of the second temple. It is used in one postexilic oracle in Jeremiah (33:11), and in Psalms 106 (the only case outside the fifth "book"), 107, 118, and 136. It also occurs in many of the Chronicler's prayers (Ezra 3:11; 1 Chr 16:34,41; 2 Chr 5:13; 7:3,6; 2 Chr 20:21).

congregation is divided up into three groups, whereas in Psalms 124 and 129 it is addressed as a whole. Whether this means that the other groups were not present, not directed to speak, or simply subsumed into "Israel" is not clear. It seems likely that such directives belonged to the liturgical life of the second temple, but more than this would press the evidence too far.

It is fairly clear, then, that at least three of the RFs (עֹשֵׂה שָׁמַיִם וָאָרֶץ, מֵעַתָּה וְעַד־עוֹלָם, and יְבָרֶכְךָ יהוה מִצִּיּוֹן), and possibly all six, belonged to worship at the temple in Jerusalem. At least three seem to belong to the second temple period (עֹשֵׂה שָׁמַיִם, יֹאמַר־נָא יִשְׂרָאֵל וָאָרֶץ, and שָׁלוֹם עַל־יִשְׂרָאֵל). I have argued above that redaction is the best explanation of the repetition of these RFs in the Songs of Ascents. It is reasonable to hypothesize, on these bases, that the RFs were part of a redactional effort to give cohesiveness and a Jerusalemite flavor to songs that originally had no such flavor, and that this occurred during the late postexilic period (see Chap. 4). It remains to be seen whether this hypothesis will be sustained by the presence of other redactional elements that give evidence of similar goals.

Other Redactional Elements

The question that must now be addressed is whether elements other than the RFs can be isolated in the Songs of Ascents as redactional. If one can isolate further instances of redactional activity that also appear to be Jerusalemite in origin, this will support the hypothesis of a deliberately Jerusalemite redaction.

One of the clearest examples of redactional activity in the Songs of Ascents is in Psalm 128. Verses 1-4 are concerned solely with the prosperity that comes to the יְרֵא יהוה. The first line introduces this theme, the next three lines elaborate on the blessing, and the fourth summarizes, "Behold, for so is the man blessed who fears YHWH," leading one to posit that this was the original conclusion of the saying. Verse 5a is the RF יְבָרֶכְךָ יהוה מִצִּיּוֹן, and has no balancing line. Verse 5b elaborates on the blessing that comes from Zion by adding the blessing, "May you enjoy the prosperity of Zion all the days of your life." Verse 6 reiterates the theme of sons as a blessing, perhaps in order to bind the addition to the original more securely. Verses 1-4 are clearly a wisdom saying about the prosperity that comes to the one who "fears YHWH." It is probable that a redactor has added vv. 5-6 in order to put that fear (and its consequent blessing) in the context of loyalty to the cultus centered in Jerusalem.

Another fairly clear example of redaction is Ps 130:7-8. These two lines clearly apply an individual petition as an object lesson for "Israel."[25] One thus immediately suspects redactional activity. But there is also evidence from the meter. In contrast to the terse, rhythmical nature of vv. 1-6, these verses seem quite prosaic. The psalm begins with a single line of 3:3 verse, which is followed by three 3:2 bicola and two 2:2:2 tricola. The latter cola are formed around the repetition of two elements: קוה (technically with different subjects but the same referent) in the first two tricola of v. 5, and שֹׁמְרִים לַבֹּקֶר in the last two tricola of v. 6. The same type of reapplication of an individual petition for community purposes appears at the end of Psalm 131, which is accompanied by the RF מֵעַתָּה וְעַד־עוֹלָם. It is not entirely clear whether these additions are Jerusalemite, but it is certainly possible to understand them as such.

Psalm 129 contains the addition of a line that is separable from the rest of the psalm on formal and thematic bases. The individual "I" speaks throughout the psalm, except when quoting the words of others (v. 8). It laments an oppressive situation and curses "the wicked" for creating that situation. The language and imagery used are those of individual complaint, and in particular, the language of mourning.[26] Two elements intrude to change the song from an individual complaint and imprecation to a corporate one. First, the RF at the beginning יִשְׂרָאֵל יֹאמַר־נָא accomplishes this admirably by predisposing the reader to think nationalistically rather than individually. Second, v. 5 introduces the element "haters of Zion." As I argued in the exegesis of this psalm, v. 5 is quite probably redactional, since it not only introduces this corporate element but also introduces military imagery into a poem that otherwise consists purely of agricultural imagery. Analysis

---

[25]For a fuller argument for the individual character of vv. 1-6, see Chap. 2, pp. 89-90.

[26]See Crüsemann, *Hymnus und Danklied*, 168-173.

therefore shows that the Jerusalemite tendencies in the RFs may also be found in other redactional elements in the collection.

Whole Psalms Added by the Redactor

The Jerusalemite tendencies found in the RFs and in discrete redactions of individual psalms may also be discerned in whole psalms, particularly those at the end of the collection. With the exception of Psalm 122 and of demonstrably redactional elements, Psalms 120-131 are strikingly devoid of Zion imagery. Psalms 132-134, on the other hand, have Zion as a central focus. The latter are also atypical in length. I therefore propose that there is a nucleus collection of non-Jerusalemite materials, to which are added psalms that fit with the Jerusalemite redactor's concerns.

It is a truism that major additions are more likely to occur at the beginning or the end of a pericope than in the middle of one. This may derive from the difficulty with which writing could be erased in the ancient world (more difficult in some media than in others).[27] Perhaps the same consideration can explain the concentration of apparently added materials at the end of the collection.

Psalm 132 is the psalm most obviously out of place in the Songs of Ascents, as recognized by the majority of commentators who write on the collection as a whole. It is double the length of most of the other songs, it advocates royal ideology much more strongly than do the other psalms in the collection,[28] and perhaps belongs to an earlier time than the other songs. The language of Psalm 132 is also apparently different from that in the other songs. The form שֶׁנָא in Ps 127:2 becomes the more standard שְׁנַת (or שְׁנָת if one accepts the BHS's suggestion). The relative pronoun אֲשֶׁר occurs in v. 2, one of only two instances of that pronoun in the Songs of Ascents (elsewhere, with the exception of Ps

---

[27] I do not think there is sufficient evidence to say what sort of medium the songs might originally have been written on. Seybold (*Wallfahrtspsalmen*, 60-61) believes that the original psalms were votive inscriptions placed in the Jerusalem temple, which are found and redacted at a later time.

[28] Cf. the several mentions of David, the title מָשִׁיחַ in vv. 10 and 17, and the notion that "YHWH has chosen Zion."

127:5, which probably uses אֲשֶׁר for reasons of assonance, it is -שֶׁ).
Conversely, although Psalm 132 advocates a clear Jerusalemite royal
ideology, it seems to do so in the language of north-Israelite sources.
YHWH is called אֲבִיר יַעֲקֹב (an epithet that is reminiscent of the El
epithet at Ugarit), which is elsewhere only used in northern literature. I
have therefore proposed (see Chap. 2, p. 106) that Psalm 132 deliberately
uses northern imagery and language in order to make its case for
Jerusalemite primacy.

Psalms 133 and 134 seem to have similar aims. Psalm 133
explicitly ties the prosperity of the North to that of Zion (see Chap. 2, p.
120). It does this in three different ways. First, the phrase שֶׁבֶת אַחִים
גַּם־יָחַד implies this at the outset. Second, the person of Aaron is
primarily a northern figure. Third, the fact that the "dew of Hermon"
falls on Zion makes the connection strong indeed. Finally, the last line
in the psalm makes the meaning explicit by emphasizing that it is at Zion
that YHWH has "commanded the blessing." One would be hard pressed
to associate more northern images with the prosperity of Jerusalem in so
few lines. Psalm 134 seems to operate in the same way, and this is
reinforced by the concluding formulae (both RFs) יְבָרֶכְךָ יהוה מִצִּיּוֹן
and עֹשֵׂה שָׁמַיִם וָאָרֶץ. Psalms 133 and 134 as whole compositions put
in short form what it seems that the collection Songs of Ascents is
arguing: it makes Zion the source of all blessing for the country round
about.

Psalms 120-122 are to the beginning of the collection what Psalms
132-134 are to the end of it. Together with the latter, these psalms
function to frame the collection. Psalm 122 is thoroughly Zionistic in
much the same way that Psalm 132 is Zionistic. More importantly, it
uses north-Israelite language as a rhetorical device with which to present
its Zionistic points. Like the rest of the Songs of Ascents, it uses -שֶׁ
rather than אֲשֶׁר (vv. 3,4), despite the fact that the assonance with
יְרוּשָׁלַם might make the latter more suitable.[29] The psalm seems to
appeal to northern sensibilities by employing the archaic designation
"Tribes of Yah" and "Congregation of Israel" (עֲדַת יִשְׂרָאֵל, according
to the emendation I have proposed; see Chap. 2, p. 44, trans. note d) for

---

[29]This element of assonance plays on the consonants of the name "Jerusalem," as
has been demonstrated by Alonso-Schökel and Strus ("Salmo 122," 234-250).

the pilgrims (v. 4).[30] Also like Psalm 132, Psalm 122 offers a nostalgic view of the kingship of David as a reason for desiring and praying for Jerusalem's good. The rhetoric targets non-Jerusalemites and tries to convince them that Jerusalem deserves both their prayers and their pilgrimages. This, as I see it, is essentially the purpose of the Songs of Ascents as a whole, and specifically also of Psalm 132.

HISTORY OF THE REDACTION PROCESS

The above analysis makes noticeable an important fact: There is a remarkable concentration of Zion imagery located within a relatively small part of the collection. Much of the material in which the Zion imagery is located is secondary, and this is demonstrable apart from the Zion imagery itself. A summary of the nucleus and redactional strata as I have identified them is presented below in Table 2 for the convenience of the reader. The most natural explanation for these phenomena is that there existed a nucleus of songs from a non-Jerusalemite setting, and that these songs were later redacted into a cycle of songs that made Zion the central focus.

The Character of the Nucleus Group

The group of songs at the heart of the Songs of Ascents is distinctive in several regards. First, the language and poetic style of these songs are different from those of any other group of Hebrew poems. Second, their theme is decidedly different from the theme of the collection of Songs of Ascents as it now stands. Third, there is evidence that this nucleus group existed as a collection prior to its redaction by a Jerusalemite editor. The distinctiveness of this collection in these regards both confirms the hypothesis that their original form was non-

---

[30]Norman K. Gottwald (*The Tribes of Yahweh: A Sociology of the Religion of Liberated Israel, 1250-1050 B.C.E.* [Maryknoll, New York: Orbis Books, 1979] 243-244) believes, in my view rightly, that Psalm 122 here preserves "very ancient terminology."

Jerusalemite (although not anti-Jerusalemite) and allows for further exploration of their character.

Table 2.—Summary of Nucleus and Redactional Materials in
the Songs of Ascents

Psalm Number	Preredactional Verses	Redactional Verses
120	all	none
121	none	all
122	none	all
123	1-4[1]	4b (gloss?)
124	1-7	8
125	3-5a[2]	1-2, 5b
126	all	none
127	all	none
128	1-4	5-6
129	1-4, 6-8	5
130	1-6	7-8
131	1-2	3
132	none	all
133	none	all
134	none	all

[1] The numbering of verses for each psalm excludes the superscript, which I regard as the work of the redactor.

[2] The phrase אֶת־פֹּעֲלֵי הָאָוֶן (v. 5aγ) may be a gloss.

Poetic and Dialectal Character

Mitchell Dahood has said that the Songs of Ascents "teem with dialectal elements still too little understood for emendation."[31] These dialectal elements constitute powerful evidence for the songs' popular

---

[31]Dahood, *Psalms*, 3:196.

character, and probably give evidence of a north Israelite provenance for the nucleus group.[32] Several items in particular constitute evidence for the northern provenance of this group. First, the particle -שֶׁ almost completely replaces אֲשֶׁר as the relative pronoun (except Ps 127:5).[33] This is a known element of north Israelite dialect.[34] Likewise, the adverbial use of רַבַּת is found only in Ps 65:10 outside the Songs of Ascents, but four times within it.[35] Table 3 lists the unusual linguistic features in the Songs of Ascents. From this list it is clear that the language of these songs is not standard Jerusalemite Hebrew, and in fact fits much better with what little is known about north Israelite dialect.

The literary character of the nucleus group is that of popular oral poetry. That this is the case finds support not only in the linguistic oddities described above, but also in the style itself. Two elements in particular—the brevity and the repetitiveness of the songs—support this view.

William Watters has compared the use of formulaic expressions in Hebrew poetry with that from similar societies. He finds brevity to be a primary feature of popular oral poetry:

> While it has been found from field studies that even the average person in an oral verse-making society can compose short poems, the longer poems, considered national treasures by the people, are performed only by the skilled, professional versemakers, expert in their craft.[36]

---

[32]At the very least it may be said that many of the songs in the nucleus group probably have a northern provenance. See the discussion of individual psalms in Chap. 2 above; see also Chap. 4, pp. 159-163.

[33]The particle -שֶׁ occurs ten times in the Songs of Ascents out of only nineteen in the entire Psalter. Other than in Ps 127:5, the relative pronoun אֲשֶׁר occurs only in Ps 132:2, which in my view is not part of the nucleus group.

[34]It can also be explained as a late element, since it is common in Middle Hebrew, and in late biblical texts such as Qohelet and Song of Songs (Kutscher, *History*, 30-31), but this does not seem likely because few other features of very late biblical Hebrew are present in these texts. On the other hand, Frank Moore Cross and David Noel Freedman (*Studies in Ancient Yahwistic Poetry* [SBLDS 21; Missoula, MT: Scholars Press, 1975] 41, n. 27) show that -שֶׁ can be genuinely archaic.

[35]On this adverbial use see Joüon, *Grammaire de l'hébreu biblique*, 128-129.

[36]William R. Watters, *Formula Criticism and the Poetry of the Old Testament* (BZAW 138; Berlin: Walter de Gruyter, 1976) 8.

Table 3.—Unusual Linguistic Features in the Songs of Ascents

Unusual Feature	Reference	Comments[1]
בַּצָּרָתָה לִּי	120:1	Cf. עוֹלָתָה in Ps 125:3. Both of these are treated as evidence of northern dialect in Chap. 4.
מִלָּשׁוֹן רְמִיָּה	120:2	Substantival apposition. One expects either מִלָּשׁוֹן רְמִיָּה (a bound construction) or מִלָּשׁוֹן רָמָה (an adjectival construction.
אוֹיָה	120:5	Normally אוֹי, this form occurs only here.
שׁכן ... עם	120:5,6	In the HB the idiom "to dwell with" is usually שׁכן ... בְּ. שׁכן ... עם occurs only here.
adverbial רַבַּת	120:6; 123:4; 129:1,2	In the first two cases the form רַבַּת + finite verb + reflexive *lamedh* appears. Cf. the use of רַב as an adverb in Ps 123:3. See Chap. 4, pp. 161-162.
אֲנִי־שָׁלוֹם וְכִי אֲדַבֵּר	120:7	The first phrase uses a noun as an adjective, and there is considerable uncertainty about the meaning of וְכִי (temporal?).
-שֶׁ	122:3,4; 123:2; 124:1,2,6; 129:6,7; 133:2,3	The particle אֲשֶׁר occurs only in Pss 127:5 (probably for assonance) and 132:2. The instances of -שֶׁ in the Songs of Ascents are nearly half of all those in the Psalter.
Construct relationship with both words definite	123:4	The LXX has τὸ ὄνειδος τοῖς εὐθηνοῦσιν, perhaps reflecting a *lamed* in the second instance, but this could equally be the translator's attempt to deal with a difficult reading.

Table 3—Continued

Unusual Feature	Reference	Comments[1]
אֲזַי	124:3-5	This form occurs only here in the HB.
נַחְלָה meaning "torrent"	124:4	The expected form is נַחַל. Cf. the other examples of final הָ as evidence of northern dialect.
לְמַעַן לֹא + finite verb	125:3	This form occurs exclusively in exilic and postexilic writings (four times in Ezekiel, once in Zechariah, and twice in Psalm 119). In classical Hebrew the expected form of the negative purposive clause is לְבִלְתִּי + impf.
עֲקַלְקַלּוֹתָם	125:5	The word עֲקַלְקַלּוֹת occurs elsewhere only in the Song of Deborah (Judg 5:6), which may be evidence of northern provenance.
שֵׁנָא	127:2	Compare שְׁנַת in Ps 132:4.
הִנֵּה כִי־כֵן	128:4	The expression is redundant.
סְלִיחָה	130:4	Elsewhere only in Neh 9:17 (plural), although the verb סלח is relatively common in the exilic period and after.[2]
גָּמַל	131:2	The only use of גָּמַל in the HB with a meaning not having to do with retribution.

[1] For detailed discussion, the reader should see the relevant discussions in Chap. 2.

[2] According to Kutscher (*History*, 128) the noun pattern qĕtîlâ is increasingly common in late biblical Hebrew, and in Middle Hebrew is nearly the exclusive formation for a verbal noun.

Watters' statement applies only by implication, of course, since it does not necessarily follow that short poems are composed by amateurs. Coupled with the almost solely non-professional concern of the songs, however, Watters' observation provides supporting evidence for the popular character of the songs. The brevity of the Songs of Ascents is striking. In contrast to the prolixity of Psalm 119, which immediately precedes the collection, only one of the songs (Psalm 132) exceeds ten lines, and there are good reasons to regard it as part of the redactional material. Indeed, as noted above, the average length of a song in the Songs of Ascents is strikingly shorter than that of the other psalms in the Psalter, and there are only 14 other psalms as short as the average length of a song in the Songs of Ascents (including Psalm 132).[37]

A second feature of popular oral poetry is repetitiveness. Oral poets use this repetitiveness primarily because of metrical[38] or artistic concerns. In my opinion it is precisely this repetitiveness that led Gesenius to propose that מַעֲלוֹת in the superscript referred to "step parallelism." Although repetition also occurs in the redactional layer, it is more pronounced in the nucleus group.

World View of the Nucleus Group

The universe presumed by the nucleus group is, as we shall see, quite different from that of the redactional materials. Life consists of everyday experiences like farming (Ps 126:5-6), having and rearing children (Pss 127:3-5; 128:1-4), and surviving controversy with one's enemies (Psalms 127:5; 129). Contact with God is for the purpose of seeking success in these arenas. Particularly prominent in the nucleus group is the prayer for deliverance from enemies or thanksgiving for that deliverance. These prayers are couched in individual language, even when reinterpreted in a more communitarian framework (cf. Psalms 124 and 129). In contrast to the redactional materials, life centers on the family and small community, rather than on Zion and Jerusalem.

---

[37]See Seybold, *Wallfahrtspsalmen*, 20.
[38]Culley, *Oral Formulaic Language*, 10-18.

Theology of the Nucleus Group

Related to world view are the various theological notions found in the nucleus group. I have broken the discussion of theological understandings down into three spheres that appear in this context to be especially significant, in that they contrast sharply with the theological concerns of the redactional materials. They are not exhaustive, but rather provide points of comparison between the two literary groupings. The three areas are (1) metaphors for God; (2) the sorts of actions God is either expected to perform or thought already to have performed; and (3) the location of God's dwelling.

(1) Strictly speaking, the nucleus group uses only one metaphor for God: the idea of master or owner. This metaphor occurs in Psalms 123 and 130. Psalm 123, as we have seen in Chap. 2, treats the metaphor at length. The relationship between God and people is precisely that of master (אָדוֹן) and slave (עֶבֶד), or mistress (גְּבֶרֶת) and maidservant (שִׁפְחָה). The speakers depend on God for deliverance as a slave depends on a merciful master. The collocation of the ideas of God's overlordship and God's grace is also present in Psalm 130. There אֲדֹנָי occurs twice as an epithet of YHWH (the only instance of a divine appellation other than יהוה in the nucleus group). Like Psalm 123, Psalm 130 makes a strong plea to YHWH for grace, and the appeal is on the basis of a relationship in which YHWH is obligated by feudal responsibility.

(2) The action of God in the nucleus group may be divided into three categories: rescuing the speaker from trouble, exacting retribution on the wicked, and granting fertility. Each of these is of course quite consistent with the Israelite concepts expressed in many psalms. What is remarkable about these ideas of God's action is the fact that God is thought to act primarily for the benefit of good individuals and small groups, and not so much for the benefit of the larger community.[39]

---

[39]In this we perhaps have a microcosm of the Psalter as a whole: the earlier material is more individual and later material is more communal. My findings vis-à-vis the Songs of Ascents thus tend to support, in a very small way, the theories of Erhard S. Gerstenberger (*Psalms: Part I with an Introduction to Cultic Poetry* [FOTL 14; Grand Rapids, Michigan: Eerdmans, 1988] 5-22), and not to support

Psalm 127 provides an excellent example. There God not only "builds a house," but "guards a city," provides food (this much, at least, is certain in v. 2), and grants sons. Each of these spheres of activity is a benefit primarily for the individual and the small group (cf. v. 5, in which the group is made smaller than the city itself). Psalm 126 requests, on the basis of Zion's prosperity, that God restore the prosperity of what seems to be an outlying community. These ideas of God's action contrast sharply with those of the redactional materials, where God's action takes place on behalf of "Israel" as a whole, or of the Davidic king, but not on behalf of individuals or small groups.

(3) In the nucleus songs God's dwelling place is not a matter of concern. Only once (Ps 123:1) is the concept mentioned. This passage has God dwelling in the sky (בַּשָּׁמַיִם). The lack of emphasis (at least) on the earthly location of God's dwelling contrasts starkly with the heavy emphasis on Jerusalem as the place where God dwells in the redactional materials (which is not to say that the redactional materials reject God's dwelling in heaven). Psalm 122 is an obvious example. There the fact of God's dwelling in Jerusalem (Ps 122:1-2) is almost subsumed into concern for Jerusalem itself. Concern for Jerusalem is surely also a primary motive in Psalm 132. Psalms 133 and 134 likewise focus on Zion, and specifically on the Temple. These thematic observations illustrate the disparity between the basic outlook implied in the nucleus group and that implied in the redactional envelope and the additions to the nucleus group.

Was the Nucleus Group Originally a Unity?

In the above discussion I have not assumed that there was an original unity to the nucleus group, despite the fact that the label "nucleus group" might seem to imply this. It is possible that the redactor collected the songs concurrently with their being edited. It is also possible that the group existed as a collection prior to its being redacted. Is there evidence that points to one hypothesis rather than the other?

Mowinckel's belief that the materials of the cultus are earliest, with individual psalms being a "democratization" of those psalms.

Much of the evidence has already been treated in other contexts, and it will suffice to recall it in this one. The first piece of evidence to consider is that there is a high degree of thematic continuity.[40] Few of the songs in the nucleus group concern themselves at all with Jerusalem or Zion; this may be one of the "defects" the redactor seeks to redress. Only Psalms 125 and 126 mention Jerusalem at all. In the former there is serious question whether the first two verses (in which Jerusalem is mentioned) belonged originally with the remaining three verses. In the latter, Zion receives mention, but in a context that sees Zion as different from the community that uttered the psalm. The Jerusalem/Zion element finds no other expression in the nucleus group. Nor is there any element of "salvation history" in these psalms, a theme that dominates Psalm 132 and appears also in Psalm 122. The ritual procession, a theme that appears in both Psalms 122 and 132, is altogether absent from the nucleus songs. The ideas that do find expression there are (1) concern for fertility and blessing in the family or small town setting, and (2) prayer against oppressors. These are rather generic categories and should not be weighted too heavily; nevertheless the thematic continuity of the nucleus group is striking.

A second datum, conversely, weighs against the hypothesis that the nucleus group was originally a unity: the genres of the songs in the nucleus group differ widely from one another. Psalm 120 is an open-ended complaint, making no plea for help, only lamenting the situation of the complainant. Psalms 123 and 125 petition God for specific action against those who treat "us" with contempt, on the one hand, and against "those who make their way crooked" on the other (despite the lack of specific petition, Psalm 120 may also be placed in this group). Psalm 126 is a petition that agricultural prosperity extend, not just to Zion, but to the present community as well. Psalm 129 is a general imprecation against the wicked. Psalms 127 and 128 have the character of wisdom sayings, especially if one assigns Ps 128:5-6 to the redactor. Psalms 130 and 131 are affirmations of innocence (or at least relative innocence) and trust in God. Psalm 124 is a thanksgiving for deliverance from enemies.

---

[40]Cf. the findings of Harry Peter Nasuti (*Tradition History and the Psalms of Asaph* [SBLDS 88; Atlanta, GA: Scholars Press, 1987]) with respect to the Asaphite psalms.

This lack of coherence in genre is hardly decisive, however, for other known collections (such as the Asaphite and Korahite psalms) are similarly diverse.

Third, there is a high degree of stylistic similarity among the nucleus songs. The comparable length of the songs is only one aspect of this stylistic comparability. Many songs utilize the same idioms. The structure רַבַּת + feminine singular verb + reflexive לְ + נֶפֶשׁ occurs in both Pss 120:6 and 123:4. Aramaisms are relatively common, and in one case (שְׁנָא in Ps 127:2), is spelled with the more common Hebrew form in the redactional materials (שְׁנַת > שֵׁנָה in Ps 132:4, although it should be noted that the word is not in construct). Another frequent device in the nucleus group is the so-called "step parallelism." This phenomenon occurs in Psalms 124, 126, 127, 130, and 131. Finally, the meter of the nucleus songs (with the exception of Psalm 125) is regular, with 3:2 being most prominent. Taken separately, none of these stylistic observations is decisive. Together, they are perhaps enough to support a theory of the original unity.

The evidence discussed above is not sufficient to prove conclusively either that the nucleus group existed as a unit prior to the redaction of the Songs of Ascents or that it was the redactor who collected them. Their relative homogeneity does tend to lead in the direction of the former, but it is at least possible that the redactor designedly collected songs that derived from similar *mileux*. Whether the redactor collected them or not, though, this person shaped them both individually and collectively into something quite new: a pilgrim psalter.

The Redactor's World View and Theology

Even a brief examination of the RFs and their placement reveals that the redactional materials are coherent and purposeful. This observation leads naturally to the question, What was the redactor's purpose? The program of the redactor may be analyzed according to world view and theological outlook, which are certainly related to one another and correspond to the categories under which the nucleus group was analyzed.

Whereas for the poets of the nucleus group life revolved around the small, local community and the individual, the redactor's world view is considerably broader in its scope, extending both temporally and spatially, and having little concern for the individual. It is the redactor who provides with pan-Israelite reinterpretations the purely individual statements of trust found in Psalms 130 and 131. The same may be said of Psalms 129 and 124. The additions to Psalm 125 are especially interesting. In the main body of the psalm, vv. 3-5a, the language is that of individual retribution. No nationalism or even broad communitarianism is present here. God simply "does good to those who are good," and casts out the evildoers. Verses 1-2 (which end with the RF מֵעַתָּה וְעַד־עוֹלָם), along with the concluding v. 5b (the RF שָׁלוֹם עַל־יִשְׂרָאֵל), take this fragment and apply it so that God's people as a whole become the equivalent of "the righteous." Like Zion/Jerusalem in vv. 1-2 (which belongs to this same redactional layer), God's people would not be moved. In these cases we have clear examples of part of the redactor's program: to make the songs usable for the community at large.

In the redactional materials the focus shifts away from the small community to Israel as a whole. Corresponding to this shift is an emphasis on Jerusalem, both in its religious and in its political aspects. Jerusalem now becomes the true source of the blessing sought in the nucleus group. Psalm 128:1-4, part of the nucleus group, celebrates the blessing that comes to the man (גֶּבֶר) who "fears YHWH," and the redactional addition in vv. 5-6 transforms that statement, so that the blessing received not only has to do with children, but also with "enjoying the prosperity of Jerusalem all the days of your life." The blessing both comes from Zion (יְבָרֶכְךָ יהוה מִצִּיּוֹן) and benefits Zion. Psalm 122 places the focus so strongly on Jerusalem itself that YHWH nearly fades into the background. The reasons for Jerusalem's ascendancy in Psalm 122 are both religious (vv. 1,4,9) and nationalistic (vv. 2,3,5-8). A similar combination of religious and nationalistic concerns is present in Psalm 132, where the focus slowly shifts from David to the city as a whole and its present Davidic king. Along the way it is stated that Zion is the proper location of worship, since it is the place God has "desired" (vv. 13-14). Various North Israelite elements are incorporated in the psalm, but these elements are subservient to the essentially Jerusalemite purpose. A similar phenomenon occurs—much more clearly—in Psalm 133, where Aaron (a figure from North Israelite legend) and Mt. Hermon (a mountain in the north) both contribute metaphorically to the blessing that is said to "descend" on Zion. Zion occurs only once in the nucleus group (Ps 126:1), and there it serves merely as an example of the prosperity that the speakers wished existed in their community. In the redactional materials Zion is the "navel of the earth" from which God's blessing goes forth and to which people should come to receive that blessing.

A third broadening of world view is a temporal one. It is truly striking that none of the nucleus songs contains any (to the ancient reader) historical reference, whereas in the redactions such references occur no fewer than seven times (a conservative estimate). The nucleus songs are, to a large degree, atemporal; the redactional layers introduce ideas of temporality in several ways. The RF מֵעַתָּה וְעַד־עוֹלָם (Pss 121:8; 125:2; 131:3) certainly leads in this direction, but this is not the only case. Psalm 121 has God as the creator of heaven and earth in primordial time. God is therefore not bound by ordinary temporal concerns, such as sleep (vv. 3-4) or time of day (v. 6,8). God is Israel's guardian who protects from all kinds of calamity at all times, and whose protection extends as far into the future as creation was in the past (v. 8b). Psalm 122, on the other hand, makes historical reasons the basis for present response. One makes pilgrimage to Jerusalem and prays for it because that is where "the tribes of Yah" had made pilgrimage, because that is where the political power had been located, and because its walls are worthy (Cf. Psalms 46, 48). Psalm 132 is so replete with historical references that many scholars have seen it as a kind of alternate version of the ark narrative. Psalm 132 bases its request for assistance from God on David's action in the past, and on a prophetic oracle that God had indeed chosen both David and Zion, and would therefore rescue both. In stark contrast to the nucleus group, the redactional materials are pervaded with a sense of time's significance, both in terms of historical precedent and in terms of temporal philosophy.

It should now be clear that the redactional materials are thoroughly different from the nucleus group in terms of *Weltanschauung*. The nucleus group is composed of songs whose place is in the workaday life of farmers and other laborers. They are almost completely unconcerned with the world outside this subsistence lifestyle. Israel's tradition of historical inquiry finds no place here, nor does the tradition of Jerusalem's importance. The community extended, with few if any exceptions in this literature, only to the family and close associates with whom even subsistence farmers must deal. There is no "Israel" as a political, religious, ethnic, or social reality. One of the redactor's central purposes in editing (or collecting and editing) these songs was to broaden the world view so that it included the political and religious union that the redactor wished to promote. With the editing finished and this view established, the collection Songs of Ascents became a sort of devotional handbook for pilgrims.

A Psalter for Pilgrims

Now it is perhaps possible to return to the question raised in Chap. 1: the meaning of the superscript. This redactional study clarifies the nature of the Songs of Ascents as a unit in that it clarifies the historical process by which it was formed. The redactor took a group of agrarian—and perhaps north Israelite (see Chap. 4, pp. 159-169)—songs and performed two, or possibly three, operations on them. First, the redactor edited them with a series of formulae (the RFs) and other additions that cemented them together both with one another and with the whole psalms that frame the collection. To some degree, these additions also disguised the songs' specific character, making them more useful for the general public. Second, an editorial frame (Psalms 121-122; 132-134) was added that put these songs in the context of pilgrimage. Third, the redactor or someone else displaced one of the nucleus songs to the first of the collection because it apparently depicted the agony of someone living in exile.[41] As a whole, then, the Songs of Ascents not only depict but make a case for pilgrimage from outlying areas to Jerusalem.

It is therefore probable that the redactor who gave this shape to the collection is also the person who added the superscript שִׁיר הַמַּעֲלוֹת.

---

[41]Allen (*Psalms 101-150*, 148) similarly states that the relevance of Psalm 120's inclusion at the beginning of the collection "seems to lie in a re-interpretation of v. 5. It became a vehicle for the homesickness of devout expatriate Jews."

In this case the proper meaning for the superscript would be "Songs of Pilgrimage," as is commonly stated. But this meaning of the superscript has two nuances previously unnoticed: first, the songs acquire this meaning only after they have been (assembled and) edited into a whole and labeled as such; and second, this editing process fits into a particular cultural milieu and has particular goals within that milieu. The former has been the subject of the present chapter. The latter is the subject of the next chapter.

CHAPTER IV

THE SOCIOHISTORICAL PLACE OF THE SONGS OF ASCENTS

I argued in Chap. 3 that the Songs of Ascents owe their character as a unit to a redactional effort. In this final chapter I shall try to fit both the nucleus of songs that existed prior to that effort and the redactions themselves into fairly specific historical and social milieux. The purpose of this chapter is not to prove beyond doubt that the Songs of Ascents derived from these milieux (I have doubts about whether this is ever possible with ancient poetry), but rather to make a case for the plausibility of this reconstruction. The amount and quality of available evidence make stronger claims impossible.

THE MILIEU OF THE NUCLEUS GROUP

In the following section I shall attempt to describe the various kinds of evidence that, taken together, may help to determine the provenance of the nucleus group. None of the lines of reasoning is sufficient by itself to do this, but their cumulative effect should be accorded some weight. If the lines of evidence make it possible to infer an approximate provenance for the songs, it may be possible to supplement these data with what is known about the surroundings in which they were first spoken. The lines of evidence may be categorized under the rubrics of linguistic evidence, hints about the geographical setting, evidence of cultural structures, and temporal evidence.

Linguistic Evidence

Any attempt to adduce particular linguistic characteristics as evidence of culture or of time period must proceed cautiously; the present collection is too small to provide an adequate sample of the language spoken by those who wrote the songs. But perhaps it will provide a line of reasoning that can be added to other lines of reasoning to infer a place and a time. My attempt to infer something from the linguistic character of the songs is bounded by two methodological restrictions: I deal here only with phenomena that occur repeatedly in the Songs of Ascents, and that are rare or absent in the remainder of the HB (or localized in a single stratum of it). In this way I hope both to limit the discussion and to isolate phenomena that distinguish this corpus from standard Hebrew usage. Table 3 (pp. 147-149) cites a variety of other examples of unusual linguistic forms in the Songs of Ascents, many of which are found in the nucleus group. These peculiarities provide important information about the dialectal character of the songs. I have selected the following examples as especially informative.

One interesting feature is the prominence of -שֶׁ as the relative pronoun which, being prominent in both the nucleus group and the redactional layer, provides important, albeit ambiguous, information about the date of each. In fact the relative pronoun אֲשֶׁר occurs only twice in the entire collection: in Pss 127:5 and 132:2. The latter is part of what I have identified as a redactional layer; in the former there is a strong possibility that the reason for its use lies in its assonance with אַשְׁרֵי in the same line. Other than these two examples, the relative pronoun is exclusively -שֶׁ, which occurs six times in the nucleus group and four times in the redactional materials. The particle could be evidence of late date or of northern provenance (or both).[1] Given the

---

[1]The general rule is that the particle is either an example of north-Israelite Hebrew in any period or south-Israelite Hebrew in later periods. In Middle Hebrew the particle -שֶׁ is the exclusive relative pronoun (Kutscher, *History*, 125). The development is to some degree reflected in the following statistics. The particle occurs four times in the book of Judges, all in stories about north Israel, alongside אֲשֶׁר. In Jonah the preferred word is אֲשֶׁר (12 occurrences), but -שֶׁ occurs three times. Similarly, Lamentations has four instances of -שֶׁ and nine instances of אֲשֶׁר. In Qohelet the usages of אֲשֶׁר (89 instances) and -שֶׁ (70 instances) are approximately equal. In Song of Songs the latter has completely replaced the former, with the

prevalence of -שֶׁ in the redactional materials, it would be claiming too much to state that this word is evidence of a north-Israelite provenance for the nucleus group, although that possibility remains open.

A second noteworthy feature, however, is on somewhat firmer ground. Throughout the nucleus group there is a marked tendency for words to end in ת- that in standard Hebrew would end in ה-. The adverb רַבַּת occurs four times in the nucleus group, and very rarely elsewhere in the HB.[2] Alternative forms of the adverb also occur in the HB (רַבָּה or רַב),[3] and although they are equally rare they seem to be located mostly in texts that are identifiably Judean. Thus the adverb רַבַּת may well be evidence of north-Israelite provenance. In Randall Garr's survey of inscriptional materials, he states that the *-at* adverbial ending has been replaced both in Hebrew inscriptions and in the inscriptions from Deir ʿAllā with the ending *ā*. The older *-at* ending survives only in Byblian and standard Phoenician (not in Aramaic!). He further posits that the shift probably happened independently, rather than as a result of one dialect's having influence on another.[4] Together with the nearly total absence of this adverb from the rest of the HB,[5] this datum may be taken

---

exception of the superscript. In the Psalms, -שֶׁ occurs only in "Book 5," which is probably the last part of the Psalter to have achieved fixed form (Wilson, *Editing of the Hebrew Psalter*, 120-121). Some of these examples may of course result from concerns of meter or other unknown concerns, but these factors would not explain the fact of its nearly complete dominance in the Songs of Ascents.

[2]Pss 120:6; 123:4; 129:1-2. Elsewhere it occurs only in Ps 65:10 and possibly Ezek 24:12 (the text of the latter is uncertain).

[3]The adverb רַבָּה occurs in Pss 62:3; 78:15; 89:8; רַב occurs in Pss 18:15; 123:3. According to BDB (p. 913a) the form רַבַּת is an Aramaism, although this seems far from certain. In any case the use of רַב in Ps 123:3 (with רַבַּת in the following line) implies that a certain amount of variation is possible within a single dialect.

[4]W. Randall Garr, *Dialect Geography of Syria-Palestine, 1000-586 B.C.E.* (Philadelphia, PA: University of Pennsylvania Press, 1985) 60-61; cf. p. 94, where north-Israelite inscriptions have a final ת as the absolute feminine singular ending and Judean inscriptions have a final ה. This shows the ת/ה shift to be a fairly regular feature that can distinguish north-Israelite dialect from Judean dialect.

[5]It would not be difficult to make a case that Psalm 65, the only other certain instance of the adverb, is of northern origin. Several features argue in this direction. First, Zion is mentioned only in the first verse, a natural place for an interpretative identification of an otherwise unspecified temple. Second, the usual שָׁנָה appears as שְׁנַת (v. 12), which belongs to the same phenomenon as רַבַּת, and is probably a northernism. Third, the language of grain production probably argues for a northern

as evidence in favor of a northern, and perhaps also of an agrarian (isolated and therefore less susceptible to change in language), provenance.

A third distinctive feature of the dialect is the use of an accusative (?) case ending when feminine nouns in הָ‍ follow the preposition בְּ. This phenomenon occurs twice in the nucleus group, in Pss 120:1 and 125:3.[6] The use of this form with place names occurs elsewhere in the HB (Num 33:22,33; Judg 14:2; Jer 52:10; Ruth 4:11; cf. בְּאֶפְרָתָה in Ps 132:6), but these two are the only occasions of the form other than in place names in the HB. It is possible that this phenomenon is related to the phenomenon of absolute feminine nouns ending in ה discussed above; the accusative ending may have survived in this dialect as a result of its not having shifted to the ending in הָ‍. If this is correct, then this case ending corroborates the hypothesis that the nucleus songs derive from a north-Israelite agrarian provenance.

Geographical References

The most obvious geographical references in the nucleus group are those of Psalm 120, which mentions both Meshek and Qedar as places where the supplicant has sojourned. If these names referred to "Arabian tribes," it would locate Psalm 120 in the southern Transjordanian Plateau. The names, however, are probably to be taken as proverbial for "haters of peace," rather than as specific references to "Arabian tribes," and so provide no real clue to the geographic setting of the psalm. The psalm also uses the image of "coals of broom plants," which chiefly grow in the coastal sand dunes of the Philistian plain and semi-arid areas of southern Palestine and the Transjordan. The story of Elijah probably

---

provenance, as does the prominence of a river (vv. 9-10). The tendency to end feminine absolute nouns in ה occurs several other times in the Songs of Ascents as well (cf. קָרְמָה in Ps 129:6; שְׁנַת in Ps 132:4). In any case the regularity with which רַבַּת occurs is striking, especially in light of the word's rarity.

[6]The preposition בְּ followed by a feminine noun in הָ‍ also occurs in the nucleus group, however (Ps 126:5,6). Certainly one must grant that any spoken dialect will not be a "pure" dialect, but will include features that are on their way out of the dialect and other features that are on their way into the dialect. Even so, the presence of the more standard Hebrew ending in הָ‍ advises caution.

implies that the plants were known also in the north (1 Kgs 19:4-5), but in any case the imagery—especially if Meshek and Qedar were taken as Arabian tribes—would seem more likely to argue for either a southern or a transjordanian setting rather than for a north-Israelite one. Similarly, Ps 126:5 uses "wadis [אֲפִיקִים] in the negev" as an image of the restoration of fertility. This at least implies familiarity with desert life, although it could be either transjordanian imagery or southern imagery, and is not necessarily southern (Apheq and Aphiq appear commonly among northern place names[7]). The agricultural imagery of Psalm 126, in any case, would seem to derive from a more fertile region.

Cultural Indications

The nucleus group provides a few hints about the cultural milieu of those who produced them. One piece of evidence is the sort of farming techniques that seem to be presupposed: Psalm 126 appears to presume northern farming techniques rather than southern ones. The noun אֲלֻמָּה "sheaf" is used elsewhere only in Genesis 37, in the story of Joseph. The preferred word in the HB is עֳמָרִים. The different terminology may imply different techniques of harvesting: If KB is correct that עֳמָרִים refers to stalks that are cut off right behind the ears of grain, and that אֲלֻמָּה is a full sheaf (as seems to be implied in Genesis 37),[8] then the difference between the two terms might be the difference between small-scale harvesting by hand or knife and larger-scale harvesting by sickle. The latter would fit better with the situation in the north, where plots of farmed land were larger, with less dependence on terraced landscape,

---

[7]The place names Aphiq and Apheq are usually thought to mean "stronghold" (BDB, 67-68), whereas the word in Psalm 126 is naturally enough supposed to mean "strong current" (both deriving from the root אפק). The three sites usually identified with the biblical names above are Tell Ras el-ᶜAin (approximately 20 miles southwest of Samaria), Tell Kurdaneh (approximately seven miles south of Acco), and Tell Fiq (approximately two miles north of Hippos, three miles east of the Lake of Galilee). Each of these is located on seasonal streams in foothill regions of the north Israelite highlands. The absence of this place name in southern Israel suggests that the word is northern. See May, Hunt and Hamilton, *Oxford Bible Atlas*, 62-63, 94-95. On the methodology of using place names as evidence of dialectal vocabulary, cf. Kutscher, *History*, 54-55.

[8]KB, עֳמָר I, p. 717.

and the sickle therefore more efficient; the small terraces in the south, together with a climate less suitable for large-scale grain production, may have made this form of reaping unnecessary.[9] The words are used too seldom in the HB to corroborate this hypothesis with distributional evidence,[10] but the distribution as it stands certainly does not controvert it.

Two of the songs in the nucleus group imply the setting of a walled city. Psalm 127 implies this in both parts of the song. In v. 1b the statement that "if YHWH does not guard a city, the guard stays awake uselessly" implies a walled city both in its use of the word עִיר and in the fact that there is a guard (for the verb שָׁקַד in the guarding of a city cf. Jer 5:6). The same is implied in the fact that one's sons contest with enemies "in the gate."[11] Psalm 130 may also imply the milieu of the walled city in its image of שֹׁמְרִים לַבֹּקֶר, which probably refers to

---

[9]Referring to Yehud during the Persian era, Grabbe (*Judaism from Cyrus to Hadrian*, 1:121) states,

> The best of the farmland was no longer within the borders of the province. The Shephelah had long been taken away, and even the southern area of Judah was now in the hands of Edomites or Arabs. Most of the country was made up of the Judean hill country. The soil and climate were suitable for vineyards and olive orchards. The tax system may also have tended to create specialization in crops which could be sold for cash rather than grown for the subsistence of residents, but grain production would have been low in any case and may have been insufficient for the needs of the people themselves.

Grabbe's assertion may go too far in saying that Yehud may not have been able to produce enough grain for itself (Avi Ofer, Judean Highlands Project, in a private communication of 30 January 1994, has stated emphatically that Grabbe is wrong about this). Nevertheless it is a truism that the farther south one goes the more limited agriculture is in scope.

[10]Cf. also the use of the verb עָמַר in Ps 129:7, where the context is small-scale reaping (of "grass of the rooftops") rather than harvesting as such.

[11]According to the findings of John Wright ("A Tale of Three Cities: Urban Gates, Squares, and Power in Iron Age II, Neo-Babylonian, and Achaemenid Israel," Society of Biblical Literature Annual Meeting, Sociology of the Second Temple Group (New Orleans, LA: 17 November 1990), the gate in the Achaemenid era has ceased to be the place in which juridical disputes are conducted; those functions are transferred to the square. If Psalm 127 derives from the Persian era, then the changed function of the city gate might be further evidence for the non-forensic character of the image in v. 5 (see Chap. 2, p. 67, textual note g).

guards on night duty who anticipate the morning as the time of their reprieve. Psalm 128 may also presume the life of the city, in that the house in which the wife stays seems to have multiple rooms (implied by the phrase יַרְכְּתֵי בֵיתֶךָ). The images of city life in these texts may be little more than figures of speech; yet such figures of speech are likely to be drawn from the everyday life (although not necessarily the direct experience) of the speaker.

Psalm 126 presents two items of interest for the historian of Israelite religion: the glorification of God among the nations and the practice of "weeping" in connection with agricultural fertility. There is little attestation for this practice because the Jerusalemite editing of the HB for the most part eliminated references to it other than negative ones.[12] The one exception is the story of Jephthah (Judges 11), in which the hero must sacrifice his daughter to fulfill a vow, and she is said to wander over the hills weeping for two months. This is probably an historicization of an older myth that had its counterpart in a ritual performed by Israelite women in later times, in which they would wander the hills weeping for four days (the incongruity of time spent weeping is evidence that the historicization of the myth and the practice are independent). It is clear that such a practice of women weeping during the months of death, or weeping for Tammuz (Ezek 8:14), is a survival of ancient fertility ritual.[13] What is less clear is that this ritual is present in Psalm 126. Here it is presumably men who weep (the verbs and participles are masculine, although no explicit subject is named), and they do so at the time of planting rather than during the fallow

---

[12]Flemming Friis Hvidberg (*Weeping and Laughter in the Old Testament: A Study of Canaanite-Israelite Religion*, ed. F. Løkkegaard, rev. ed. [Leiden: E. J. Brill, 1962] 98-137) argues that a large number of texts in the HB contain disguised references to the "Canaanite" fertility ritual of weeping for the dead god and expressing joy at his revival. Especially with regard to Psalm 126, he sees the following features as clearly demonstrating a background in folk religion: (1) a general sense of infertility, and a hope for fertility; (2) the (admittedly general) terms "tears," "weep," and "carry" are all associated with Baal's burial; (3) "Laugh" and "rejoice" are associated with Baal's revival.

[13]On the interpretational issues, see J. Alberto Soggin, *Judges, A Commentary* (Old Testament Library; Philadelphia, PA: Westminster, 1987) 213-219. See also J. Cheryl Exum, "The Tragic Vision and Biblical Narrative: The Case of Jephthah," in *Signs and Wonders: Biblical Texts in Literary Focus,* ed. J. Cheryl Exum (*Semeia*; Atlanta: Scholars Press, 1989) 59-83.

months. The Ezekiel passage makes clear that the practice of weeping in connection with fertility rites continues in exilic Israel, and it would therefore be plausible to see it in Psalm 126. On the other hand, even if this is the background, it has been so thoroughly de-mythologized that the majority of commentators perceive the weeping and joy merely as symbols of "strenuous seedtime and happy harvest."[14] If a fertility ritual of some sort is alluded to in Psalm 126, this datum would be good evidence that the psalm came from outside the priestly establishment at Jerusalem (implied by Ezekiel's negative reference to it), reinforcing the plausibility of my interpretation that Psalm 126 is prayed by non-Jerusalemites who see Jerusalem's restoration from outside.

The second item, that Psalm 126 is an example of the tradition in which foreign nations glorify YHWH on account of Israel's restoration (cf., e.g., Isaiah 60), provides further evidence about the religious system of the community that prayed this song, if it is a unity as I believe it to be. This motif is characteristic of the Persian period; most notably it serves as a justification for Persian hegemony (in the form of Yehudite governors) over the area: if the restoration of Zion is glorious enough to cause this kind of laudatory speech among the nations, it must be glorious indeed![15] As I understand it, the community that heard the rhetoric enshrined in the first lines does not accept it as a matter of fact, however. The skepticism is implied, first of all, in the statement that the restoration was ephemeral, having the nature of a dream. It is focused more strongly in the prayer that God restore in actuality what the rhetoric implies. The restoration of Zion's fortunes is a source of hope, to be sure, but it is hope that must be realized in restored fortunes for the praying community. This implies that at least some people in outlying communities thought of Zion as normative for their lives as well.

---

[14]Quote from Hans Walter Wolff, *Anthropology of the Old Testament* (trans. Margaret Kohl; Philadelphia, PA: Fortress Press, 1974) 84. Cf. Keet, A Study of the Psalms of Ascents, 53.

[15]Morton Smith (*Palestinian Parties and Politics that Shaped the Old Testament* [London: SCM, 1987] 69-72) regards this theme as evidence of the "popular, synchretistic piety" (62) of the masses who were not deported to Babylon. His basis for this conclusion is that it seems to imply that some foreigners had already been converted to worship of YHWH, which presupposes the ideology he identifies as synchretistic. If he is right about this, it would be yet another piece of evidence for the popular character of the nucleus songs.

Despite the critique implied in Psalm 126, the redactor did not find it necessary to edit it, perhaps because of this ideological predisposition.

Time Frame

Those songs in the nucleus group that can be dated all probably stem from the Persian period. The date of none of them is certain (it seldom is with psalms), nor is it possible in any case but one (Psalm 120) to be more specific than the very general "Persian period" identification. Nevertheless, if these songs may tentatively be seen together as stemming from a common milieu (see Chap. 3, pp. 152-154), then their collective witness is somewhat stronger.

To summarize the evidence presented in Chap. 2, the following psalms from the nucleus group seem to be more or less datable: Psalms 120, 125, 126, and 130. Psalm 120 refers to two people groups, Meshek and Qedar, that are widely separated from one another (the former probably in Anatolia and the latter in the Transjordan and perhaps southern Palestine). Because of their geographical remove from one another, they are best seen as symbolic references to particularly troublesome neighbors, but the time in which the use of these symbols together would have had this meaning is probably the early- to middle-fifth century BCE, with the caveat that the symbolic usage could have survived for a while after the particular situations that gave rise to it disappeared. Three pieces of evidence point to a postexilic provenance for the nucleus part of Psalm 125. First, two matters of vocabulary point to a postexilic date. The word צַדִּיקִם occurs rarely in datable preexilic literature (Exod 23:8; Isa 5:23, both of which in juridical contexts) and is quite common in datable postexilic literature, especially in wisdom literature; with the definite article it occurs elsewhere only in Qohelet. Second, the phrase לְמַעַן לֹא partially replaces לְבִלְתִּי as the indicator of negative purpose in the exilic and later periods. The latter continues to be used, but the former never occurs in preexilic literature. Third, the implication of vv. 3-5a is that a "wicked" power has political domination over "the inheritance of the righteous." Although such would not be the understanding of Nehemiah with regard to the Persian domination, it may very well have been the view of the indigenous population with regard to the Persian governors in Jerusalem and Samaria. Coupled with the distinction between "those who are at ease" and the praying community, the psalm may presume an increasing tendency on the part of rich landowners to take over the lands of their less fortunate neighbors, so that the ideology portrayed here has a background in Jubilee ideology.[16] As a less likely alternative, it would also fit with the period of Greek (probably Seleucid rather than Ptolemaic, since toleration seems to have been the norm for the latter) domination. Psalm 126 also points to a postexilic date. Its relationship to the book of Joel certainly indicates this, whether that relationship is that of literary dependence or of a common milieu. Indeed, if Beyerlin is right that the psalm depends on the written book of Joel for its ideas,[17] this would fix the date of the psalm as somewhat later than the early fourth century; otherwise it merely points to the Persian period. The theme of the glorification of YHWH among the nations would also fit with such a date. The presence of the late noun סְלִיחָה in Ps 130:4 may perhaps be adduced as evidence of a postexilic date for Psalm 130, although there is little else about the psalm to corroborate this. Contrary to those interpreters who place these songs in the preexilic period,[18] the bulk of the evidence argues in favor of a postexilic setting for the nucleus group.

Summary of Evidence from the Nucleus Group

The internal evidence from the nucleus group that might allow one to posit a milieu in which they might have been composed is admittedly scanty. The problem is complicated by the fact that there is no way to be certain that the songs were originally unified. In the above discussion I

---

[16]Although the takeover of lands by the rich is known to have happened at other periods in Israelite history (cf. Isa 5:8; Mic 2:1-5; Jer 17:11), it is also known and dealt with by Nehemiah (Neh 5:1-13). If one may judge from the prominence of this theme in Leviticus 25 and 27, the cancellation of debts was an important concept in some circles during the postexilic era.

[17]Beyerlin, *We Are Like Dreamers*, 46-48 and *passim* (cf. Chap. 2, p. 63).

[18]Thirtle, *Old Testament Problems*, 13-19; Hengstenberg, *Commentary on the Psalms*, 408; Dahood, *Psalms*, 3:195; Beaucamp, *Psautier*, 252.

have analyzed the evidence with the hypothesis that they were such; the conclusions remain tentative in proportion to the uncertainty of that hypothesis and to the scarcity of available evidence. Nevertheless, the evidence does not negate the hypothesis, and some conclusions may therefore be offered on that basis. The nucleus group appears to have been composed during the Persian period; at the earliest, probably the late-sixth century, or more probably the early- to mid-fifth century BCE. If one considers the addition of a gloss referring to the Greeks (if that is what is meant) in Ps 123:4, this might imply that the glossator was working some time after the middle of the fifth century (and therefore that the song itself was written prior to that time), when Greek marauders and mercenaries became an increasing threat in the Levant, or some time before the beginning of the second century, when the Seleucid rulers became increasingly oppressive. The evidence also allows one to suggest that the nucleus songs were composed in the fertile north-Israelite highlands rather than in the south. One piece of evidence apparently controverts this, namely the mention of "wadis in the negev" (Ps 126:4). The word אֲפִיקִים could well have belonged to north-Israelite dialectal vocabulary, as is evident from the distribution of the name Apheq and Aphiq in north-Israelite place names. Moreover, the term "negev" does not necessarily refer to the modern region called by that name. Overall it seems safer to rely on the vocabulary, on the type of agriculture presupposed, and on the distinctive linguistic elements of the nucleus group than to rely on overt references to places, especially in light of the songs' poetic character.

THE MILIEU OF THE REDACTIONAL LAYER

Temporal Evidence

The most important data relating to the period in which the redaction took place come from the RFs themselves, since they are the best evidence of the redaction process. In Chap. 3 (pp. 137-146) I have argued that at least three of the RFs—עֹשֵׂה שָׁמַיִם, יֹאמַר־נָא יִשְׂרָאֵל

וָאָרֶץ, and שָׁלוֹם עַל־יִשְׂרָאֵל—are postexilic, probably belonging to the late Persian period.[19] Although the other four RFs cannot be dated with as much certainty, neither do they provide evidence for a time earlier than this. Indeed, if the hypothesis is accepted that the nucleus material is from the Persian period, one would hardly expect that the redactional elements would be earlier than this; nevertheless, it does seem that the redactor is using expressions that are *au courant* rather than archaistic.

The next most important area to consider is the redactional additions to songs in the nucleus group, because these additions are almost as probably from the hand of the redactor of the collection as are the RFs. The ending of Psalm 130 is instructive in that it reinterprets the song, originally an individual expression of piety, as a promise of divine forgiveness for those who wait for it. This promise may be compared with the very similar program in Chronicles, where even Manasseh is allowed to repent and find divine forgiveness. Needless to say, this theme is not absent in preexilic writings, but it becomes most prominent in the postexilic community, which had to struggle with the assertion of the prophets and of the Deuteronomic History that the exile happened as a result of the people's wickedness. The addition to Psalm 131, likewise, reinterprets an individual's prayer of humility as an example for "Israel" as a whole to follow.

The communalizing (one might even say "nationalizing") tendency of the redactional layer finds expression in several other cases as well. Psalms 124 and 129 both begin in the same way, with "let Israel now say," which reinterprets a thanksgiving song of the small community (Psalm 124) and an individual petition (Psalm 129) as national songs. The thanksgiving of Psalm 124 becomes national and, by the addition of עֹשֵׂה שָׁמַיִם וָאָרֶץ celebrative of the divine world order. Indeed, this reinterpretation practically transforms the monster imagery of v. 3 and the water imagery of vv. 4-5 into a narration of the *Chaoskampf*, the defeat of chaos and subsequent establishment of the divine order. Because the creation of world order is nearly always tied to the

---

[19]Especially the RF שָׁלוֹם עַל־יִשְׂרָאֵל, being common on Rabbinic literature and otherwise unknown in the HB, is best seen as very late (see Chap. 3, p. 139).

establishment of political power,[20] this transformation may imply an attempt to construe the governor in Jerusalem as an appointee not only of Persia but of God.[21]

The time of the redactional effort seems to have been one of some degree of "foreign" opposition to the circles in which the redactor operated. Ps 129:5, for example, transforms an individual's curse against oppressors (the language is too metaphorical to specify what sort of enemies they were) into a curse against "those who hate Zion." This phrase occurs only here in the HB, but the response to their hatred implies that it is primarily a metaphor for military or political threat, rather than mere feelings of animosity. The threat is against Zion, a term that in the Songs of Ascents is used to refer to the place by that name, rather than to the gathered community.[22] The redactional additions to the nucleus group not only curse these opponents but also try to reassure the community that the efforts of such opponents will fail, as in the beginning of Psalm 125 (cf. the assertion that help is from YHWH in Pss 121:2 and 124:8). This community consists not only of persons who dwell in Jerusalem, but also of those who may "enjoy the prosperity of Jerusalem" while away from the city (cf. Ps 122:6-9). This implies that Jerusalem has some degree of hegemony over outlying areas.

A third type of evidence comes from the whole psalms identified as redactional additions to the collection (Psalms 121-122 and 132-134). I think it likely that the redactor was the author of these songs. This cannot be established with certainty, however, and the temporal evidence from these songs is therefore less weighty than that of the RFs and the redactional additions to nucleus songs. Nevertheless some indicators of date are pertinent to the discussion. The Jerusalem of these psalms includes a functional temple, walls (Ps 122:7), and city gates (Ps 122:2). If the preceding discussion is accepted (making the redactional layer postexilic), it follows that the redaction took place at some point after the mission of Nehemiah in 445 BCE. On the other hand, Psalm 132 was probably written before Chronicles was written, since a paraphrase of

---

[20]Mowinckel, *Psalmenstudien*, 2:*passim*.

[21]On the prevalence of such legitimizing techniques, see Jon L. Berquist, *Judaism in Persia's Shadow: A Social and Historical Approach* (Minneapolis, MN: Fortress Press, 1995) Chaps. 10 and 13.

[22]*Contra* Beyerlin, *We Are Like Dreamers*, 37; Harman, "Psalm 126," 76.

parts of it appears in Solomon's prayer of the temple's dedication (2 Chr 6:41-42). It was also probably written after the Deuteronomistic History, since the statement in v. 12 probably presumes the development of that corpus.[23]

The power structure implied in Psalm 132, and to some extent also in Psalm 122's nostalgia about the "house of David," implies a time of emphasis on secular rather than priestly authority, although to what extent this dichotomy continues to exist in the Persian Period is a matter of some dispute. The only explicit reference to priests is in Psalm 132, where their own power comes as a result of God's blessing the royal line. Simon de Vries has studied the references to Moses and David in the book of Chronicles, concluding that the Chronicler associates David with Levites and Moses with Aaronid priests to the end that the former are given preeminence in the cult.[24] If his thesis is accepted as correct (and it would seem to corroborate, for example, the increase of Levitical power in Chronicles), then the primacy of David and the subordinacy of priests[25] might imply Levitical authorship for the redactional materials. It might also imply a time in which there was a Davidic pretender to the gubernatorial office, although there were probably not many governors of Persian Yehud from the Davidic line (Zerubbabel is the exception, and in any case it does not appear that he made messianic claims[26]).

If my interpretation of Psalm 133 is correct, then it provides an important datum: the redactional materials would belong to a period in which there is an effort underway to make Jerusalem a center not only for Yehud but for northern Israelites as well. Several efforts of this sort

---

[23]Kruse, "Psalm cxxxii," 285.

[24]Simon de Vries, "Moses and David as Cult Founders in Chronicles," *JBL* 107 (1988) 619-639.

[25]In point of fact the opposite seems to have been the case. The "second temple period" is characterized by the increase of power for the priests—especially of the High Priest—and diminution of power for the Levites, with the latter "caring for the fabric of the temple structure and similar mundane duties but not presiding at the altar" (Grabbe, *Judaism from Cyrus to Hadrian*, 1:145). Such a reconstruction also fits well with the emerging picture of how the book of psalms seems to have achieved its present form; that the psalms contain scarcely any reference to the sacrificial cultus implies that the Levitical singers of the "second temple period," who were probably responsible for the psalm tradition, saw no need to do so.

[26]Grabbe, *Judaism from Cyrus to Hadrian*, 1:77-79.

are known to have happened following the fall of Samaria to the Assyrian army in 722 BCE. Hezekiah evidently took steps in this direction (2 Kgs 18:22; 2 Chr 30:1), as did Josiah (2 Kgs 23:1-23; 2 Chr 34:1-7). The evidence is against such an early date for the redactional layer, however. It is also probable that Nehemiah made overtures to the north-Israelite farmers (it seems to have been one of the sources of Tobiah's opposition), and it is of course possible, even likely, that later governors of Yehud about whom we have no information could have done the same.

The redactional materials seem to date to some time during the Persian period. The existence of temple and walls need not give a *terminus ante quem* of 445 BCE, the year of Nehemiah's mission, although this is certainly possible.[27] Neither is a *terminus post quem* readily available in the redactional materials. The implication that the community of Zion might be threatened could reflect the growing turmoil as the Persian empire declined, but they could equally reflect a variety of situations about which we have less information. The desire to bring northern Israelites into the sphere of Zionistic influence, as reflected directly in Psalms 132 and 133 and indirectly in the redaction of the Songs of Ascents as such, could belong to Zerubbabel's or Nehemiah's attempts to do this, but they could equally well belong to one of the periods about which we have virtually no information. Considering the nature of the sources, there is considerable evidence that the struggle for Jerusalemite influence in the region of Samaria took place in several periods. In any case it is certainly not surprising that such might have been the case. To summarize, then: although we are

---

[27]I accept the early date of Ezra's return (458 BCE), on the basis of Grabbe's summary of arguments in favor of this date (*Judaism from Cyrus to Hadrian*, 1:90-90). When Ezra comes he finds the walls of Jerusalem already built (Ezra 9:9). Indeed, it is difficult to imagine that they would not have been rebuilt at some point following the Babylonian destruction, perhaps by Zerubbabel, since Jerusalem from that point on operates as a provincial capital. The report that Nehemiah hears about Jerusalem (Neh 1:3) would hardly be news to him if the destruction referred to was the Babylonian destruction. For this reason several scholars have proposed that there was a wall built before Nehemiah's time, but that this wall was destroyed in the suppression of Inaros' rebellion (465-455 BCE) or one of the other rather frequent rebellions of the early fifth century (Grabbe, *Judaism from Cyrus to Hadrian*, 1:93-94).

not able to posit a specific period for the redaction of the Songs of
Ascents on the basis of the internal evidence, it is reasonable to suppose
that the redaction happened at some point in the Persian period; and
since our general knowledge of the social structure of that period is
somewhat more complete, perhaps consideration of this social structure
will provide some clues.

Social and Historical Setting

*Political Relationships between Jerusalem
and the Surrounding Areas*

The books of Ezra and Nehemiah mostly portray a situation in
which the province of Yehud, with Jerusalem at its center, was the only
authentic continuation of Israelite culture in postexilic Palestine.
Tobiah, whose name is Yahwistic, is portrayed as an "Ammonite
servant." Sanballat, whose name is Assyrian but whose sons have
Yahwistic names, rules Samaria as a foreigner (a Horonite). Ezra
portrays "the people of the land" as being opposed to the divine law that
is "in the hand" of Ezra. Yet there are occasional hints in Ezra-
Nehemiah that this was far from being a factual presentation. These
hints receive confirmation in the broader corpus of Persian-era biblical
literature. In the next few pages I shall try to present what seems to be
something of a scholarly consensus about some of the historical and
social realities of Persian-era Yehud that relate to the Songs of Ascents.
The aim is to elaborate on the picture that has begun to emerge in the
above discussion, and to see whether such elaboration helps to clarify
the setting of the Songs of Ascents.

When Cyrus, king of Media and Persia, succeeded in overthrowing
the Babylonian king Nabonidus, one of his earliest acts was apparently
to insure that the local religious institutions of the conquered regions
received state sanction. It was a policy that continued in later times.[28]

---

[28]Under Cyrus this support seems to have been minimal, allowing exiles to
return and rebuild if they desired to do so. Under Darius I (during whose reign the
temple was actually reconstructed), and for Yehud especially under Artaxerxes I

This state support had two primary purposes: first, it sought to reinterpret local religious traditions in ways that would legitimate the Persian overlordship; second, it utilized the old local religious structures for imperial logistical operations, such as the appraisal of goods, collection of taxes, gathering of intelligence, and enforcement of imperial law. Persian government was thoroughly hierarchical. Each descending level of the hierarchy was responsible for specified smaller parts of the whole, and received this authority from the next higher level. An elaborate system of ritualized behavior surrounded upper-level rulers (emperor, satraps, and governors), clearly marking them as important persons and setting them apart from the general populace. Thus the realm of religion and the realm of politics interpenetrated one another in significant ways. Indeed this had always been the case in the ancient Near East; what was new was the combination of indigenous religious traditions with imperial political structures.

Yehud was a small province, or perhaps a subprovince, within the satrapy of *Ebir-Nari* ("Beyond the [Euphrates] River"). Judging by the lists in Ezra and Nehemiah, the district of Yehud refers to the area within about a fifteen-mile radius of Jerusalem, somewhat farther to the south and not so far to the north. It included Bethel to the north, Azekah to the west, and Beth-Zur to the south. The book of Nehemiah stylizes this area as "Judah and Benjamin," clearly seeing it as the continuation of the preexilic southern kingdom, which was the true Israel according to the Chronicler; but it was not so extensive as was monarchical Judah, especially to the south. On the other hand, it included some of the Israelite highlands that in the divided monarchy were counted as belonging to the northern kingdom. The crops of this area were chiefly grapes and olives grown on terraced hillsides. Some cereals were also grown in the valleys; once the fields were harvested, grain farmers allowed them to be grazed by small cattle, which created a symbiotic relationship between pastoralists and farmers. But agriculture (which, strictly speaking, refers only to grain production) seems to have lost some of its importance in Persian Yehud, perhaps as a result of imperial tax structures. It is possible that Yehudite farmers were unable to

---

(who probably commissioned Ezra and almost certainly commissioned Nehemiah), official Persian support reached much higher levels.

produce enough grain to supply themselves; the increasing tendency is to produce crops such as grapes and olives, which could be preserved and either sold for cash or traded to people from neighboring areas for grain.

The population of Jerusalem in this period outstripped that of any of the other cities in Yehud. Jerusalem itself became an urban center, the residents of which relied mainly on sources other than farming to earn a living.[29] The list in Nehemiah 11 indicates that many of Jerusalem's inhabitants may have been representatives of the smaller towns (probably the land-owning aristocracy, whose livelihood was maintained by peasant workers) and personnel connected with the temple. Nehemiah's bringing of these "representatives" (according to the list, 10% of the returnees from Babylon) to Jerusalem may have been in order to insure his power base in Jerusalem. The population of Jerusalem was, generally speaking, not an agrarian but an urban population. They were the wealthy, artisans, merchants, governmental officials (including Persian military personnel, at least during some periods), and temple personnel. Jerusalem, in other words, was heavily dependent upon its satellite cities for production of food.

The book of Ezra portrays the returning exiles as constitutive of "Israel." It opposes these "Israelites" to the "people of the land" in ways that deliberately recall the Joshua narratives (Ezra 9:1-14).[30] These "people of the land" are viewed by the writer as Canaanites, not authentic Israelites. One of Ezra's chief concerns is the definition of the Yehudite community (which he calls "Israel"); only those who could prove that their ancestors had returned from Babylon were included in the definition. In historical fact, however, the "people of the land," or most of them at any rate, were the descendants of Israelite people who had not been deported by the Babylonians and Assyrians. This situation is reflected in the fact that these people come to Zerubbabel during the early attempts to rebuild the temple and ask to assist in the effort (Ezra 4:1-4), "for we worship your God as you do, and have been sacrificing to [God] since the time of Esarhaddon the king of Assyria, who made us

---

[29]See Charles Edward Carter, "A Social and Demographic Study of Post-Exilic Judah" (Ph. D. diss., Duke University, 1992).

[30]Robert P. Carroll, "The Myth of the Empty Land," *Semeia* 59 (1992) 84-85.

move here."[31] The view of the author is that these people could not be authentic Israelites, since all of them had been deported, but rather they must be people brought by "Esarhaddon the king of Assyria." More probably, however, these people were simply Yahwists from Samaria who were descended from the vast majority of ancient Israelites, most of whom never had been deported. In such a context both their speech and the writer's interpretation of it make sense.

Religious Relationships with Surrounding Areas

Jerusalem was not the only center of Jewish cultus in the Persian period.[32] We know of another—known to and presumably approved by the authorities in Jerusalem—at the garrison of Jewish mercenaries on the island of Elephantine in Egypt. That this sanctuary did not include a sacrificial cultus probably derives from Persian or Egyptian scruples more than from Jerusalemite ones.[33] Moreover, in the correspondence between Elephantine and Jerusalem, it is stated that the permission to rebuild and operate a temple there was also being sought from Samaria. There are two possible explanations for this: (1) that Samaria was the capital of the province of which Yehud was actually a subprovince, and therefore had political authority over Jerusalem, and (2) that Samaria and Jerusalem were both religious centers, and had equal claim to authority when it came to authorizing Jewish worship at Elephantine. The first of these seems unlikely because, even if Samaria had legal auhority over Yehud, it would not follow that Samaria would have legal jurisdiction over a Jewish installation in Egypt. Moreover, it is known from later periods that a cultus has developed at Samaria, and it is reasonable to think that it may have been in operation during this period. So we know

---

[31]I read וְלֹא אֲנַחְנוּ זֹבְחִים, as suggested by BHS on good grounds. The *aleph* is probably either a result of dittography or an early attempt to "correct" the text.

[32]I use the term "Jewish" in a generic sense—referring to any groups descended from ancient southern Israelites and maintaining a sense of identity with the region and with the historical Israel—rather than in its specific religious meaning.

[33]Gösta Ahlström, *The History of Ancient Palestine*, 2d ed. (Minneapolis, MN: Fortress, 1994), 871.

that Jerusalem was not the only center of worship during the Persian era, and we know that, at least under one leader, this was not considered particularly threatening.[34] It is also at least plausible that another center of Israelite tradition exists in Samaria during this period.

On the other hand, it seems that Jerusalem has primary place as a center of Yahwistic worship for at least some diasporic Jews. By the first century CE, of course, pilgrimage to Jerusalem has become common not only for local people, but for Jews from all around the Mediterranean (cf. Acts 2:5). This does not seem to have been common practice until the end of the Hasmonean era, but it does demonstrate the tendency of diasporic Judaism to orient itself toward Jerusalem.[35] This is confirmed both by the Elephantine correspondence and by incidental references in the biblical materials.

Several passages in the Persian-era biblical materials imply that persons outside Yehud concerned themselves with the temple at Jerusalem. If one accounts for the bias of the writer against the "people of the land," then such an idea is certainly implied in Ezra 4:1-4, in which people from Samaria offer to help Zerubbabel with the rebuilding of the temple. Admittedly this portion of Ezra is somewhat less than reliable for historical information, since its source is not clear.[36] It must have been considered plausible at the time of writing, however, that people from Samaria might come and offer to assist in building the temple. Indeed one can hardly imagine the author recounting such a story—even a rewritten one—if there were not some compelling reason (such as its appearance in a source) for doing so. The book of Zechariah implies that at the time of Zerubbabel there was an effort to extend the influence of Jerusalem to its Davidic boundaries. At the beginning of Zechariah 7, envoys come from Bethel to ask whether they should

---

[34]Malachi has God saying, "my name is great among the nations; and in every place incense is burned to my name, a clean offering, for my name is great among the nations, says YHWH of Hosts" (Mal 1:11). This seems clearly to refer to Jewish sacrificial worship, or at least worship using incense, in the diaspora.

[35]Safrai, *Wallfahrt*, 9.

[36]Grabbe, *Judaism from Cyrus to Hadrian*, 1:30-32. One could perhaps also cite Ezra 6:16, in which "the people of Israel," who are different from the "returned exiles," celebrate at the dedication of the temple. This, too, probably authentically represents the time of Zerubbabel, who seems to have been more open to Israelites who had not been in exile.

continue their practice of fasting in memory of Jerusalem's destruction "70 years" previously.[37] What is particularly striking here is the total acceptance of these Bethelites, despite the fact that they were not returned exiles. Further, the story is an example from the earliest period of the restoration (probably, that is, before Jerusalem's territory included Bethel) of north Israelites seeking divine guidance at Jerusalem. Other oracles of Zechariah also imply a thrust to bring northern Israelite people under Zerubbabel's governance. This seems to be presupposed by Zechariah's making Messianic claims for him (although there is some doubt about whether he claimed such himself), and is made explicit in the claim that God's coming blessing would apply both to "the house of Judah" and "the house of Israel" (Zech 8:13).

Another important factor to consider in this period is the identity of the priesthood, and of religious officials in general. The history of the various cultic officials is a tangled one, and not one that I hope to be able to present here, but I do think that it is important to discuss the issues that are of central importance in the Persian era. Clearly there were priests who had continued operating the Jerusalem cultus during the Babylonian period. This is implied in a variety of exilic writings, including Lamentations and Ezekiel; the writing of polemics against priests on the one hand (Lam 4:13,16), and Levites on the other (Ezek 44:10; 48:11), probably means that the authors of these works were disgruntled with functioning priestly groups, not simply judging groups for past actions. These groups were apparently deposed by, or perhaps subsumed into, the community of returned exiles at the time of Zerubbabel.

The portrayal of the Davidic-Solomonic temple in Chronicles, it is generally assumed, provides a good picture of what the Persian-era cultus was like, rather than of what the preexilic cultus was like. In the relevant narratives, the primary groups are known as priests, Levites, singers, gatekeepers, and "temple servants" (נְתִינִים). Ezekiel's stern denunciations of the "Levitical priests" and consequent elevation of Zadokites does not seem to have been influential; the בְּנֵי צָדוֹק are

---

[37]*Contra* David L. Petersen (*Haggai and Zechariah 1-8: A Commentary* [OTL; Philadelphia: Westminster, 1984] 281), it seems quite natural to read Zech 7:2 as a reference to people coming from Bethel.

never mentioned in the work of the Chronicler, except in the singular with the literal meaning "the son of Zadok" in Solomon's time. Priests as a class are descendants of Aaron, rather than of Zadok. Few passages provide any hint about the distinction between priests and Levites. Those that do seem to imply a subordinate role for the Levites (2 Chr 8:14); on the other hand, Levites generally receive less criticism than do priests (2 Chr 24:5-6; 29:34). Gatekeepers (Korahites) are composed of both groups (2 Chr 23:4), but singers (Asaphites) are a division of the Levites (2 Chr 5:12).[38] Of more importance, however, is the increased prominence of the High Priest, who is elevated to nearly monarchical status. In Haggai and Zechariah the High Priest Jeshua and the Davidic Zerubbabel are seen as equals. That such religious officials were sometimes involved in political maneuvering is evidenced by the alliance of the High Priestly line in Jerusalem with Sanballat, the governor of Samaria (Neh 13:28). By the Greek period, perhaps several decades before then, the position of king/governor has all but disappeared, and the position of the High Priest has taken on royal overtones.

One of the truly striking aspects of Judean religion in the Persian period, at least if the extant literature is any guide, is the prominence of the issue of marriage and divorce. This issue must be understood in the context of the postexilic community's concern for order and differentiation. The Priestly writings are concerned above all with maintenance of order. The creation of order is a matter of separation between the spheres of the sacred and the profane, between clean and unclean, and, especially during and following the period of exile, between true Israelites and "Canaanites."[39] It is this perspective that dominates the work of the Chronicler. To be a member in the reconstituted Israelite community one must be able to prove one's genealogy, one's separateness from the "people of the land." The same perspective is present in Malachi, in the chastisement of those who had

---

[38]Cf. the interesting note in Neh 10:38 that Levites are the ones "who collect the tithe in all the towns where we work." Clearly this implies that administrative duties, especially with regard to taxation, were among the duties performed by Levites.

[39]Jacob Milgrom, *Leviticus 1-16* (AB 3; Garden City, NY: Doubleday, 1991) 42-51.

married "the daughter of a foreign god" (Mal 2:11), although the criticism of those who had "abandoned the wife of [their] youth" (Mal 2:14-16) might be taken as opposition to attempts, like those of Ezra and Nehemiah, to mandate divorce for all those returnees who had married natives of uncertain genealogy. It is clear that at least some returned exiles and probably most non-exilic Israelites held differing ideas of what constituted the true Israelite community (the book of Ruth, for example, presents another viewpoint).

The above description points to the fact that Persian Yehud was characterized by several groups in competition with one another. The biblical sources that have survived are mostly derived from one of those groups—the Jerusalemite priestly group—but this fact has not completely eliminated evidence of opposition from other groups. This picture must be supplemented with evidence from other sources. The Elephantine papyri and the Samaria ostraca are particularly instructive. The onomastic and epigraphical evidence indicates that the people called "people of the land" in Ezra perceived themselves as Yahwists. It follows that the division is not between Yahwists and non-Yahwists, but between one sort of Yahwism and another.

THE PURPOSE OF THE REDACTOR

I have argued above that there is good reason for seeing the redaction of the Songs of Ascents as taking place in Jerusalem during the Persian period. If this is right, what might have been the redactor's purpose in taking some songs and reinterpreting them, adding a few more songs, and creating a collection in which each member is called שִׁיר הַמַּעֲלוֹת? How might such a collection have functioned after its redaction? Such questions attempt to get at the question of the *Sitz im Leben* of the collection as a whole. Because of the uncertain and incomplete nature of knowledge about the period and the limited amount of evidence in the songs themselves, success in answering these questions depends upon the degree to which the theory is able to make sense out of the collection and relate it to the period. To claim anything beyond plausibility would be, given the nature of the evidence, to overstate the case. As I see it, the redactor wished to provide a collection of songs for use by pilgrims to the Jerusalem temple during the Persian period.

Creation of a Pilgrim Psalter

Most scholarly treatments of the Songs of Ascents have regarded the collection as a pilgrim psalter. Few of them have provided any support for this supposition apart from the superscript itself and Psalm 122 (and perhaps also parts of Psalm 132). Most noticed that, apart from these two psalms, none of the songs appeared to be particularly relevant to pilgrimage, but how a pilgrim psalter might have emerged from these songs was left largely unanswered.[40] This study has attempted to clarify how such a situation might have come about, and did so without presupposing because of the common superscript that the collection served as a psalter for pilgrims. What remains is to provide a summary of the ways in which the redactor was able to transform this rather miscellaneous group of songs into a pilgrim psalter.

Nationalization of Psalms of the Individual and of the Small Community

Perhaps the most important new direction provided by the redactor was a tendency to nationalize the songs. I do not think Seybold was right to regard any communalizing element within an individual psalm as a redactional addition. Several of the songs are communal in a non-nationalistic sense. Psalm 123, for example, speaks in the first person plural without any hint that it applies beyond the small group. It is thoroughly a unified poem. Seybold's attempt to give a redactional explanation for the variation from singular to plural fails to prove the point in light of the structural unity. Neither can Psalm 123 be considered a national psalm. The opposition between "us" and "those who are at ease" implies a sociological rather than a nationalistic

---

[40]The one exception to this is Seybold's *Wallfahrtspsalmen*, which, despite many differences, in many ways parallels my own work.

distinction,[41] and the female imagery of the psalm implies a background in folk religion. Similarly, although Psalm 126 speaks of Zion, it does so from the perspective of outsiders and is concerned primarily with the prosperity of a local community.

Some psalms make this nationalization quite explicit. Psalm 124, less the redactional elements of verses 1 and 8, appears to be a song that could be applied in almost any circumstance in which a group had been rescued, and could therefore be applied to a national deliverance. Whether it is the ease with which such a song could be reapplied, or whether for some reason the redactor felt it necessary to provide a corrective, the ambiguity concerning who the speaker is receives clarification at the redactional level, with "Israel" being the speaker. Psalm 125 is nationalized in even more concrete ways. The addition of a paean to Jerusalem and Zion at the beginning of the psalm predisposes one to read it nationally, as does the closing formula "Peace be upon Israel." These two redactional additions surround material deriving from popular wisdom that, although not antithetical to nationalism, primarily relates to individual retribution. In this respect Psalm 125 closely parallels Psalm 128, where the redactional addition also relates the prosperity of individual persons to that of Zion and Jerusalem. The redactional additions to Psalms 130 and 131 both make individual expressions of piety as examples for "Israel" to follow.

The nationalizing tendency that occurs at the level of individual psalms also takes place at the level of the collection as a whole. The redactor accomplishes this first of all by appeal to the sacred history to establish the primacy of Jerusalem in Psalms 122 and 132. The nucleus songs, indeed the remainder of songs in the collection, are remarkably devoid of any sacred history; but in these two songs that history plays a primary role. The sacred history narrated in both of them is that of the Davidic monarchy. In Psalm 122 that history provides the reason why "the tribes of Yah" have made pilgrimage to Jerusalem, in both historical and contemporary times. That pilgrimage results in the fact that those present "seek the welfare of Jerusalem" both for the sake of its

---

[41]Cf. Norman K. Gottwald, "Sociohistoric Horizons of the Psalms," in *The Hebrew Bible: A Socio-Literary Introduction* (Philadelphia, PA: Fortress Press, 1985) 537-541.

inhabitants and for the sake of the temple within its walls. The same structure exists in Psalm 132. There the history of David's "efforts" in bringing the ark to Jerusalem serves as the motivation for God to answer the prayer and bless the city. In both of these psalms, in other words, there is an argument for present blessing in response to past faithfulness. Such arguments are common in the Psalter, but these two are the only songs in the Songs of Ascents that appeal to this tradition. Thus Psalms 122 and 132 surround the nucleus collection (less Psalm 120, which I believe was displaced to the beginning of the collection for reasons that will be discussed below), and supply for it a nationalistic and Jerusalem-oriented framework.

Jerusalem as the Source of Blessing

Alongside the general tendency to nationalize the collection is the more specific tendency to see in Jerusalem an *omphalus mundi*, a center from which God's blessing flows forth.[42]   As with the general nationalizing tendency, this more specific argument appears both in the redactional additions to nucleus songs and in the redactional framework for the collection. The nucleus part of Psalm 128 (vv. 1-4) is a wisdom saying about, or a blessing pronounced upon, an individual "who fears YHWH." The language is that of family life: proper relationship to YHWH (namely that of "fear") yields fertility in both farm and family. The redactional addition (vv. 5-6) asserts that such fertility derives ultimately from worship at Zion, so that "delighting in the prosperity of Jerusalem" is bound up with "seeing one's grandchildren." Blessing flows forth from Zion, coming upon individuals who fear YHWH, so that ultimately שָׁלוֹם comes upon all Israel.

Just as the nationalistic tendencies of the redactional additions to nucleus songs receive clarification and justification in the historicism of Psalms 122 and 132, so the centralization of blessing finds its best statement in the redactional Psalm 133. This psalm makes use of northern imagery and terminology in order to say that the blessing of the

---

[42]Mircea Eliade, *The Myth of the Eternal Return; or, Cosmos and History* (Princeton, NJ: Princeton University Press, 1971) 6-27.

north (the "good oil," the "beard of Aaron," and the "dew of Hermon") has been transferred to Zion. It is on Zion (and not some other place; v. 3b) that God has bestowed extraordinary blessing and life.

There are two primary characteristics of the *omphalus mundi* idea as it appears in these songs, as well as in religious literature from around the world. We have seen the first characteristic, that such places are seen as spatial centers, so that the blessing goes out from them to the rest of the earth. The second characteristic is that such places are seen as being outside of time. They are not of this world, but rather manifest the character of "otherness," belonging to the divine world. The atemporal character of Jerusalem as the *omphalus mundi* manifests itself in several expressions in the redactional layer. The blessing comes from God "from now and forever more" (מֵעַתָּה וְעַד־עוֹלָם; Pss 121:8; 125:2; 131:3). Likewise, the blessing is identified as "life forever" (הַחַיִּים עַד־הָעוֹלָם; Ps 133:3). Such expressions should be seen as deriving from the atemporal character of the temple as the place where time ceases to exist. Psalm 121 should perhaps be seen as a combination of the blessing that comes through the non-spatial and atemporal character of this place. It never mentions Zion, but it has both the element of timelessness (vv. 6,8b) and the element of non-spatiality (vv. 1-2,8a). It holds both together for the purpose of protection, rather than precisely of blessing; but surely the two cannot be divorced from one another.

Pilgrimage and the "Shape" of the Collection

To summarize the discussion so far, not only is there a tendency to nationalize the songs so that they become songs for "Israel"; there is also a tendency to make Jerusalem and Zion the center of that reality, the source of all blessing. The argument proceeds from the assumption that Israel exists and lives its life in places other than Zion to the assertion that it must find its hope for life and fertility precisely at Zion. In essence, although there is no outright statement that non-Jerusalemites are expected to make pilgrimage (possibly excepting Psalm 122), the whole thrust of the redactional materials is an implicit argument for it. Indeed, the two songs that provide a frame for the entire collection,

Psalms 120 and 134, reinforce this implicit argument with a sort of narrative structure of pilgrimage. Psalm 120 decries a situation that, although not necessarily diasporic, certainly reminds one of the diaspora. The complainant laments having dwelled long "in Meshek" and "among the tents of Qedar." Psalm 134 has the worshiper being blessed by the priests at the temple in Jerusalem. This quasi-narrative framework throws new light on the other songs of the redactional layer as well. Psalm 121 becomes a song for safe keeping on the journey; Psalm 122 becomes a celebration of the end of the journey and entry into the city; Psalm 132 becomes the ritual procession up to the temple following the pilgrimage proper; Psalm 133 becomes a celebration of common life in the city during the procession; and Psalm 134 ends the collection in the temple courts and receiving God's blessing.

The Use of the Songs of Ascents

That this narrative structuring is the work of the redactor is relatively clear. What is also clear is that this narrative framework is a redirection, a reinterpretation, of songs that came from elsewhere, possibly from small towns in north Israel. The question that must finally be addressed is, Why? What is it about the nucleus songs that makes them important enough to edit and transmit in a new context? Why did they need reshaping before they could be transmitted? How did the editor intend for this collection to be used?

I believe that the answer to these questions lies with the rhetorical character of the collection. The songs themselves mention a variety of concretely identifiable regions, from the Negev in the extreme south to Mt. Hermon in the extreme northern part of what had been Israel, and even as far away as Qedarites in Arabia and Meshek near the Black Sea. Not only places named but also sociological indications presuppose various locations. Viewed as a piece of rhetoric, the central point of the Songs of Ascents would seem to be that Jews in all of these locations— and by extension, Jews wherever they are—must look to Jerusalem as the source of their prosperity. If this is correct, then the nucleus songs would seem to have been included *because* they were folk songs from outside Jerusalem. The nucleus songs pray for God's blessing, seek

God's curse against enemies, and assure that it is only with God's help that prosperity can come about; the redactor asserts that God's help is primarily available at Jerusalem. In order to accomplish this task the editor reshaped them, both by editing several of the individual songs and, perhaps more significantly, by framing them in a new interpretative context. This appropriation of folk songs would have been a powerful rhetorical tool in an effort to convince Israelites from outlying areas to make pilgrimage to Jerusalem.[43]

The use of folk traditions by centralized powers in order to provide a *mythos* for the state is of course not new in the Persian era. It is precisely a program of this sort that is carried out by the Yahwistic and Elohistic authors of the Pentateuchal sources. It seems probable to me that the so-called "library of Asshurbanipal" seeks to accomplish similar ends in its accumulation and revision of folk traditions from various parts of the Assyrian empire. It is probably impossible, therefore, to argue that a program of this sort is *characteristically* Persian; on the other hand, other cases of this phenomenon during the Persian era[44] demonstrate that such a program is certainly possible in the Persian era. It is known, in other words, that redactors sometimes made use of local religious traditions to support centralization of power. It seems to me likely that this type of program is what underlies the redaction of the Songs of Ascents.

---

[43]One's motivations are of course seldom a simple matter. I think it likely that the redactor had benign intentions in editing the collection in this manner. It seems obvious, but perhaps should be stated forthrightly, that empires also provide real and lasting benefits, and that political rhetoric need not necessarily be self-serving. Moreover, it seems likely that to some degree the community(ies) that prayed the nucleus songs already felt some connection to Zion and Jerusalem (cf. Psalm 126); otherwise there would be little force to the redactor's argument.

[44]Analogous phenomena include the declaration of Cyrus in support of, and claiming support from, local religious manifestations; Deutero-Isaiah's application of messianic titles to Cyrus; Haggai's use of popular religious questions in support of rebuilding the temple; and the Chronicler's application of "Canaanite" versus "Israelite" to the new political situation.

BIBLIOGRAPHY

Ackroyd, Peter R. *Exile and Restoration: A Study of Hebrew Thought of the Sixth Century B.C.* OTL. Philadelphia: Westminister, 1968.

_____. *Israel Under Babylon and Persia.* Oxford: Oxford University Press, 1986.

Aejmelaus, Anneli. *The Traditional Prayer in the Psalms.* BZAW, no. 167. Berlin: Walter de Gruyter, 1986.

Aharoni, Yohanan. "'Arad: Its Inscriptions and Temple." *BA* 31 (1968): 2-32.

_____. *The Land of the Bible: A Historical Geography.* Revised ed. Philadelphia: Westminster, 1979.

Ahlström, Gösta W. *The History of Ancient Palestine.* 2d ed. Minneapolis, MN: Fortress, 1994.

_____. *Joel and the Temple Cult of Jerusalem.* Leiden: E. J. Brill, 1971.

Albright, William Foxwell. "Notes on Psalms 68 and 134." In *Interpretationes ad Vetus Testamentum pertinentes Sigmund Mowinckel*, ed. Land Ogkirke, 1-12. Oslo: Fabritius & Sonner, 1955.

Alden, Robert. "Chiastic Psalms (III): A Study in the Mechanics of Semitic Poetry in Psalms 101-150." *JETS* 21 (1978): 199-210.

Aletti, Jean-Noël, and Jaques Trublet. *Approche poétique et théologique des psaumes.* Paris: Initiation, Editions du Cerf, 1983.

Alexander, Joseph A. *The Psalms.* Edinburgh: Andrew Elliott, 1864.

Allen, Leslie C. *Psalms 101-150.* WBC, ed. John D. W. Watts, and Ralph P. Martin, no. 21. Waco, TX: Word Books, 1983.

Alonso-Schökel, Luis, and Andrzej Strus. "Salmo 122: Canto al nombre de Jerusalén [sic]." *Bib* 61 (1980): 234-250.

Alter, Robert. *The Art of Biblical Poetry.* New York: Basic Books, 1985.

Althann, Robert. "Does ʾet (ʾaet) sometimes signify 'from' in the Hebrew Bible?" *ZAW* 103 (1991): 121-124.

Andersen, Francis I., and A. Dean Forbes. *Spelling in the Hebrew Bible*. BibOr, no. 41. Rome: Pontifical Biblical Institute, 1986.

Anderson, Arnold Albert. *The Book of Psalms*. NCB. Grand Rapids, MI: Eerdmans, 1972; reprint, softback, 1981.

Anderson, Bernhard W. *Out of the Depths: The Psalms Speak for Us Today*. Philadelphia: Fortress, 1970; reprint, 1974.

Anderson, George W. "Israel: Amphictyony: ʿam; ḳāhāl; ʿēḏâh." In *Translating and Understanding the Old Testament: Essays in Honor of Herbert G. May*, ed. Harry Thomas Frank, and William L. Reed, 135-151. Nashville: Abingdon, 1970.

Arconada, R. "Psalmus 129 (130) «De profundus» retentus, emendatus, glossatus." *VD* 12 (1932): 213-219.

Armfield, H. T. *The Gradual Psalms, a treatise on the fifteen Songs of Degrees with Commentary*. London: J. T. Hayes, 1874.

Asensio, Félix. "El Salmo 132 y la 'lámpara' de David." *Greg* 38 (1957): 310-316.

Auffret, Pierre. "Essai sur la structure littéraire du Psaume 133." *Biblische Notizen: Beiträge zur exegetischen Diskussion* 27 (1985): 22-34.

Auffret, Pierre. *La sagesse a bâti sa maison: Études de structures littéraires dans l'Ancien Testament et spécialment dans les Psaumes*. OBO, no. 49. Göttingen: Vandenhoeck & Ruprecht, 1982.

Auffret, Pierre, and David J. A. Clines translator. "Note on the Literary Structure of Psalm 134." *JSOT* 45 (1989): 87-89.

Baethgen, Friedrich. *Die Psalmen, übersetzt und erklärt*. HAT, Series 2, no. 2. Göttingen: Vandenhoeck & Ruprecht, 1904.

Balentine, Samuel E. *Prayer in the Hebrew Bible: The Drama of Divine-Human Dialogue*. OBT. Minneapolis: Fortress, 1993.

Banton, Michael, ed. *Anthropological Approaches to the Study of Religion*. Association of Social Anthropologists Monographs, no. 3. London: Tavistock Publications, 1966.

Barnes, O. L. *A New Approach to the Problem of the Hebrew Tenses*. Oxford: Thornton, 1965.

Barr, James. *Comparative Philology and the Text of the Old Testament, With Additions and Corrections*. Winona Lake, IN: Eisenbrauns, 1987.

_____. "Specimen Profile of One Book: The Book of Psalms." In *The Variable Spellings of the Hebrew Bible*, 212-215. Schweich Lectures of the British Academy, 1986. Oxford: Oxford University Press, 1989.

_____. *Variable Spellings of the Hebrew Bible*. Schweich Lectures of the British Academy, 1986. Oxford: Oxford University Press, 1989.

Baumann, Eberhard. "Struktur-Untersuchen im Psalter II." *ZAW* 62 (1950): 140-144.

Beaucamp, Évode. "L'unité du recueil des montées: Psaumes 120-134." *Studium Biblicum Franciscanum, Liber anuus* 29 (1979): 73-90.

_____. *Le Psautier*. Vol. 2, *Ps 73-150*. SB, series 8 (traduction), no. 114. Paris: J. Gabalda, 1979.

Bee, R. E. "The Textual Analysis of Psalm 132: A Response to Cornelius B. Houk." *JSOT* 6 (1978): 49-53.

Bellinger, William H., Jr. *Psalmody and Prophecy*. JSOTSup, no. 27. Sheffield: JSOT Press, 1984.

_____. *Psalms: Reading and Studying the Book of Praises*. Peabody, MA: Hendrickson, 1990.

Berger, Peter L. *The Sacred Canopy: Elements of a Sociological Theory of Religion*. New York: Doubleday, 1967.

Berlin, Adele. *Biblical Poetry Through Medieval Jewish Eyes*. Indiana Studies in Biblical Literature. Bloomington, IN: Indiana University Press, 1991.

_____. *The Dynamics of Biblical Parallelism*. Bloomington, IN: Indiana University Press, 1985.

_____. "On the Interpretation of Psalm 133." In *Directions in Biblical Hebrew Poetry*, ed. Elaine R. Follis, 141-147. JSOTSup 40. Sheffield: Sheffield Academic Press, 1987.

Berquist, Jon L. *Judaism in Persia's Shadow: A Social and Historical Approach*. Minneapolis, MN: Fortress, 1995.

Beyerlin, Walter. "Die Toda der Heilsvergegenwärtigung in den Klageliedern des Einzelnen." *ZAW* 79 (1967): 208-224.

_____. *Rettung der Bedrängten in den Feindpsalmen der Einzelnen auf institutionelle Zusammenhänge untersucht*. Göttingen: Vandenhoeck & Ruprecht, 1970.

_____. *We Are Like Dreamers: Studies in Psalm 126*. Translated by Dinah Livingstone. Edinburgh: T. & T. Clark, 1982.

_____. *Weisheitliche Vergewisserung mit Bezug auf den Zionskult: Studien zum 125. Psalm*. OBO 68. Göttingen: Vandenhoeck & Ruprecht, 1985.

_____. *Wider die Hybris des Geistes: Studien zum 131. Psalm*. SBS 108. Stuttgart: Katholisches Bibelwerk, 1982.

_____. *"Wir sind wie Traumende": Studien zur 126. Psalm*. SBS, no. 89. Stuttgart: Katholisches Bibelwerk, 1978.

Bird, Phyllis. "The Place of Women in the Israelite cultus." In *Ancient Israelite Religion: Essays in Honor of Frank Moore Cross*, ed. Jr. Patrick D. Miller, Paul D. Hanson, and S. Dean McBride, 397-419. Philadelphia: Fortress, 1987.

_____. "Women's Religion in Ancient Israel." In *Women's Earliest Records from Ancient Egypt and Western Asia*, ed. Barbara J. Lesko, 283-298. Brown Judaic Studies, 166. Atlanta: Scholars Press, 1989.

Birkeland, Harris. *Evildoers in the Book of Psalms*. Oslo: Jacob Dybwad, 1955.

Bishop, John. "God's Gift of Sleep." *ExpTim* 90 (1979): 339-341.

Blakeney, E. H. "Psalm 121,1-2." *ExpTim* 56 (1944/5): 111.

Blenkinsopp, Joseph. "The Mission of Udjahorresnet and Those of Ezra and Nehemiah." *JBL* 106 (1987): 409-421.

Bloemendaal, Willem. *The Headings of the Psalms in the East Syrian Church.* Leiden: E. J. Brill, 1960.

Borger, Riekele. "Zu שוב שבות/ית." *ZAW* 66 (1954): 315-316.

Bosniak, Jacob, ed. *The Commentary of David Kimhi on the Fifth Book of the Psalms CVII-CL, edited on the basis of Manuscripts and Early Editions of the fifteenth and sixteenth centuries in the Library of Jewish Theological Seminary of America.* New York: Bloch, 1954.

Bovet, Félix. *Les Psaumes de Maaloth: Essai d'explication.* Paris: Neuchatel, 1889.

Boylan, Patrick Canon. *Psalms: A Study of the Vulgate Psalter in the Light of the Hebrew Text.* St. Louis: B. Herder, 1931.

Braslavi, Joseph. "תהלים קל״ג, נ כטל חרמון שיורד על הררי ציון." *Bet Mikra* 49 (1972): 143-145.

Braude, William G. *Midrash on Psalms.* Vol. 2. Yale Judaica Series, no. 13. New Haven: Yale University Press, 1959.

Breckelmans, C. H. W. "Psalm 132: Unity and Structure." *Bijdragen, Tijdschirft voor filosofie en theologie* 44 (1983): 262-265.

_____. "Some Translation Problems. Judges 5:29, Psalm 120:7, Jona 4:4, 9." *OTS* 15 (1969): 170-176.

Brennan, J. P. "Some Hidden Harmonies in the Fifth Book of the Psalms." In *Essays in Honor of Joseph P. Brennan*, ed. R. F. McNamara. Rochester, NY: St. Bernard's Seminary, 1976.

Briggs, Charles Augustus, and Emilie Grace Briggs. *A Critical and Exegetical Commentary on the Book of Psalms.* ICC, no. 15. New York: Charles Scribner and Sons, 1906.

Bright, John. *Jeremiah.* Anchor Bible, no. 21. Garden City, New York: Doubleday, 1965.

Brin, Gershon. "The Significance of the Form *Mah-ṭṭob*." *VT* 38 (1988): 462-465.

Broshi, Magen. "Estimating the Population of Ancient Jerusalem." *BARev* 4 (1978): 10-15.

Broyles, Craig C. *The Conflict of Faith and Experience in the Psalms.* JSOTSup, ed. David J. A. Clines, and Philip R. Davies, no. 52. Sheffield: JSOT Press, 1989.

Brueggemann, Walter. *Abiding Astonishment: Psalms, Modernity, and the Making of History.* Literary Currents in Biblical Interpretation. Philadelphia: Westminster/John Knox, 1991.

_____. "Bounded by Obedience and Praise: The Psalms as Canon." *JSOT* 50 (1991): 63-92.

_____. *Israel's Praise: Doxology Against Idolatry and Ideology.* Nashville: Fortress, 1988.

_____. *The Message of the Psalms, A Theological Commentary*. Augsburg Old Testament Studies. Minneapolis: Augsburg, 1984.

Buss, Martin. "The Psalms of Asaph and Korah." *JBL* 82 (1963): 382-392.

_____. "The Idea of Sitz-im-Leben—History and Critique." *ZAW* 90 (1978): 157-170.

Bussby, F. "A Note on שֶׁנָּא in Ps. CXXVII 2." *JTS* 35 (1934): 306-307.

Buttenweiser, Moses. *The Psalms, Chronologically Treated, with a New Translation*. Library of Biblical Studies. New York: KTAV, 1969.

Calès, J. *Le livre des Psaumes*. Paris: Beauchesne, 1936.

Calvin, John. *Calvin's Commentaries*. Vol. 5, *A Commentary on the Book of Psalms*. Translated by James Anderson. Grand Rapids, MI: Eerdmans, 1949.

Carroll, Robert P. "The Myth of the Empty Land." In *Ideological Criticism of Biblical Texts*, ed. David Jobling and Tina Pippin, 79-93. Semeia: An Experimental Journal for Biblical Criticism. Atlanta: Scholars Press, 1992.

Carter, Charles Edward. "A Social and Demographic Study of Post-Exilic Judah." Ph.D. dissertation, Duke University, 1992.

Cartledge, Tony W. "Conditional Vows in the Psalms of Lament: A New Approach to an Old Problem." In *The Listening Heart: Essays in Wisdom and the Psalms in Honor of Roland E. Murphy, O. Carm.*, ed. Kenneth G. Hoglund, 77-94. JSOTSup, vol. 58. Sheffield: JSOT Press, 1987.

Cassuto, Umberto. *A Commentary on the Book of Genesis*. Vol. 1, *From Adam to Noah*. Translated by Israel Abrahams. Jerusalem: Central Press, 1961.

Ceresko, Anthony R. "Psalm 121: A Prayer of a Warrior?" *Bib* 70 (1989): 496-510.

_____. "The Sage in the Psalms." In *The Sage in Israel and the Ancient Near East*, ed. John G. Gammie, and Leo G. Perdue, 217-230. Winona Lake, IN: Eisenbrauns, 1990.

Chadwick, Henry. *Early Christian Thought and the Classical Tradition: Studies in Justin, Clement, and Origen*. New York: Oxford University Press, 1966.

Charlesworth, James H. "Jewish Hymns, Odes, and Prayers (ca. 167 B.C.E.-135 C.E.)." In *Early Judaism and Its Modern Interpreters*, ed. Robert A. Kraft, and George W. E. Nickelsburg. The Bible and Its Modern Interpreters. Atlanta: Scholars Press, 1986.

Childs, Brevard S. *Introduction to the Old Testament as Scripture*. Philadelphia: Fortress, 1979.

_____. *Memory and Tradition in Israel*. SBT, no. 37. London: SCM, 1962.

_____. "Psalm Titles and Midrashic Exegesis." *JSS* 16 (1971): 137-150.

Clarisse, Theodoro Adriano. *Psalmi Quindecim Hammaäloth, Philologice et Critice Illustrati*. Lugduni Batavorum: H. W. Hazenberg, 1819.

Clark, Mary T. "'Introductory Note' to *Homiles on the Psalms*." In *Augustine of Hippo: Selected Writings*, 197-198. New York: Paulist, 1984.

Clements, Ronald Ernest. *In Spirit and in Truth: Insights from Biblical Prayers.* Atlanta: John Knox, 1985.

_____. *Isaiah 1-39.* NCB, ed. Ronald E Clements (OT), and Matthew Black (NT). Grand Rapids, MI: Wm. B. Eerdmans, 1980.

_____, ed. *The World of Ancient Israel: Sociological, Anthropological, and Political Perspectives.* Cambridge: Cambridge University Press, 1989.

Clines, David J. A. "Psalm Research Since 1955: I. The Psalms and the Cult." *TynBul* 18 (1967): 103-126.

Closen, Gustav E., S.J. "Gottvertrauen und Selbstbescheidung in der Lehre der Schrift des Alten Bundes." *GL* 15 (1940): 187-197.

Cody, Aelred. *A History of Old Testament Priesthood.* AnBib, no. 35. Rome: Pontifical Biblical Institute, 1969.

Cohen, A. *The Psalms: Hebrew Text, English Translation and Commentary.* Hindhead, Surrey: Soncino, 1945.

Cooper, Alan. "The Absurdity of Amos 6:12a." *JBL* 107 (1988): 725-727.

Cooper, Charles M. "Jerome's «Hebrew Psalter» and the New Latin Version." *JBL* 69 (1950): 233-244.

Cornill, C. H. "Psalm 130." In *Festschrift für Karl Budde zum siebzigsten Geburtstag am 13. April 1920,* ed. Karl Marti, 38-42. BZAW, no. 34. Giessen: Alfred Töpelmann, 1920.

Cox, Samuel. *The Pilgrim Psalms: An Exposition of the Songs of Degrees.* London: Daldy, Ibister, 1874.

Craigie, Peter C. "Psalm 113." *Int* 39 (1985): 70-74.

_____. *Psalms 1-50.* WBC, ed. John D. W. Watts, and Ralph P. Martin, no. 19. Waco, TX: Word Books, 1983.

Crenshaw, James L. *Old Testament Wisdom: An Introduction.* Atlanta: John Knox, 1981.

_____. "Research in Wisdom Literature: Retrospect and Prospect." Paper presented to the Israelite and Early Christian Wisdom Section, Society of Biblical Literature Annual Meeting, New Orleans, LA, 1990.

_____. *A Whirlpool of Torment: Israelite Traditions of God as an Oppressive Presence.* OBT. Philadelphia: Fortress, 1984.

Crim, Keith. *Royal Psalms.* Richmond, VA: John Knox, 1962.

Croft, Steven J. L. *The Identity of the Individual in the Psalms.* JSOTSup, no. 44. Sheffield: JSOT Press, 1987.

Cross, Frank Moore. *Canaanite Myth and Hebrew Epic.* Cambridge: Harvard University Press, 1973.

_____, and David Noel Freedman. *Studies in Ancient Yahwistic Poetry.* SBLDS, no. 21. Missoula, MT: Scholars Press, 1975.

Crüsemann, Frank. *Studien zur Formgeschichte von Hymnus und Danklied in Israel.* Neukirchen: Neukirchener Verlag, 1969.

Culley, Robert C. *Oral Formulaic Language in the Biblical Psalms.* Toronto: University of Toronto Press, 1967.

Dahood, Mitchell. "The Aleph in Psalm CXXVII 2 šēnāʾ." *Or* 44 (1975): 103-105.

_____. *Psalms I (1-50).* Anchor Bible, no. 16. Garden City, NY: Doubleday, 1965.

_____. *Psalms II (51-100).* Anchor Bible, no. 17. Garden City, NY: Doubleday, 1968.

_____. *Psalms III (101-150).* Anchor Bible, no. 17A. Garden City, NY: Doubleday, 1970.

Daiches, Samuel. "Psalm 127. 2. A New Explanation." *ExpTim* 45 (1933-34): 24-26.

Dalman, Gustaf Hermann. *Arbeit und Sitte in Palästina.* 7 vols. Beitrage zur Förderung christlicher Theologie, series 2, no. 33. Gütersloh: C. Bertelsman, 1928-1942; reprint, Hildesheim: Georg Olms Verlagsbuchhandlung, 1964.

Davies, Eryl W. "Inheritance Rights and the Hebrew Levirate Marriage." *VT* 31 (1981): 138-144, 257-268.

Day, John. "Asherah in the Hebrew Bible and Northwest Semitic Literature." *JBL* 105 (1986): 386-408.

de Boer, Pieter Arie Hendrik. "Psalm CXXXI 2." *VT* 16 (1966): 287-292.

de Rossi, Johann Bernhard. *Variae lectiones Veteris Testamenti librorum.* Vol. 4. Amsterdam: Philo, 1970.

de Vries, Simon. "Moses and David as Cult Founders in Chronicles." *JBL* 107 (1988): 619-639.

de Wette, Wilhelm Martin. *Kommentar über die Psalmen.* Breslau: Herrmann Kelsch, 1885.

de Witt, John. *Psalms: A New Translation, with Introductory Essay and Notes.* New York: Anson D. F. Randolf and co., 1891.

Deiss, Lucien. "Le lectionnaire dominical: le psaume graduel." *Assemblées du Seignor (2d series)* 3 (1968): 49-72.

Deissler, Alfons. *Die Psalmen.* Düsseldorf: Patmos, 1963.

Delamare, J. "Les Psaumes des montées, Jérusalem, commentés par S. Augustine." *Verbum Salutis* 81 (1949): 478-493.

Delcor, Mattias. "Zum Psalter von Qumran." *BZ* 10 (1966): 15-29.

Delekat, L. "Probleme der Psalmenüberschriften." *ZAW* 76 (1964): 280-297.

Delitzsch, Franz. *Commentary on the Old Testament in Ten Volumes by C. F. Keil and F. Delitzsch.* Vol. 5, *Psalms.* Translated by Francis Bolton. Grand Rapids, MI: Eerdmans, 1871; reprint, 1988.

Dentan, Robert C. "An Exposition of an Old Testament Passage." *JBR* 15 (1947): 158-161.

Descamps, Albert. "Genres littéraires du Psautier. Un état de la question." In *Le Psautier: Ses origines. Ses problèmes littéraires. Son influence.*, ed. Robert DeLanghe, 73-88. Études présentées aux XIIe Journées Bibliques (29-31 doȗt 1960). Louvain-Leuven: Publications Universitaires et Institut Orientaliste, 1962.

Deurloo, Karel. "Gedächtnis des Exils—Psalm 120-134." *Theologie und Kirche* 55 (1992): 28-34.

Devreesse, Robert. *Les anciens commentateurs grecs des Psaumes.* Studia e testi, no. 264. Vatican City: Biblioteca apostolica vaticans, 1970.

Dietrich, E. L. שׁוּב שְׁבוּת. *Die endzeitliche Wiederstellung bei den Propheten.* BZAW, no. 40. Gießen: Alfred Töpelmann, 1925.

Donner, Herbert. "Psalm 122." In *Text and Context: Old Testament and Semitic Studies for F. C. Fensham*, ed. W. Classen, 81-91. JSOTSup 48. Sheffield: JSOT Press, 1988.

Drijvers, Pius. *The Psalms: Their Structure and Meaning.* New York: Herdner and Herdner, 1965.

Driver, Godfrey Rolles. "Notes on the Psalms. II. 73-150." *JTS* 44 (1943): 12-23.

_____. *Problems of the Hebrew Verbal System.* Edinburgh: T. & T. Clark, 1936.

Duhaime, J. L. Review of *Le Psautier*, by Évode Beaucamp. In *VT* 31 (1981): 493-498.

Duhm, Bernhard. *Die Psalmen.* 2d ed. HKAT, no. 14. Tübingen: J. C. B. Mohr (Paul Siebeck), 1922.

Durham, John I. "שָׁלוֹם and the Presence of God." In *Proclamation and Presence: Old Testament Essays in Honour of Gwynne Henton Davies*, ed. John I. Durham, and J. R. Porter, 272-293. Macon, GA: Mercer University Press, 1983.

Eerdmans, B. D. *The Hebrew Book of Psalms.* OTS, no. 4. Leiden: E. J. Brill, 1947.

Ehrlich, Arnold B. *Die Psalmen: neu übersetzt und erklärt.* Berlin: M. Poppelauer, 1905.

Eisenbeis, Walter. *Die Wurzel שׁלם im Alten Testament.* Berlin: Walter de Gruyter, 1969.

Eissfeldt, Otto. "Psalm 121." In *Kleine Schriften*, ed. Rudolf Sellheim, and Fritz Maass, 494-500. Vol. 3. Tübingen: J. C. B. Mohr [Paul Siebeck], 1966.

_____. "Psalm 132." In *Kleine Schriften*, ed. Rudolf Sellheim, and Fritz Maass, 481-485. Vol. 3. Tübingen: J. C. B. Mohr [Paul Siebeck], 1966.

Eliade, Mircea. *The Myth of the Eternal Return; or Cosmos and History.* Translated by Willard R. Trask. Princeton: Princeton University Press, 1971.

Emerton, J. A. "Meaning of *šēnāʾ* in Psalm CXXVII 2." *VT* 24 (1974): 15-31.

Enciso, J. "Los titulos de los Salmos y la historia de la formación der Saltero." *EstBib* 13 (1954): 135-166.

Engnell, Ivan. "The Book of Psalms." In *A Rigid Scrutiny: Critical Essays on the Old Testament*, 68-122. Nashville: Vanderbilt University Press, 1969.

Estes, Daniel J. "Like Arrows in the Hand of a Warrior (Psalm CXXVII)." *VT* 41 (1991): 304-311.

Ewald, Heinrich. *Allgemeines über die hebraeische Poesie und über das Psalmenbuch*. Die Dichter des alten Bundes, part 1. Göttingen: Vandenhoeck & Ruprecht, 1939.

_____. *Die poetischen Bücher des alten Bundes: Zweiter Theil: Die Psalmen*. Göttingen: Vandenhoeck & Ruprecht, 1833.

Exum, J. Cheryl. "The Tragic Vision and Biblical Narrative: The Case of Jephthah." In *Signs and Wonders: Biblical Texts in Literary Focus*, ed. J. Cheryl Exum, 59-83. Semeia: An Experimental Journal for Biblical Criticism. Atlanta: Scholars Press, 1989.

Falkenstein, Adam, and Wolfram von Soden. *Sumerische und akkadische Hymnen und Gebete*. Zurich: Artemis, 1953.

Feldman, Louis H. "Josephus's Portrait of Hezekiah." *JBL* 111 (1992): 597-610.

Fisch, Harold. *Poetry With a Purpose: Biblical Poetics and Interpretation*. Bloomington, IN: Indiana University Press, 1988.

Fishbane, Michael. *Biblical Interpretation in Ancient Israel*. Oxford: Clarendon, 1985.

Fitzmyer, Joseph A. *The Aramaic Inscriptions of Sefire*. BO 19. Rome: Pontifical Biblical Institute, 1967.

Fleming, Daniel E. "'House'/'City': An Unrecognized Parallel Word Pair." *JBL* 105 (1986): 689-693.

Franken, Handricus Jacobus. *The Mystical Communion with YHWH in the Book of Psalms*. Leiden: E. J. Brill, 1954.

Freedman, David Noel. "Divine Names and Titles in Early Hebrew Poetry." In *Magnalia Dei: The Mighty Acts of God*, ed. Frank Moore Cross. Garden City, NY: Doubleday, 1976.

Freehof, Solomon B. *The Book of Psalms: A Commentary*. Cincinnati: Union of American Hebrew Congregations, 1938.

Fretheim, Terence E. "Psalm 132: A Form-Critical Study." *JBL* 86 (1967): 289-300.

Gammie, John G. *Holiness in Israel*. OBT. Minneapolis: Augsburg Fortress, 1989.

Garr, W. Randall. *Dialect Geography of Syria-Palestine, 1000-586 B.C.E.* Philadelphia: University of Pennsylvania Press, 1985.

Geertz, Clifford. "Religion as a Cultural System." In *Anthropological Approaches to the Study of Religion*, ed. Michael Banton, 1-46. Association for Social Anthropology Monographs, no. 3. London: Tavistock Publications, 1966.

Gerstenberger, Erhard S. "The Lyrical Literature." In *The Hebrew Bible and Its Modern Interpreters*, ed. Douglas A. Knight, and Gene M. Tucker, 409-444. The Bible and Its Modern Interpreters. Philadelphia: Fortress, 1985.

_____. *Psalms: Part I with an Introduction to Cultic Poetry*. FOTL, no. 14. Grand Rapids, Michigan: Eerdmans, 1988.

_____, Konrad Jutzler, and Hans Jochen Boecker. *Die Psalmen in der Sprache unserer Zeit: Der Psalter und die Klagelieder eingeleitet, übersetzt und erklärt*. Neukirchen: Neukirchener Verlag, 1972.

Gese, Hartmut. "Die Entstehung der Büchereinteilung des Psalters." In *Wort, Lied und Gottesspruch. Beiträge zu Psalmen und Propheten. Festschrift für Joseph Ziegler*, ed. Joseph Schreiner, 57-64. Forschung zur Bibel 2. Würzburg: Echter-Verlag, 1972.

Gesenius, Wilhelm. *Thesaurus philologicus criticus linguae Hebrae et Chaldae Veteris Testamenti*. 2d ed. Lipsiae: Fr. Chr. Wil. Vogelius, 1839.

Gevirtz, Stanley. *Patterns in the Early Poetry of Israel*. Oriental Institute, University of Chicago Studies in Ancient Oriental Civilization, no. 32. Chicago: University of Chicago Press, 1973.

Gibson, John C. L. *Canaanite Myths and Legends*. 2d ed. Edinburgh: T. & T. Clark, 1978.

Glueck, Nelson. *Rivers in the Desert*. London: Weidenfeld and Nicholson, 1959.

Goeke, Hugo. "Gott, Mensch und Gemeinde in Ps 123." *BibLeb* 13 (1972): 124-128.

Gonzáles, Angel. *El Libro de los Salmos: Introducción, versión y commentario*. Biblioteca Herder: Sección de Sagrada Escritura, no. 73. Barcelona: Editorial Herder, 1966.

_____. "Concordia fraterna." *CB* 18 (1961): 228-298.

Gordon, Cyrus H. "North Israelite Influence on Postexilic Hebrew." *IEJ* 5 (1955): 85-88.

Gottwald, Norman K. *The Hebrew Bible: A Socio-Literary Introduction*. Philadelphia: Fortress, 1985.

_____, ed. *Social Scientific Criticism of the Hebrew Bible and Its Social World: The Israelite Monarchy*. Semeia, no. 37. Society of Biblical Literature, 1986.

_____. *The Tribes of Yahweh: A Sociology of the Religion of Liberated Israel, 1250-1050 B.C.E.* Maryknoll, NY: Orbis Books, 1979.

Goulder, Michael D. *The Psalms of the Sons of Korah*. JSOTSup, no. 20. Sheffield: JSOT Press, 1982.

Grabbe, Lester L. *Judaism from Cyrus to Hadrian*. Vol. 1, *The Persian and Greek Periods*. Minneapolis: Fortress, 1992.

Greer, Rowan A. *Origen*. New York: Paulist, 1979.

Grossberg, Daniel. *Centripetal and Centrifugal Structures in Biblical Poetry*. SBLMS, ed. Adela Yarbro Collins, and E. F. Campbell, no. 39. Atlanta: Scholars Press, 1989.

_____. "The Disparate Elements of the Inclusion in Psalms." *HAR* 6 (1982): 97-104.

Gunkel, Hermann. *Einleitung in die Psalmen: Die Gattungen der religiösen Lyrik Israels.* 3d ed. Translated by Ed. Joachim Begrich. Göttingen: Vandenhoeck & Ruprecht, 1966.

_____. *Die Psalmen, übereßt und erklärt.* HKAT, no. 2. Göttingen: Vandenhoeck & Ruprecht, 1926.

_____. "Psalm 133." In *Festschrift für Karl Budde zum siebzigsten Geburtstag am 13. April 1920,* ed. Karl Marti, 69-74. BZAW, no. 34. Giessen: Alfred Töpelmann, 1920.

Habel, Norman C. "'Yahweh, Maker of heaven and Earth': A Study in Tradition Criticism." *JBL* 91 (1972): 321-337.

Haglund, Erik. *Historical Motifs in the Psalms.* ConBOT, no. 23. Lund: C. W. K. Gleerup, 1984.

Hamp, Vinzenz. "Der Herr gibt es den Seinen im Schlaf, Ps 127,2d." In *Wort, Lied und Gottesspruch. Beiträge zu Psalmen und Propheten. Festschrift für Joseph Ziegler,* ed. Joseph Schreiner, 71-79. Forschung zur Bibel 2. Würzburg: Echter Verlag, 1972.

Hanson, Paul D. *The People Called: The Growth of Community in the Bible.* San Francisco: Harper and Row, 1986.

Harman, Allan M. "The Setting and Interpretation of Psalm 126." *RefThR* 44 (1985): 74-80.

Haupt, Paul. "On the Penitential Psalm 'De Profundis'." *Hebraica* 2 (1885): unsure.

Hayes, John H. *Understanding the Psalms.* Valley Forge, PA: Judson, 1976.

_____, and J. Maxwell Miller. *A History of Ancient Israel and Judah.* Philadelphia: Westminster, 1986.

Hengstenberg, Ernst W. *Commentary on the Psalms.* 2d ed. Vol. 3. Translated by John Thomson and Patrick Fairbairn. Edinburgh: T. & T. Clark, 1854.

Herder, Johann Gottfried. *The Spirit of Hebrew Poetry.* Translated by James Marsh. Burlington: Edward Smith, 1833.

Hess, Richard S. "Hebrew Psalms and Amarna Correspondence from Jerusalem: Some Comparisons and Implications." *ZAW* 101 (1989): 249-265.

Higgins, A. G. McL. Pearce. "A Metrical Version of Psalm 127." *CQR* 166 (1965): 425.

Hillers, Delbert R. "Ritual Procession of the Ark and Ps 132." *CBQ* 30 (1968): 48-55.

Hirsch, Samson Raphael. *The Psalms.* New York: Philipp Feldheim, 1966.

Hitzig, Ferdinand. *Die Psalmen, uebersetzt und ausgelegt.* Leipzig and Heidelburg: C. F. Winter'sche Verlagshandlung, 1863.

Hockey, F. "Cantica graduum. The Graduel Psalms in Patristic Tradition." *Studia Patristica* 10 (1970): 355-359.

Hoglund, Kenneth. "The Achaemenid Context." In *Second Temple Studies: 1. Persian Period,* ed. Philip R. Davies, 53-72. JSOTS, no. 117. Sheffield: Sheffield Academic Press, 1991.

_____. "Material Culture of the Persian Period and the Sociology of the Second Temple Period." Paper presented to the Sociology of the Second Temple Period Group, Society of Biblical Literature Annual Meeting, New Orleans, 1990.

Holladay, William L. *The Psalms through Three Thousand Years: Prayerbook of a Cloud of Witnesses.* Minneapolis: Fortress, 1993.

Hopkins, David C. *The Highlands of Canaan: Agricultural Life in the Early Iron Age.* SWBA, ed. James W. Flanagan, no. 3. Decatur, GA: Almond, 1985.

Houk, Cornelius B. "Psalm 132, Literary Integrity, and Syllable-Word Structures." *JSOT* 6 (1978): 41-48.

_____. "Psalm 132: Further Discussion." *JSOT* 6 (1978): 54-57.

Howard, David M., Jr. "Editorial Activity in the Psalter: A State-of-the-Field Survey." *WW* 9 (1989): 274-285.

Howell, James C. "Jerome's Homiles on the Psalter in Bethlehem." In *The Listening Heart: Essays in Wisdom and the Psalms in Honor of Roland E. Murphy, O. Carm.*, ed. Kenneth G. Hoglund et al. JSOTSup, vol. 58. Sheffield: JSOT Press, 1987.

Hulst, Alexander Reinard. "Psalm 126." In *Herr, tue meine Lippen auf: Eine Predigthilfe*, ed. Georg Eichholz, 567-577. Vol. 5. 2d ed. Wuppertal-Barmen: Emil Müller, 1961.

Humbert, Paul. "'Étendre le main' (note de lexicographie hébraïque)." *VT* 12 (1962): 383-395.

Hupfeld, Hermann. *Die Psalmen. Übersetzt und ausgelegt.* Vol. 3,4. Gotha: Friedrich Andreas Perthes, 1860, 1862.

Hurvitz, Avi. "אימתי נטבע בעברית הצירוף ׳שלום על ישראל׳." *Leš* 27/28 (1964): 297-302.

_____. "Wisdom Vocabulary in the Hebrew Psalter: A Contribution to the Study of 'Wisdom Psalms'." *VT* 38 (1988): 41-51.

Huwiler, Elizabeth F. "Patterns and Problems in Psalm 132." In *The Listening Heart: Essays in Wisdom and the Psalms in Honor of Roland E. Murphy, O. Carm.*, ed. Kenneth G. Hoglund, 199-215. JSOTSup, vol. 58. Sheffield: JSOT Press, 1987.

Huyck, Mary Cecilia. "Psalm-City: A Study of Psalm 127." *Worship* 40 (1966): 510-519.

Hvidberg, Flemming Friis, and ed. F. Løkkegaard. *Weeping and Laughter in the Old Testament: A Study of Canaanite-Israelite Religion.* Revised ed. Translated by Niels Haislund. Leiden: E. J. Brill, 1962.

Hyman, Semah Cecil. "Pilgrimage." *EncJud* 13 :510-519.

Irsigler, Hubert. "'Umsonst ist es, dass ihr früh aufsteht...': Psalm 127 und die Kritik der Arbeit in Israels Weisheitsliteratur." *Biblische Notizen: Beiträge zur exegetischen Diskussion* 37 (1987): 48-72.

Jauss, Hannelore. *Tor der Hoffnung: Vergleichsformen und ihre Funktion in der Sprache der Psalmen.* Europäische Hochschulschriften; Series 23, Theologie, no. 412. Frankfurt am Main; New York: Peter Lang, 1991.

Jellicoe, Sidney. *The Septuagint and Modern Study.* Oxford: Oxford University Press, 1968; reprint, Winona Lake, IN: Eisenbrauns, 1989.

Jenni, Ernst. Review of *Die Wallfahrtspsalmen: Studien zur Entstehungsgeschichte von Psalm 120-134*, by Klaus Seybold. In *TRu* 46 (1981): 98-99.

_____. "Zu den doxologischen Schlussformeln des Psalters." *TZ* 40 (1984): 114-120.

Jeremias, Jörg. *Das Königtum Gottes in den Psalmen. Israels Begegnung mit dem kanaanäischen Mythos in den Jahwe-König-Psalmen.* FRLANT, no. 141. Göttingen: Vandenhoeck & Ruprecht, 1987.

_____. "Lade und Zion. Zur Enstehung der Ziontradition." In *Probleme biblischer Theologie. G. von Rad zum 70. Geburtstag*, ed. Hans Walter Wolff, 183-198. Munich: C. Kaiser, 1971.

Jirku, Anton. *Altorientalischer Kommentar zum Alten Testament.* Hildesheim: H. A. Gerstenberg, 1972.

Jobling, David, Peggy L. Day, and Gerald T. Shepherd, eds. *The Bible and the Politics of Exegesis.* Cleveland, OH: Pilgrim, 1991.

_____, and Tina Pippin, eds. *Ideological Criticism of Biblical Texts.* Semeia, no. 59. Atlanta: Scholars Press, 1992.

Johnson, Aubrey R. *Sacral Kingship in Ancient Israel.* Cardiff: University of Wales, 1967.

Joüon, Paul. *Grammaire de l'hébreu biblique.* Graz, Austria: Akademischen Druck, 1965.

Kaiser, Walter J., Jr. *The Journey Isn't Over: The Pilgrim Psalms for Life's Challenges and Joys.* Grand Rapids, MI: Baker Book House, 1993.

Kautsch, E. *Gesenius' Hebrew Grammar.* Revised by A. E. Cowley. 2d ed. Oxford: Clarendon, 1910; reprint, 1983.

Keel, Othmar. "Kultische Brüderlichkeit — Ps 133." *FreibZ* 23 (1976): 68-80.

_____. *The Symbolism of the Biblical World: Ancient Near Eastern Iconography and the Book of Psalms.* New York: Seabury, 1978.

Keet, Cuthbert C. *A Study of the Psalms of Ascents: A Critical and Exegetical Commentary upon Psalms CXX to CXXIV.* London: Mitre, 1969.

Keller, Carl. "Les «béatitudes» de l'ancien testament." In *Hommage Wilhelm Vischer*, ed. Jean Cadier, 88-100. Montpellier: Causse, Graille, Castelnau, 1960.

Keßler, Hans. *Psalmen für die zweite Auflage überseßt und ausgelegt.* Vol. 1. Kurzgefaßter Kommentar zu den heiligen Schriften, A. Altes Testament, no. 6. Munich: C. H. Bech'sche Verlagsbuchhandlung, 1899.

Kidner, Derek. *Psalms 73-150: A Commentary on Books 3-5 of the Psalms.* Tyndale Old Testament Commentaries. London: Inter-Varsity Press, 1975.

Kilian, Rudolf. "»Tau« in Ps 110,3 — ein Misverständnis?" *ZAW* 102 (1990): 417-419.

Kimhi, David. *The Commentary of Rabbi David Kimḥi on Psalms CXX-CL.* Translated by and Trans. Joshua Baker and Ernest W. Nicholson. Cambridge: Cambridge University Press, 1973.

Kirkpatrick, A. F. *The Book of Psalms.* CBC. Cambridge: Cambridge University Press, 1902; reprint, 1939.

Kissane, E. J. *The Book of Psalms.* 2 vols. Dublin: Browne and Nolan, 1953/54; reprint, in one volume, 1964.

Kitchen, K. A. *Ancient Orient and Old Testament.* Downers Grove, IL: Intervarsity Press, 1966.

Kittel, Bonnie Pedrotti. *The hymns of Qumran: Translation and Commentary.* SBLDS, no. 50. Missoula, MT: Scholars Press, 1980.

Kittel, Rudolf. *Die Psalmen, übersetzt und erklärt.* 4th ed. KAT, no. 13. Leipzig: A. Deichertsche Verlagsbuchhandlung, 1922.

Knierim, Rolf. "Criticism of Literary Features, Form, Tradition, and Redaction." In *The Hebrew Bible and its Modern Interpreters,* ed. Douglas A. Knight, and Gene M. Tucker, 123-165. Philadelphia: Fortress, 1985.

Knight, George A. F. *The Psalms.* Vol. 2. The Daily Study Bible. Philadelphia: Westminster, 1982.

Koehler, Ludwig, and Walter Baumgartner, eds. *Lexicon in veteris testamenti libros.* 2d ed. Leiden: E. J. Brill, 1958.

Kraus, Hans-Joachim. "Der lebendige Gott." *Biblisch-theologische Aufsätze* (1972): 1-36.

——————. *Die Psalmen.* 5th ed. 2 vols. BKAT, no. 15. Neukirchen: Neukirchener Verlag, 1978.

——————. *Psalms 1-59.* Translated by Hilton C. Oswald. Minneapolis: Augsburg, 1988.

——————. *Psalms 60-150.* Translated by Hilton C. Oswald. Minneapolis: Augsburg, 1989.

——————. *Theology of the Psalms.* Translated by Keith R. Crim. Minneapolis: Augsburg, 1986.

——————. *Worship in Israel: A Cultic History of the Old Testament.* Translated by Geoffrey Buswell. Oxford: Basil Blackwell, 1966.

Kroon, J. "Ita filii excessorum." *VD* 11 (1931): 42.

——————. "Sicut torrent in austro (Ps. 125,4)." *VD* 10 (1930): 337.

Kruse, Heinz. "Psalm cxxxii and the Royal Zion Festival." *VT* 33 (1983): 279-297.

Kugel, James L. *The Idea of Biblical Poetry: Parallelism and its History.* New Haven: Yale University Press, 1981.

Kuntz, J. Kenneth. "The Canonical Wisdom Psalms of Ancient Israel--Their Rhetorical, Thematic, and Formal Dimensions." In *Rhetorical Criticism: Essays in Honor of James Muilenburg*, ed. Jared J Jackson, and Martin Kessler, 186-222. Pittsburgh Theological Monograph Series, vol. 1. Pittsburgh: Pickwick, 1974.

Kurzke, Hermann. "Saekularization oder Realization: Zur Wirkungsgeschichte von Psalm 130 ("De profundis") in der deutschen Literatur von Luther bis zur Gegenwart." In *Liturgie und Dichtung*, ed. H. Becker, and R. Kaczynski, 67-89. Vol. 2. St. Ottilien: EOS Verlag Erzabtei St. Ottilien, 1983.

Kutscher, Eduard Yecheskel. *A History of the Hebrew Language*. Ed. Raphael Kutscher. Leiden: E. J. Brill, 1982.

Laato, Antti. "Psalm 132 and the Development of the Jerusalemite/Israelite Royal Ideology." *CBQ* 54 (1992): 49-66.

Langdon, Stephen Herbert. *Sumerian Liturgies and Psalms*. Publications of the Babylonian Section, no. 10/4. Philadelphia: University of Pennsylvania Museum, 1919.

Lewis, Clive Staples. *Reflections on the Psalms*. New York: Harcourt, Brace & World, 1958.

Liebreich, Leon J. "The Songs of Ascents and the Priestly Blessing." *JBL* 74 (1955): 33-36.

Limburg, James. "Psalm 121: A Psalm for Sojourners." *WW* 5 (1985): 180-187.

Lipiński, Eduard. *La Royauté de Yahwé dans la poésie et le culte de l'ancien Israël*. Brussels: Paleis der Academiën, 1968.

_____. "Macarismes et psaumes de congratulation." *RB* 75 (1968): 321-367.

Loewenstamm, Samuel E. "The Formula *mē ʿattā wěʿad ōlām*." In *Comparative Studies in Biblical and Ancient Oriental Literatures*, 166-170. AOAT, no. 204. Neukirchen-Vluyn: Neukirchener Verlag, 1980.

Lohfink, Norbert. *Lobgesänge der Armen: Studien zum Magnifikat, den Hodajot von Qumran, und einigen späten Psalmen*. Stuttgart: Katholisches Bibelwerk, 1990.

Loretz, Oswald. *Die Psalmen: Beitrage der Ugarit-Texte zum Verständnis von Kolometrie und Textologie der Psalmen*. AOAT, no. 207. Neukirchen: Neukirchener Verlag, 1979.

Lowth, Robert M. *Lectures on the Sacred Poetry of the Hebrews*. Vol. 2. London: St. Paul's Churchyard, 1787; reprint, New York: Garland, 1971.

Luther, Martin. *A Commentary on the Psalms Called Psalms of Degrees; in which, among other interesting subjects, the scriptural doctrine respecting the divinely instituted and honorable estate of matrimony is explained and defended, in opposition to the Popish errors of monastic seclusion and enforced celibacy*. Translated by Henry Bull. London: Thomas Vautroullier, 1577; reprint, London: W. Simpkin and R. Marshall, 1899.

Maertens, Thierry. *Jérusalem. cité de Dieu (Ps. 120-128)*. Bruges: Abbaye de Saint-André, 1954.

Magne, J. "Répétitions de mots et exégèse dans quelques Psaumes et le Pater." *Bib* 39 (1958): 177-197.

Maillot, Alphonse. "Israël, sompte sur le Seigneur (Ps 131)." *BVC* 77 (1967): 26-37.

_____, and André Lelièvre. *Les Psaumes, commentaires.* Genève: Labor et Fides, 1969.

Mannati, Marina. "Les Psaumes Graduels consistuent-ils un genre littéraire distinct, l'intérieur du psautier biblique?" *Sem* 29 (1979): 85-100.

Margalit, Baruch. "The Meaning and Significance of Asherah." *VT* 40 (1990): 264-297.

Marrs, Rick R. "A Cry From the Depths (Ps 130)." *ZAW* 100 (1988): 81-90.

_____. "Psalm 122,3.4: A New Reading." *Bib* 68 (1987): 106-109.

_____. "The *Šyry-Hmᶜlwt* (Psalms 120-134): A Philological and Stylistic Analysis." Ph.D. Diss., Johns Hopkins University, 1982.

Matthews, Victor H. *Manners and Customs in the Bible.* Peabody, MA: Hendrickson Publishers, 1988.

_____, and Don C. Benjamin. *The Social World of Ancient Israel, 1250-587 BCE.* Peabody, MA: Hendrickson, 1993.

May, Herbert G., G. N. S. Hunt, and R. W. Hamilton, eds. *Oxford Bible Atlas.* 3d ed. Revised by John Day. New York: Oxford University Press, 1984.

Mayes, Andrew David Hastings. *Deuteronomy.* NCB, ed. Ronald E. Clements. Grand Rapids, MI: William B. Eerdmans, 1979.

Mays, James Luther. "The David of the Psalms." *Int* 50 (1986): 143-155.

_____. "The Place of the Torah-Psalms in the Psalter." *JBL* 106 (1987): 3-12.

McCann, J. Clinton, Jr. "The Psalms as Instruction." *Int* 46 (1992): 117-128.

_____. *A Theological Introduction to the Book of Psalms: The Psalms as Torah.* Nashville: Abingdon, 1993.

McCarthy, Charlene B. "Psalm 132: A Methodological Analysis." Diss., Marquette University, 1968.

McClellan, William H. "Obscurities in the Latin Psalter (Ps. 126,4b)." *CBQ* 5 (1943): 345-349.

McKay, John W. "Psalms of Vigil (Daybreak)." *ZAW* 91 (1979): 229-247.

McKenzie, Stephen L. *The Chronicler's Use of the Deuteronomistic History.* HSM, no. 33. Atlanta: Scholars Press, 1984.

Meyers, Carol L. "David as Temple Builder." In *Ancient Israelite Religion: Essays in Honor of Frank Moore Cross*, ed. Jr. Patrick D. Miller, Paul D. Hanson, and S. Dean McBride, 357-376. Philadelphia: Fortress, 1987.

_____. "The Roots of Restriction: Women in Early Israel." In *The Bible and Liberation: Political and Social Hermeneutics*, ed. Norman K. Gottwald, 289-306. Maryknoll, NY: Orbis, 1983.

Meyers, Eric M. "Priestly Language in the Book of Malachi." *HAR* 10 (1987): 225-37.

Michel, Diethelm. *Tempora und Satzstellung in den Psalmen.* Bonn: Bouvier, 1960.

Milgrom, Jacob. *Leviticus 1-16.* AB, no. 3. Garden City, NY: Doubleday, 1991.

Miller, James E. "Dreams and Prophetic Visions." *CBQ* 53 (1991): 401-404.

Miller, Patrick D., Jr. *Interpreting the Psalms.* Philadelphia: Fortress, 1986.

_____. "Psalm 127—The House that Yahweh Builds." *JSOT* 22 (1982): 119-132.

_____. "Psalm 130." In *Interpreting the Psalms*, 138-143. Philadelphia: Fortress, 1986.

_____. Review of *Die Wallfahrtspsalmen: Studien zur Entstehungsgeschichte von Psalm 120-134*, by Klaus Seybold. In *CBQ* 42 (1980): 110-111.

_____. "Synonymous-Sequential Parallelism in the Psalms." *Bib* 61 (1980): 256-260.

Morgenstern, Julius. "Psalm 121." *JBL* 58 (1939): 311-323.

_____. "Psalm 126." In *Homenaje a Millás-Vallicrosa*, 109-118. Vol. 2. Barcelona: Consejo Superior de Investigaciones Cientificas, 1956.

Mowinckel, Sigmund. *Psalmenstudien.* 6 vols. Oslo: Kristiana, 1921-1924; reprint, Amsterdam: P. Schippers, 1961.

_____. "Notes on the Psalms." *ST* 13 (1959): 134-165.

_____. *The Psalms in Israel's Worship.* Nashville: Abingdon, 1962.

Mühlenberg, Ekkehard. *Psalmenkommentare aus der Katenüberlieferung.* Vol. 2. Patristische Texte und Studien, no. 16. Berlin: Walter de Gruyter, 1977.

Muilenburg, James. "The Linguistic and Rhetorical Uses of the Particle כִּי in the Old Testament." *HUCA* 32 (1961): 135-160.

_____. "A Study in Hebrew Rhetoric." In *Congress Volume*, 97-111. VTSup, no. 1. Leiden: E. J. Brill, 1953.

Murphy, Roland E. "A Consideration of the Classification 'Wisdom Psalms'." In *Congress Volume*, 156-167. VTSup, no. 9. Leiden: E. J. Brill, 1962.

_____. "The Psalms." In *JBC*, 569-602.

Nasuti, Harry Peter. *Tradition History and the Psalms of Asaph.* SBLDS, no. 88. Atlanta: Scholars Press, 1987.

Neale, J. M., and R. F. Littledale. *A Commentary on the Psalms from Primitive and Medieval Writers.* London: Joseph Masters & Co., 1883.

Nel, Philip. "Psalm 132 and Covenant Theology." In *Text and Context: Old Testament and Semitic Studies for F. C. Fensham*, ed. W. Classen, 183-191. JSOTSup, no. 48. Sheffield: JSOT Press, 1988.

Nemoy, Leon. "Salmon Ben Jehoram's Commentary on Psalms 42-72." *JQR* 48 (1957): 58-66.

Nickelsburg, George W. E. *Jewish Literature Between the Bible and the Mishnah: A HIstorical and Literary Introduction.* Philadelphia: Fortress, 1981.

Norin, Stig. "Ps. 133. Zusammenhang und Datierung." *ASTI* 9 (1978): 90-95.

Nuñez, A. Gonzalez. "Cual torrentes del Nuguev (Salmo 126)." *EstB* 24 (1965): 349-360.

Oesterley, W. O. E. *A Fresh Approach to the Psalms.* New York: Charles Scribner's Sons, 1937.

_____. *The Psalms, translated with text-critical and exegetical notes.* London: SPCK, 1962.

Okinga, Boyo G. "An Example of Egyptian Royal Phraseology in Psalm 132." *Biblische Notizen: Beiträge zur exegetischen Diskussion* 11 (1980): 38-42.

Ollenburger, Ben C. *Zion, the City of the Great King: A Theological Symbol of the Jerusalem Cult.* JSOTSup, no. 41. Sheffield: Sheffield Academic Press, 1987.

Owen, John. *A Practical Exposition of the CXXXth Psalm: wherein the nature of the forgiveness of sin is declared, the truth and reality of it asserted, and the case of a soul distressed with the guilt of sin, and relieved by a discovery of forgiveness with God, is at large discoursed.* Salem, NY: Dodd & Rumsey, 1806.

Pascual, Bartolomé. "Dos notas al Saltero." *Estudios Ecclesiasticos* 34 (1960): 134-135; 645-655.

Perdue, Leo G. *Wisdom and Cult: A Critical Analysis of the Views of Cult in the Wisdom Literatures of Israel and the Ancient Near East.* SBLDS, no. 30. Missoula, MT: Scholars Press, 1977.

Perowne, J. J. Stewart. *The Book of Psalms: A New Translation, with Introductions and Notes, explanatory and critical.* 3d ed. Andover: Warren F. Draper, 1898.

Petersen, David L. *Haggai and Zechariah 1-8: A Commentary.* OTL. Philadelphia: Westminster, 1984.

Pfeiffer, Robert H. "The Fear of God." *IEJ* 5 (1955): 41-48.

Planas, Francisco. "Brevas notas a los salmos 127, 11 y 8." *CB* 32 (1975): 279-281.

_____. "Notas a los Salmos 119, 120 y 123." *CB* 34 (1977): 61-66.

Pollock, P. H. "Psalm 121." *JBL* 59 (1940): 411-412.

Porter, J. Roy. "The Interpretation of 2 Samuel vi and Psalm 132." *JTS* 5 (1954): 161-173.

Porúbčan, Štephan. "Psalm 130, 5-6." *VT* 9 (1959): 322-323.

Power, E. "Sion or Siʾon in Psalm 133 (Vulg 132)?" *Bib* 49 (1922): 342-349.

Praetorius, F. "Bemerkungen zu der ŠEr hammaꜥalōt." *ZDMG* 71 (1917): 389-390.

Preß, Richard. "Der zeitgeschichtliche Hintergrund der Wallfahrtspsalmen." *TZ* 14 (1958): 401-415.

Preuss, Horst Dietrich. "Die Psalmenüberschriften in Targum und Midrasch." *ZAW* 71 (1959): 44-53.

Pritchard, James B., ed. *Ancient Near Eastern Texts Relating to the Old Testament*. 3d ed. Princeton: Princeton University Press, 1969.

Puech, Émile. "Fragments du Psaume 122 dans un manuscrit hébreu de la Grotte IV." *RevQ* 9 (1978): 547-554.

Qimron, Elisha. *The Hebrew of the Dead Sea Scrolls*. Atlanta: Scholars Press, 1986.

Quell, G. "Struktur und Sinn des Psalms 131." In *Das ferne und das nahe Wort. Festschrift für L. Rost*, ed. Fritz Maass, 173-185. Berlin: Alfred Topelmann, 1967.

Raabe, Paul R. *Psalm Structures: A Study of Psalms With Refrains*. Sheffield: JSOT Press, 1990.

_____. "Deliberate Ambiguity in the Psalter." *JBL* 110 (1991): 213-227.

Rahlfs, Alfred. *ʿani und ʿanav in den Psalmen*. Göttingen: Dieterich, 1892.

Rasker, Albert Jan. "Psalm 121." In *Herr, tue meine Lippen auf: Eine Predigthilfe*, ed. Georg Eichholz, 76-84. Vol. 5. Wuppertal-Barmen: Emil Müller, 1961.

Rendsburg, Gary A. *Linguistic Evidence for the Northern Origin of Selected Psalms*. SBLMS, no. 43. Atlanta: Scholars Press, 1990.

Reuss, Ed. "Chants de pèlerinage: petit psautier des pèlerins du second temple." *Nouvelle revue de théologie (n.s.)* 1 (1858): 273-311.

Ridderbos, Nic. H. *Die Psalmen: stilistische Verfahren und Aufbau mit besonderer Berücksichtigung von Ps 1-41*. BZAW, no. 117. Berlin and New York: Walter de Gruyter, 1972.

Rinaldi, G. "*ʿim* 'con' una diviniṭ." *BeO* 10 (1968): 68.

Robinson, Aubrey. "Do Ephratha and Jaar Really Appear in Psalm 132:6?" *ZAW* 86 (1974): 220-222.

Robinson, Aubrey. "The Meaning of rî and the Dubiety of the Form harrê and its variants." *VT* 24 (1974): 500-504.

Rogerson, J. W., and J. W. McKay. *Psalms*. CBC. Cambridge: Cambridge University Press, 1977.

Rose, A. "Chant de pèlerinage, Jérusalem (Psalm 122)." *AS* 73 (1962): 7-17.

Rose, A. "Le Psaume 126 (125). Joie d'un peuple que son Dieu fait revivre." *Feu Nouveau* 9 (1966): 16-26.

Rosenstiehl, Jean M. "Un commentaire du Psaume 133, l'époque intertestamentaire." *RHPR* 59 (1979): 559-565.

Rost, Leonard. "Ein Psalmenproblem." *TLZ* 93 (1968): 241-246.

Rotherham, Joseph Bryant. *Studies in the Psalms*. Cincinnati: Standard Publishing Company, n.d.

Ruppert, Lothar. "Klage oder Bitte? Zu einer neuen Sicht der individuellen Klagelieder." *BZ* (n.s.) 33 (1988): 252-255.

Sabourin, Leopold. *The Psalms: Their Origin and Meaning.* Staten Island, NY: Alba House, 1969.

Safrai, Shmuel. *Die Wallfahrt im Zeitalter des zweiten Tempels.* Forschungen zum jüdisch-christlichen Dialog, no. 3. Neukirchen-Vluyn: Neukirchener Verlag, 1981.

Sailhamer, John H. *The Translational Technique of the Greek Septuagint for the Hebrew Verbs and Participles in Psalms 3-41.* New York: Peter Lang, 1991.

Sanders, James A. *The Dead Sea Psalms Scroll.* Ithaca, NY: Cornell University Press, 1967.

──────────. *The Psalms Scroll of Qumrân Cave 11 (11QPsᵃ).* DJD, no. 4. Oxford: Clarendon, 1965.

Sawyer, John F. A. "An Analysis of the Context and Meaning of the Psalm-Headings." *Transactions of the Glasgow University Oriental Society* 22 (1967-68): 26-38.

Scammon, John H. "Changes of Interpretation of the Psalms in One Man's Lifetime." *ANQ* 12 (1971): 91-98.

Schmidt, Hans. *Das Gebet der Angeklagten im AT.* BZAW, no. 49. Giessen: Alfred Töpelmann, 1928.

──────────. "Grüsse und Glückwunsche im Psalter." *TSK* 103 (1931): 141-150.

──────────. *Die Psalmen.* HAT, no. 15. Tübingen: J. C. B. Mohr, 1934.

Schmidt, Werner H. "Gott und Mensch in Ps. 130: Formgeschichtliche Erwägungen." *TZ* 22 (1966): 241-253.

Schreiner, Joseph. "Wenn nicht der Herr für uns wäre! Auslegung von Psalm 124." *BibLeb* 10 (1969): 16-25.

Schuller, Eileen M. *Non-Canonical Psalms from Qumran: A Pseudepigraphic Collection.* HSS, no. 28. Atlanta: Scholars Press, 1986.

──────────. "The Psalm of 4Q372 1 within the Context of Second Temple Prayer." *CBQ* 54 (1992): 67-79.

Schulß, W. *Die Psalmen.* Kurzgefaßter Kommentar zu den heiligen Schriften Alten und Neuen Testaments sowie zu den Apokryphen, A. Altes Testament, ed. Hermann Strack and Otto Böckler, no. 6. Nördlingen: C. H. Beck'schen Buchhandlung, 1888.

Schwantes, Milton. "A herenca de Jave: meditando o Salmo 127." 27 (1987): 175-180.

Schwarzschild, Roger. "Syntax of אֲשֶׁר in Biblical Hebrew with Special Reference to Qoheleth." *HS* 31 (1990): 7-39.

Segal, Alan. "Heavenly Ascent in Hellenistic Judaism, Early Christianity and Their Environment." In *ANRW*, 1333-94. Vol. 2, no. 23. Berlin: Walter de Gruyter, 1980.

Seidel, Hans. Review of *"Wir sind wie Träumende": Studien zum 126. Psalm,* by Walter Beyerlin. In *TLZ* 106 (1981): 741-742.

_____. Review of *Die Wallfahrtspsalmen: Studien zur Entstehungsgeschichte von Psalm 120-134*, by Klaus Seybold. In *TLZ* 106 (1981): 742-744.

_____. "Wallfahrtslieder." In *Das Lebende Wort: Beiträge zur kirchlichen Verkündigung Festgabe für Gottfried Voigt zum 65. Geburtstag*, ed. Hans Seidel, and Karl-Heinrich Bieritz, 26-40. Berlin: Evangelische Verlagsanstalt, 1982.

Sellers, Ovid R. "The Status and Prospects of Research Concerning the Psalms." In *The Study of the Bible Today and Tomorrow*, ed. Harold R. Willoughby, 129-143. Chicago: University of Chicago Press, 1947.

Seybold, Klaus. "The Asaph Psalms." Paper presented to the Book of Psalms Consultation, Society of Biblical Literature Annual Meeting, New Orleans, LA, 1990.

_____. *Die Psalmen: Eine Einführung.* Urban-Taschenbücher, no. 382. Stuttgart: W. Kohlhammer, 1986.

_____. "Die Redaktion der Wallfahrtspsalmen." *ZAW* 91 (1979): 247-268.

_____. *Die Wallfahrtspsalmen: Studien zur Entstehungsgeschichte von Psalm 120-134.* Biblisch-Theologische Studien, no. 3. Neukirchen: Neukirchener Verlag, 1978.

Sheppard, Gerald T. "Theology and the Book of Psalms." *Int* 46 (1992): 143-155.

Shoemaker, H. Stephen. "Psalm 131." *RE* 85 (1988): 89-94.

Simon, Uriel. *Four Approaches to the Book of Psalms: From Saadiah Gaon to Abraham Ibn Ezra.* Albany, NY: SUNY Press, 1989.

Skehan, Patrick W. "Some Short Psalms." *AER* 124 (1951): 104-109.

Slotki, I. W. "The Text and the Ancient Form of Recital of Psalm 24 and Psalm 124." *JBL* 51 (1932): 214-226.

Smith, Daniel L. *The Religion of the Landless: The Social Context of the Babylonian Exile.* Bloomington, Indiana: Meyer-Stone, 1989.

Smith, Morton. "Jewish Religious Life in the Persian Period." In *Introduction; The Persian Period*, ed. W. D. Davies and Louis Finckelstein, 162-188. The Cambridge History of Judaism, no. 1. Cambridge: Cambridge University Press, 1984.

Smith, Morton. *Palestinian Parties and Politics that Shaped the Old Testament.* 2d corrected ed. London: SCM, 1987.

Smith, Mark S. "The Psalms as a Book for Pilgrims." *Int* 46 (1992): 156-166.

Soggin, J. Alberto. *Judges, A Commentary.* 2d ed. Old Testament Library. Philadelphia: Westminster, 1987.

Speier, Salomon. "Sieben Stellen des Psalmentargums in Handschriften und Druckausgaben: 3,7; 44,17; 45,6; 49,11; 68,15.20; 126,1." *Bib* 48 (1967): 491-508.

Sperling, Uwe. *Das theophanische Jahwe-Überlegenheitslied: Forschungsbericht und gattungskritische Untersuchung der sogenannten Zionlieder.* Europäische Hochschulschriften; Series 23, Theologie, no. 426. New York: Peter Lang, 1991.

Spieckermann, Hermann. *Heilsgegenwart: eine Theologie der Psalmen.* FRLANT, no. 148. Göttingen: Vandenhoeck & Ruprecht, 1989.

Stamm, Johann Jakob, et al. *Hebräisches und Aramäisches Lexikon zum Alten Testament von Ludwig Koehler und Walter Baumgartner.* 3d ed. Leiden: E. J. Brill, 1990.

Starbuck, Scott R. A. "Like Dreamers Lying in Wait, We Lament: A New Reading of Psalm 126." *Koinonia* 1 (1989): 128-149.

Starr, Chester G. *A History of the Ancient World.* New York: Oxford University Press, 1991.

Stern, Ephraim. *Material Culture of the Land of the Bible in the Persian Period, 538-332 B.C.* Jerusalem: Israel Exploration Society, 1982.

Strauß, Hans. "'Siehe, Jahwes Erbbesitz sind Söhne': Ps 127 als ein Lied der Ermutigung in nachexilischer Zeit." In *Altes Testament und christliche Verkündigung: Festschrift für Antonius H. J. Gunneweg zum 65. Geburtstag,* ed. Manfred Oeming, and Axel Graupner, 390-398. Stuttgart: W. Kohlhammer, 1987.

Strugnell, John. "A Note on Ps. 126:1." *JTS* 7 (1956): 239-243.

Stuhlmueller, Caroll. *The Psalms.* Old Testament Message, no. 22. Wilmington, DA: Michael Glazier, 1983.

Sulah, Aryeh. "שיר המעלות' מזמורי." *Beth Mikra* 47 (1971): 457-475.

Tate, Marvin E. *Psalms 51-100.* WBC, ed. John D. W. Watts, and Ralph P. Martin, no. 20. Dallas: Word Books, 1990.

Taylor, William R., and W. Stewart McCullough. *Psalms: Introduction and Exegesis.* IB, no. 4. New York: Abingdon, 1955.

Thayer, Charles Snow. *Ueber das Verhältniss der Psalmen zu Jeremia.* Göttingen: Dieterich (W. Fr. Kästner), 1901.

Thirtle, James William. *Old Testament Problems: Critical Studies in the Psalms & Isaiah.* London: Henry Frowde, 1907.

Tournay, Raymond Jacques. *Seeing and Hearing God with the Psalms: The Prophetic Liturgy of the Second Temple in Jerusalem.* JSOTSup, no. 118. Sheffield: JSOT Press, 1991.

Tromp, Johannes. "The Text of Psalm cxxx 5-6." *VT* 39 (1989): 100-103.

Tsevat, Matitiahu. *A Study of the Language of the Biblical Psalms.* Journal of Biblical Literature Monograph Series, no. 9. Philadelphia: Society of Biblical Literature, 1955.

Tsumura, David T. "Sorites in Psalm 133,2-3a." *Bib* 61 (1980): 416-417.

Urbrock, William J. "Psalms 1-37 as a Chiastic Arrangement." Paper presented to the Psalms Group, Society of Biblical Literature Annual Meeting, Washington, DC, 1993.

van der Ploeg, Johannes P. M. "Notes sur quelques psaumes." In *Melanges bibliques et orientaux en l'honneur de M. Mathias Delcor*, ed. André Caquot, 425-430. Neukirchen-Vluyn: Neukirchener Verlag, 1985.

van der Wal, Adri J. O. "The Structure of Psalm cxxix." *VT* 38 (1988): 364-367.

VanGemeren, Willem A. "Psalm 131:2--kegamul: the problems of meaning and metaphor." *HS* 23 (1983): 51-57.

Viviers, Hendrik. "A Text Immanent Study on the Coherence of the Maʿalot-Psalms." D.D. Thesis, University of Pretoria (South Africa), 1991.

Volz, P. "Zur Auslegung von Psalm 23 und 121." *NKZ* 36 (1925): 576-585.

von Rad, Gerhard. "Die levitische Predigt in den Büchern der Chronik." *TBei* 8 (1961): 248-261.

_____. "'Righteousness' and 'Life' in the Cultic Language of the Psalms." In *The Problem of the Hexateuch and Other Essays*, 243-266. New York: McGraw-Hill, 1966.

_____. *Weisheit in Israel*. Neukirchen: Neukirchener Verlag, 1970.

Wahl, Otto. "Die Erfahrung Israels damals und heute (dargestellt an Ps 126)." In *Erfahrung als Weg: Beiträge zur Theologie und religiösen Praxis: Festschrift zur Feier des fünfzigjährigen Bestehens der Philosophisch-Theologischen Hochschule der Salesianer Don Boscos Benediktbeuern*, eds. Horacio E. Lona and Otto Wahl, 37-56. Donauwörth: Ludwig Auer, 1981.

Waltke, Bruce K. "Superscripts, Postscripts, or Both." *JBL* 110 (1991): 583-596.

_____, and Michael Patrick O'Connor. *An Introduction to Biblical Hebrew Syntax*. Winona Lake, IN: Eisenbrauns, 1990.

Wanke, Gunther. *Die Zionstheologie der Korachiten in ihrem Traditionsgeschichtlichen Zusammenhang*. BZAW, no. 97. Berlin: Alfred Töpelmann, 1966.

Wanke, Gunther. "Prophecy and Psalms in the Persian Period." In *Introduction; The Persian Period*, ed. W. D. Davies and Louis Finckelstein, 162-188. The Cambridge History of Judaism, no. 1. Cambridge: Cambridge University Press, 1984.

Watkins, Arthur Charles. *The Pilgrim Psalms: being a rendering into English of fifteen Hebrew lyrics, with an essay and some explanations*. Hannibal, NY: A. C. Watkins, 1899.

Watson, Wilfred G. E. "The Hidden Simile in Psalm 133." *Bib* 60 (1979): 108-109.

Watters, William R. *Formula Criticism and the Poetry of the Old Testament*. BZAW, no. 138. Berlin: Walter de Gruyter, 1976.

Weber, J. J. *Le Psautier, texte et commentaire, édition refondue*. Tournai: Desclée, 1968.

Weber, Max. *Ancient Judaism*. Translated and edited by Hans H. Gerth and Don Martindale. New York and London: The Free Press and Collier-MacMillan, 1952; reprint, Free Press Paperback, 1967.

Weingreen, Jacob. *Introduction to the Critical Study of the Text of the Hebrew Bible*. Oxford: Clarendon, 1982.

Weir, T. H. "Psalm 121:1." *ExpTim* 27 (1915/16): 90-91.

Weiser, Artur. *Psalms: A Commentary*. OTL. Philadelphia: Westminster, 1962.

Westermann, Claus. *Ausgewählte Psalmen: Übersetzt und erklärt*. Göttingen: Vandenhoeck & Ruprecht, 1984.

_____. "The Formation of the Psalter." In *Praise and Lament in the Psalms*, 250-258. Translated by Keith R. Crim and Richard N. Soulen. Atlanta: John Knox, 1981.

_____. *Isaiah 40-66: A Commentary*. OTL. Philadelphia: Westminster, 1965.

_____. *Living Psalms*. Translated by J. R. Porter. Grand Rapids, MI: William B. Eerdmans, 1989.

_____. *Praise and Lament in the Psalms*. Translated by Keith R. Crim and Richard N. Soulen. Atlanta: John Knox, 1981.

_____. "Psalm 130." In *Herr, tue meine Lippen auf: Eine Predigthilfe*, ed. Georg Eichholz, 606-612. Vol. 5. 2d ed. Wuppertal-Barmen: Emil Müller, 1961.

_____. *The Psalms: Structure, Content & Message*. Translated by Ralph D. Gehrke. Minneapolis: Augsburg, 1980.

Wiedermann, Gotthelf. "Alexander Alesius' Lectures on the Psalms at Cambridge, 1536." *JEH* 37 (1986): 15-41.

Willems, Gerard F. "Les psaumes dans la liturgie juive." *Bijdragen* 51 (1990): 397-417.

Williams, Ronald J. *Hebrew Syntax: An Outline*. 2d ed. Toronto: University of Toronto Press, 1976.

Willis, John T. "An Attempt to Decipher Psalm 121:1b." *CBQ* 52 (1990): 241-251.

Wilson, Gerald Henry. *The Editing of the Hebrew Psalter*. SBLDS, no. 76. Chico, CA: Scholars Press, 1985.

_____. "Qumran and the Hebrew Psalter." *TSF Bulletin* 9 (1985): 10-12.

_____. "The Shape of the Book of Psalms." *Int* 46 (1992): 129-142.

_____. "The Use of 'Untitled' Psalms in the Hebrew Psalter." *ZAW* 97 (1985): 404-413.

_____. "The Use of Royal Psalms at the 'Seams' of the Hebrew Psalter." *JSOT* 35 (1986): 85-94.

Wolff, Hans Walter. *Hosea*. Translated by Gary Stansell. Hermeneia, ed. Frank Moore Cross, et al. Philadelphia: Fortress, 1974; reprint, 1989.

_____. *Joel and Amos: A Commentary on the Books of the Prophets Joel and Amos*. Translated by Waldemar Janzen, S. Dean McBride Jr., and Charles A. Muenchow. Hermeneia, ed. Frank Moore Cross, et al. Philadelphia: Fortress, 1977; reprint, 1989.

_____. "Prophecy from the Eighth Through the Fifth Century." In *Interpreting the Prophets*, ed. James Luther Mays, and Paul J. Achtemeier, 14-26. Philadelphia: Fortress, 1987.

_____. "Psalm 122." In *Herr, tue meine Lippen auf: Ein Predigthilfe*, ed. G. Eichholz, 105-115. Vol. 5. Wuppertal-Barmen: Emil Müller, 1961.

Wright, Christopher J. H. *God's People in God's Land: Family, Land, and Property in the Old Testament*. Grand Rapids, Michigan: Eerdmans, 1990.

Wright, John R. "A Tale of Three Cities: Urban Gates, Squares, and Power in Iron Age II, Neo-Babylonian, and Achaemenid Israel." Paper presented to the Sociology of the Second Temple Group, Society of Biblical Literature Annual Meeting, New Orleans, LA, 1990.

Würthwein, Ernst. *The Text of the Old Testament: An Introduction to the Biblia Hebraica*. Translated by Erroll F. Rhodes. Grand Rapids, MI: William B. Eerdmans, 1979; reprint, 1983.

Yardeni, Ada. "Remarks on the Priestly Blessing on Two Ancient Amulets from Jerusalem." *VT* 41 (1991): 176-185.

Youngblood, Ronald. "Divine Names in the Book of Psalms: Literary Structures and Number Patterns." *JANES* 19 (1989): 171-181.

Zenger, Erich. *Ich will die Morgenröte wecken: Psalmenauslegungen*. Freiburg im Breisgau: Herder, 1991.

Zerr, B. *The Psalms: A New Translation*. New York: Paulist, 1979.

Zimmerli, Walther. *Ezekiel*. Translated by Ronald E. Clements. 2 vols. Hermeneia, ed. Frank Moore Cross, et al. Philadelphia: Fortress, 1979, 1983.

Zobel, H. -J. "יִשְׂרָאֵל *yiśrāʾēl*." In *Theological Dictionary of the Old Testament*, ed. G. Johannes Botterweck and Helmer Ringgren, 397-420. Vol. 6. Trans. David E. Green. Grand Rapids, MI: William B. Eerdmans, 1990.

INDEX OF ANCIENT AND MODERN AUTHORS

INDEX OF CITATIONS FROM BIBLICAL AND COGNATE LITERATURE

221

Psalms

136, 140 n. 24
136: 4, 95
137: 7, 100
140: 10, 33 n. 5
143: 6, 86
145: 5, 95; 5-6, 95; 9,12, 140 n. 23
146, 134, 138
147: 1, 109 n. 146

Job

10: 3, 72
19: 21, 50 n. 31
30: 26, 89
36: 11, 109

Proverbs

6: 4, 100; 17, 95
17: 15, 110 n. 150
18: 12, 95
22: 6, 108
30: 13, 95

Ruth

1: 5, 110 n. 150
2: 4, 80
4: 11, 70, 162

Song of Songs

1: 5, 37 n. 12

Qohelet

7: 1, 112
8: 14, 58

Lamentations

2: 19, 125
4: 13,16, 179

Daniel

9: 9, 91
12: 2, 118

Ezra

3: 11, 140 n. 24
4: 1-4, 176, 178
7: 9, 11

Nehemiah

1: 3, 173 n. 27
3: 7, 45
5: 1-13, 168 n. 16
10: 38, 180 n. 38
12: 32, 26
13: 14, 99; 28, 180

1 Chronicles

1: 5,17, 36
6: 17, 124 n. 196
9: 23-27, 124
19: 4, 107
22: 14, 100; 9, 140
23: 18, 124 n. 196

2 Chronicles

1: 3, 122 n. 191
2: 11, 138 n. 18
6: 41-42, 101, 172
7: 3,6, 140 n. 24
8: 14, 180
16: 4, 108
19: 2, 79 n. 79
20: 21, 140 n. 24
21: 7, 101
23: 4, 180
29: 34, 180
30: 1, 173
32: 24-26, 14
34: 1-7, 173

Apocrypha

1 Esd 6: 13, 122 n. 193
2 Esd 16: 35, 122 n. 193
Add Esth 4: 17c, 138 n. 18
Sir 1: 27, 95; 5: 5, 91; 50: 12, 110
Azar 63, 122 n. 193
Bel 5, 138 n. 18
Pr Man 2, 138 n. 18

Rabbinic Literature

b. Sukk. 51b, 14, 18
b. Sukk. 51b, 19 n. 62
t. Soṭa 7: 7, 21
Psalms Midrash, 9

GENERAL THEOLOGICAL SEMINARY
NEW YORK